GW01144878

No Tea for Dad's Army

by Patrick Emme

To John

Thank You for Your Support

Best Regards,

Patrick Emme

April 29, 2023

Copyright of Patrick Emme©

© **Godfrey Holmes**
MARCH 2015

ISBN : 978-0-9536016-5-3

All rights reserved. No part of this publication may be reproduced or transmitted in any form or by any means: electronic or mechanical, including photocopying, recording - or entered into any information storage and retrieval system -
nor may its content be incorporated into staff training programmes, without the prior permission, in writing, from the publisher.
A catalogue record of this Dictionary is available from
the British Library

NETHERMOOR BOOKS
"St. Elphin"
12 North Promenade
Withernsea
East Riding of Yorkshire
HU19 2DP

Telephone : 01964-615258
Contact the Author :
godfrey.holmes@btinternet.com

DEDICATED TO
THE UNK̂OWN WORKER
SUFFERING IN SILENCE
YET STILL STANDING AT 5

PROLOGUE

As the Civil Rights movement faded and a sectarian struggle emerged, Northern Ireland spiraled into destruction. The British Army, deployed to keep the peace and protect the Catholic communities from the initial onslaught from rabble gangs from the Orange community, was losing its shine in Green eyes and was morphing into the enemy. In a couple of short years, the Army had descended from hero to zero. The positivity that had come to the Catholic Community was changing to despair. As chaos pervades, we witness the birth of the Troubles.

This account, inspired by true events, depicts the downward spiral of a buoyant environment. It chronicles the utter despair of the province and the indelible changes that the communities had to face. Within this turmoil a law-abiding Belfast student runner is striving for a normal life and hopes of realizing his dream to compete internationally. He is focused, despite the horror that surrounds him, on maintaining his spirit and dedication to progressing his athletic performance. He comes to understand that to reach his potential he must acknowledge and adapt to his external environment.

This book is a work of fiction. Any references to historical events, real people, or real places are used fictitiously. Other names, characters, places and events are products of the author's imagination, and any resemblance to actual events, places or persons, living or dead, is entirely coincidental.

ACKNOWLEDGEMENTS

A big thank you to Lucy Mullins for the editing. I am most indebted to her devotion, perseverance, and enthusiasm in assisting me through multiple iterations of the work.

I would like to thank Rebecca Miller for the artwork. She took my memories of a mural that no longer exists and relived it on canvass. The words on the mural have been an indelible message in my mind of the new and enduring direction the Troubles took at that time.

Finally I would like to dedicate the novel to my wife and children who supported and encouraged me throughout the project. I hope this will help them understand what has framed me during the formative years of my youth.

CONTENTS

Chapter 1: Paradise Lost

Chapter 2: Blister on the Moon

Chapter 3: Relax and Stride

Chapter 4: Tearing Us Apart

Chapter 5: Three-Point Turn

Chapter 6: The Loneliness of the Long-Distance Runner

Chapter 7: Angels with Dirty Faces

Chapter 8: Saracen City

Chapter 9: Shock of the New

Chapter 10: Three Strikes

Chapter 11: Break the Chain

Chapter 12: Slán Leat

PARADISE LOST

On a quiet spring afternoon in 1971 in West Belfast, Seamus Rooney crouched behind a hedge. He eased his sports kit bag onto the ground, opened it, and began assembling the rifle components he pulled from it. Two companions, crouched next to him, were doing the same. As leader of the team, he felt a sense of pride at how efficient they were. They had been tasked with sending a message to the enemy, and he was ready for it. He nurtured the anger he felt and let it build. It would help him do what he needed to do. His assembly completed, he brushed his shoulder-length locks away from his face and aimed the rifle out onto the street.

"Shouldn't be long now," Seamus whispered to his companions.

They were all dressed in dull olive tracksuits to aid their camouflage and to appear as typical youths returning from a training workout, which they were some of the times. Seamus looked through the gunsight and out via a gap in the hedge onto the street of Gransha Park. He took a couple of deep breaths to calm himself so he could hold his rifle steady. All was quiet. He had spent several weeks casing the area for his team before he settled on this place and time. He was intimate with this street, part of a new middle class housing estate. Most of the houses were semi-detached with a front garden behind a three-foot wall, behind which was often a thick hedge or rosebush, perfect for cover, and a driveway at the side leading to a garage that abutted to the house and the garage next door. However, he had wisely chosen one of the detached houses, where there was a clear passage to the back garden and the parkland beyond.

Still looking through the gunsight, Seamus surveyed to his right from his vantage point down the gently sloping road that spread about four car widths from footpath to footpath. At about thirty yards the street dropped sharply for about another seventy yards to the Glen Road. This fitted their purpose well.

He gently turned his rifle from side to side checking the area. To the left some hundred yards the street took a sweeping ninety degree turn to the right. He noticed a Consul Cortina and a Mini Cooper parked on the street. As he eased his rifle back to the right, he saw a man carefully washing a vintage Ford Zephyr some twenty yards from the corner on the opposite side of the road. A couple of the houses closer to him, he noticed a lady in a floral frock tending to the flowers in her driveway border. Her next-door neighbor was sitting on a deck chair in her front garden flicking through a magazine in her hands. She was in conversation with the other lady. Hope they are out of the way when the fun starts, Seamus thought. Apart from that, all was quiet.

Seamus eased his rifle further to the right, and a pudgy gentleman with curly, greying auburn hair came into view as he emerged from a wooden gate of his house across the street. Just like clockwork Mr. Quinn was right on time. His two young children were bouncing around him. He bent over to kiss them, and then they ran back into the house. He proceeded down the footpath toward the steep drop to the Glen Road. Seamus kept Mr. Quinn in the crosshairs of his gunsight as he gently applied his finger to the trigger. Then he noticed him waving over to the other side of the road. He eased his gunsight around and noticed a young lady walking up the hill. Although not unexpected, it threw Seamus off. She nodded with assurance back to Mr. Quinn and continued walking. Seamus knew Siobhan. She was in the same class in school as his younger sister and was just a couple of years younger than him. He had met her a couple of times when his sister had a few of her friends over. Important that she does not see me, he thought. Siobhan was wearing the burgundy uniform of her high school. She lived several houses up the street toward the corner. Seamus glanced at his men and signaled to keep quiet as she walked closer to them on their side of the street. She passed by on the footpath. Come on. Move quickly up the street, he thought. Don't want to delay because of you.

One of Seamus's companions nudged his arm. Seamus looked down the street to his right. Mr. Quinn was almost at the brow of the hill, and then helmets appeared over the horizon. Six armed British soldiers in camouflage uniforms with vest-shaped body armor started to come into view. They were spread across the road with rifles in hand as they patrolled the street. Seamus held his breath for a few seconds as his heartbeat raced.

"This is it. Wait for my signal," Seamus said with his eyes firmly fixed on the enemy.

Mr. Quinn was now out of sight as the soldiers marched closer.

Shane McMahon was out for a run on this beautiful afternoon. He was at that point of the run where he felt his legs moving effortlessly. Injury seems to be holding up, he thought. His breathing was smooth, and he could relax and take in the spring flowers, the birds singing, and the spring air. For Shane it was paradise. Life was good. He rounded the corner on Gransha Park ready to race down the hill, and suddenly he heard a shriek of bullets. He pulled up short in horror and then stood there witnessing a surreal scene in front of him as if it were happening in slow motion. He was frozen to the spot. He heard more gunshots, but in his shocked state they sounded far away. A lady in a house across the road lay helplessly on her driveway. Shane could see blood seeping from her midriff and spreading across her frock. A lady from the neighboring house jumped up from her deck chair and began running to the wounded woman's aid, but before she made it, she was hit in her leg and went down. She tried to crawl up the driveway of her friend's house to get to her. At the same time, a man dropped his bucket of water by the car he was washing and hightailed up his driveway. A hail of bullets ploughed through his car just a few seconds later. A British soldier lay injured on the ground groaning, and others were crouched down in the middle of the street shooting in different directions. Suddenly a young woman came into view some twenty yards in front of Shane. She was running frantically toward him. Bullets were following her path and bouncing off walls and embedding in wooden gates.

"Help! Help!" she cried out.

Seeing the plight of the young woman pulled Shane out of his trance. He shook himself, took a deep breath, and kicked into action. Shane accelerated toward Siobhan. He threw his arm around her waist and pulled her toward him as they hurtled over a short wall and a neatly groomed hedge into a lush lawn, which helped break their fall. They crouched down low, Siobhan's face in his shoulder. The house was on the bend of Gransha Park, so many of the bullets came in their direction. Siobhan flinched each time a bullet hit the outside of the wall behind which they were hiding. Shane could hear bullets whizz through the short hedge above them. They held tight to each other and moved further in under the hedge. Jeez, never expected to get this close to danger, Shane thought. Hope we can get out of this. Never expected to be this close today to a young lady. Feels strange. Feels uncomfortable. Feels great. I can feel her body breathing rapidly against mine. She must be petrified. Better hold on tight to her.

Shane peeked through a gap in the hedge and could see at least two wounded soldiers spreadeagled on the ground, with their colleagues striving to get to them.

"Keep your head low! Bullets are coming our way," Siobhan said.

Shane dropped his head, and both kept low on the ground shielded by the low brick wall. The battle lasted just a few minutes, but during that time they could hear a constant ping of bullets.. Then quietness broke out. It was short lived as groans and cries of the injured ladies and soldiers could be heard. It appeared that the gunmen had left the scene. Most likely they had escaped through the fields at the back of the estate. Shane could hear walkie-talkies in the distance as the patrol called for help. The army barracks was just half a mile away so reinforcements would arrive soon.

Shane eased his clutch on Siobhan. "Are you OK?"

"Just shaken. But no wounds," she said checking herself over.

"Let's stay low just in case the shooting starts up again."

"Sure thing."

Siobhan then settled back down and huddled close to Shane still shaking. He eased his arms around her, and she gently slipped deeper into the embrace. Despite his discomfort at this intimacy Shane felt a warmth inside that he had not experienced before. After a few more minutes, the trouble had appeared to pass. Siobhan gently eased herself up.

"I think it's safe now," she said.

"Never been this close to a gun battle," Shane said.

"Me neither. Just seen the aftermath on TV."

"Frightening. Thought we were goners."

"Know what you mean. We're the lucky ones. I hear groans close by. People have been shot. Maybe some were killed."

"Yes. Ugly. I saw a couple of ladies hit across the road and a man running for his life. I think they're still alive."

"Let's hope so. Not sure about the soldiers. Some may have gone down after we jumped the hedge. Do you think we should see how they are?"

"Better stay put for a while. Could still be dangerous."

They sat up still shaken.

"Wow, wasn't expecting that much activity during my run."

"Shocking. What are you training for?"

"Cross-country. The Belfast Schools Championships are just a couple weeks off."

"Are you going to win?"

Shane paused for several seconds thrown by the question. "Aah. Not me, but I need to do well and finish most likely in the top five for my school to win the team event."

"Why not win yourself?"

"I'm just not as good as a lot of other runners, including some on my team. I'm also getting over a bad injury."

"Oh. What type of injury?"

Shane noticed that Siobhan kept the conversation going.

Maybe she's afraid the shooting will start again, he thought.

"I partially ruptured the Achilles tendon on my left heel."

"Ugh. Can you run free now?"

"Yes. Appears to be on the mend. Almost fully fit."

"I see. What school do you compete for then?"

"St. Mary's. I'm in my final year."

"So, you must be doing your A-levels soon?"

"Yes, in a couple of months. Just getting deep into revision at present. My next priority."

"Me too."

"I take it from the uniform that you're at St. Dominic's?"

"Yes."

"My sister attends there, but she'd be a couple of years behind you."

"Grand. Well, it appears that the scare is over. Must be getting back," Siobhan said.

"We should go over the road and check on the injured," Shane said.

"Sure thing."

They both rose and brushed themselves off. Shane looked over at Siobhan. In the commotion he hadn't noticed how gorgeous she was. She was sleek and tall, just a few inches shorter than his six-foot frame, and with shiny brown hair sweeping down to her waist. Moments ago, he had his arms around her without even realizing it. This must be heaven, he thought.

"May not need to help the injured," Siobhan said. "Soldiers are attending to their colleagues. Better not to interfere there. Mrs. Quinn from across the road is going to the injured ladies with blankets and pillows. Mr. Quinn isn't far behind."

"I thought he went down the hill."

"Must have come back. Why, d'ya know him?"

"Sure do. I work part-time two nights a week in his pub."

"Oh. The Eagle Inn?"

"Yes. In fact, I'm on this evening."

"Do you want to go over and speak with him?"

"Better if he doesn't see me. My father sometimes drinks in the Eagle Inn, and I'd prefer he didn't tell him about this."

"Oh, a man of mystery! Well, then you'd better get on your way."

"Yes. Not sure that I can continue my run. I'll call it a day and make my way back home."

"Where's that?"

"A couple of miles down the Falls Road just after the Falls Park, near the base of the Whiterock."

"Oh, yes, I know the area. Pass it every day for school."

Shane was now struggling for words to continue the conversation, but Siobhan seemed at ease.

"Promise to be there, next time I'm in danger?"

"If I can, of course," Shane said swallowing in his throat.

"Well in that case you can protect me on Sunday."

"What's happening on Sunday?"

"Maybe going to the Milk Bar on the Glen Road for lunch."

Shane hesitated not quite understanding. "I thought all the coffee shops around here were blown up?"

"That's why I may need protecting there just in case."

With a sudden understanding Shane looked in wonderment into her striking brown eyes. "In that case, of course I'll come," he said. Shane remembered that a local Milk Bar was still open for business on the Glen Road despite most being victims of the Troubles.

"Then let's meet at noon," Siobhan said.

"Noon, Sunday. You've got it."

In a daze, Shane wondered, Am I really having a date with this beauty? He could see that Mr. and Mrs. Quinn were now tending to the injured and heard the ambulance sirens getting louder. The medics will be here soon, he thought. He could see the uninjured army soldiers progressing up the street crouching close to the house walls and hedges as they advanced.

"When the army reinforcements come, they'll comb the area and search all houses," Siobhan said. "Most likely they'll not have their best listening skills to the fore."

"Know what you mean."

"You should go now. Cross through this back garden, then on through the gardens of the adjacent four houses, and thereafter take the main road back."

"Will do." Shane was about to run off but then turned. "Where do you live?" he asked.

"In this house."

"Oh! Noon, Sunday, this house. Got it. Please apologize to your folks from me for the damage to the hedge."

"No worries. They'll be looking for an apology first from the army for the bullet holes in the front gate. Fat chance of that!"

Although Shane had intended to do a ten-mile run that day, he decided to cut his losses and run back home. Six miles and still fully fit will do for today, Shane considered. He started off, was progressing down through the Gransha estate, and as he upped the pace, he suddenly felt a twinge in his left Achilles tendon.

"Aaah!" He limped to a standstill, untied his shoe, and rolled down his sock. "Looks like I inflamed it again," he muttered. "Damn it. Must have happened when I jumped the hedge. What a bummer. I thought I'd cracked this." He rubbed his heel gently and prodded it. "Ouch!" He kept feeling around the tendon as he muttered to himself. "The rest of the area seems OK. Sore to touch just in that spot." He eased his sock back over the heel and tied his trainer. Better take it easy back.

He found the pain eased with the slower pace. As he progressed, his mind drifted from the injury. He was thinking of the striking, cheeky young lady who had just captured his heart. Then he looked around at the barricades as he jogged down the Falls Road and realized that his brief encounter was an oasis in this desert of destruction. Before long, he had covered most of the distance back home from the Gransha estate.

Shane turned from the Falls Road onto the cul-de-sac he lived in. The street comprised two-up, two-down terraced houses with front doors adjacent to the footpaths on either side of the road. The McMahon's house had been extended to a third floor to provide a studio bedroom for his younger sister, Scarlet. After a hundred-and-fifty yards, he arrived at his front door. He opened it, removed his running shoes in the entrance hallway, and progressed the short walk to the kitchen at the back of the house. The door was open, and he was greeted by his mother Lily, who was busy putting away the groceries she had just bought into a stand-alone glass-fronted cupboard. He looked down on the short, slim figure of his mother, leaned down, and kissed her. "Hi, Mom."

"Hi, Son. Did you have a good run?"

"Yes, went well."

"How's your Achilles?"

"Tweaked it a bit."

"Will you be OK for the big race in a couple of weeks?"

"Hope so. I'll see what that specialist says when we go there during the week."

"Yes. Good idea."

Lily then put on an apron over her breezy light-blue frock and started to prepare vegetables for a soup for the family dinner. Shane moved to the parlor a few yards along the hallway. He opened the door. His father Brendan was at home sitting in his favorite chair by the coal fire, warming his hands while listening to the wireless radio.

"Hi, Da."

"Hi, Son. How did the run go?"

"Tweaked my Achilles a bit. I'll need to take it easy running for a while."

Brendan turned down the volume on the radio. "Oh, hope it recovers for the big race."

"Hope so."

"I heard on the radio there was a gun battle up the Glen. I hope you were nowhere near that," Brendan said.

"Heard it from a distance. Sounded like it was at Gransha."

"That's a relief. Sounded like it was a reenactment of the gunfight at the O.K. Corral. Glad you weren't near."

"That's Belfast these days."

"Yes, isn't it just? Maybe you could ask John Quinn about it when you see him in case he knows more. If anyone knew what went on, he would."

"Yes, Da. I'll speak with him this evening when I clock in."

Shane moved to the hallway and shouted out that he was going for a shower. He briskly ascended the staircase. He passed by the bathroom door and saw that it was shut, so he knocked.

"Will just be a minute," Scarlet yelled from inside.

He went to the bedroom where his youngest sibling, his eight-year-old brother Tyrone who shared the room with him, was lying reading a comic book in the lower bunk.

"How'd the run go, Shane? Anything exciting?"

"Yes, there was something exciting."

"What? Wow! Tell me about it."

A shout came from along the landing as Scarlet ascended the second set of stairs to her studio bedroom. "Bathroom free."

"I'll tell you downstairs, wee man," Shane said.

"Can't wait."

The shower was in fact just an attachment to the taps in the bath. It worked well and was necessary for a teen who was training regularly. It would not have been hip for him to go out smelling of sweat. Shane knew that his parents made sure that within their means their children were best looked after. Following a relieving shower Shane came back to his bedroom. It was empty. Tyrone had probably gone downstairs. Shane dried himself off and dressed. In the room were posters on the wall of the top distance runners Abebe Bikila and Dave Bedford. He had just ordered a new poster. It was of a little-known American whose work ethic in training had inspired Shane. His name was Steve Prefontaine, a student at the University of Oregon in Eugene, in the United States. Shane had a feeling that he would upset the Finns and Brits in the Olympics in Munich the following year. Shane had also just acquired a new pair of Adidas Gazelle running shoes. Shane, being Shane, had to place his mark on the shoes. He took them out of the box. Each blue shoe had three lateral white stripes on the outside. On both of the middle white stripes he neatly inscribed, Go Pre," in indelible black in, in honor of this emerging running sensation. In the corner of the room there was a rack housing two guitars, one a basic Scala, slightly smaller than full size, on which he taught others, and the second his cherished Martin guitar, ordered and delivered just a few months earlier from the manufacturing facility in Nazareth, Pennsylvania, in the States, on which he composed and occasionally played to others. In addition to those of his running heroes, he also had posters of his music heroes, Bob Dylan, Rory Gallagher, and Peter Green.

Shane came down to the parlor.

"Shane had an exciting run today," Tyrone said.

"Oh, I can't wait to hear what happened," Lily said.

Shane now felt obliged to discuss this experience. "Well, while on the run today I sort of bumped into a young lady."

"Did you know her before?"

"No. She's about the same age as me and in her final year at St. Dominic's."

"Nice to hear, Son. Will you be seeing her again soon?"

"Yeah, I'll be taking her out for lunch on Sunday."

Tyrone jumped in and sang, "Ooh, Shane's got a girlfriend."

"Well, this is just a first trip out. Nothing serious."

Lily gave Shane a knowing glance.

"I'll be meeting her at noon so I'll attend an earlier Mass."

Brendan had a puzzled look. "How did you meet her?" he asked.

"I accidentally bumped into her while was out for a run. So I struck up a conversation."

"Stopping during a run! She must have been worth it."

"Well, you have to look at the bigger picture, Da."

"OK"

"Sounds like a good Catholic girl," Lily said with approval.

"Yeah, Mom. She lives up in posh Gransha!"

"Wow, posh Gransha!" Tyrone said with excitement.

"What's she called?" Brendan asked.

"Siobhan O'Connell."

"Ah, yes. Sure, isn't she the daughter of Joe O'Connell, who has a chemist's shop on the Upper Falls? I believe so. Very good looking I hear. Good enough to stop in a middle of a run for, I'm sure. I hear that she's a very intelligent girl too. I was talking to Joe at the Eagle Inn last week. He says she's already won a scholarship to Liverpool University to do engineering studies," Brendan said with a smile on his face.

"Sounds like just the girl for you, Son," Lily said with a beaming smile on her face.

"Yeah, Mom."

Then Scarlet piped in. "So, Shane, if she's that beautiful and intelligent, why does she want to go out with you?"

"I guess she's just lucky."

"Ha. Ha."

"Must be those dashing good McMahon looks and charm!" Brendan said. Lily sent an approving glance Brendan's way and then disappeared into the kitchen.

Brendan took Keeper, the family's lean, three-foot-tall mongrel dog, most likely a cross between a rough collie and a golden retriever, out to the back garden.

"Would you like to hear a joke?" Tyrone said.

"Of course, little man, go ahead." Shane always had time for Tyrone.

"Knock, knock."

"Who's there?" Shane said, as per the normal response to this type of joke.

"Siobhan."

Now Shane was wondering where this joke was going. "Siobhan who?"

"Siobhan your knickers your Da's coming!"

Shane rose to his feet. "You little eejit Tyrone. I'm going to brain you!" Shane then ran after Tyrone, who ran for the stairs screaming.

A shout rang out from the kitchen. "Shane, if you lay a

finger on that child, you'll have to answer to me!" It was of course Lily. Shane stopped in his tracks and returned to the parlor. Tyrone made a funny face at him.

It was important to break in new running shoes, so Shane sat down and put on his new Gazelles.

"Mom, I'm just heading off to Granda's."

"OK, Son."

"Is there anything you'd like me to take down to him?"

"Please take the lambs liver in the pantry for his dinner."

"Will do, Mom." He collected the package and headed off.

After the twenty-minute walk, Shane arrived at a row of terraced houses near Grosvenor Park, just off the Falls Road. He progressed to his grandfather's house toward the middle of the row, knocked on the door, opened it, and walked in. Joseph McKeown, Shane's grandfather, was sitting by the fireplace.

"How are you doing, son?" said Joseph while warming his hands close to the fire.

"Grand, Granda," said Shane as he moved over to the fireplace and joined Joseph and warmed his hands also.

"You seem to be limping a bit. What's up?"

"Must have twisted my ankle a bit and strained the tendon while out on a run just after lunchtime."

"Let's take a look."

Shane sat down, removed his training shoe, and his sock.

"Plump it up here on my lap."

"Hm, yes looks like a slight tear and swelling. Not major but needs to be treated. Hold on here a minute."

Joseph eased Shane's foot back down, rose, and went out to the backyard. He returned carrying a metal bucket. As he came closer Shane could see it was filled with water.

"OK. Roll your jeans up on that leg and place your foot in the water."

Shane was a bit puzzled but complied. He plunged his foot into the water. "Aah. Jeez. Mother of God. It's freezing!"

"That's the point. Now leave it there while I make a cup of

tea and hear how you got on during the week with the physical therapist I recommended."

"You mean that I have to continue with this torture?"

"Remember. No pain, no gain."

"So, remind me, Granda, when was it you became a physio?"

"Oh, that's a long story. First, let me put the kettle on for a cup of tea."

Joseph went into the kitchen to make a pot of tea for them both. He then came back and sat down beside Shane while the kettle was heating.

"OK, your foot should've been in there long enough now."

Joseph dried Shane's foot in a towel. "Hold on a minute." Joseph then went upstairs to his bedroom and came back with his physio bag. "OK. Leg please."

Shane once again placed his foot on Joseph's knee.

"Extend your ankle." Joseph then applied a long sticky tape from under his heel, up and over Shane's Achilles tendon and onto his calf muscle. "Now, try to flex the ankle."

"Can't get it all the way."

"Great. We're good."

"I see. That'll prevent it from overstretching."

"You got it. Now, here's what you need to do. When you arrive home, grab a bucket, fill it with cold water, and put it in your backyard. After work tonight, grab the bucket. Then put a plastic bag over the foot covering all the tape so as not to get it wet. Then plunge the foot in the water for four to five minutes as we just did."

"Got it, Granda."

"When you shower, cover the foot. Do the cold treatment tomorrow morning and then evening. On Sunday follow each cold treatment with a basin of hot water, for about four minutes. Do that through Tuesday. This is the 'hot and cold' treatment."

"Oh yes, heard of it. Will do. Can I continue training?"

"Don't see any reason why not but take it easy until you see the physio. On Wednesday, is it?"

"Yes. I have one appointment this Wednesday evening and

then my last one the following Wednesday."

"Leave the tape on for your Wednesday meeting. However, explain to him what happened and what treatment we've done. See what he recommends."

"Will do. Thanks, Granda."

"Now, put your sock and shoe back on and walk up and down."

Shane walked up and down the parlor.

"How does it feel? Any pain?"

"Feels good. No pain."

"So, Granda. Back to my question on when you became a physio."

"Well, the physio work was not my first profession. I was an insurance salesman. However, when the big depression hit in the thirties, I realized I needed a backup plan."

"Were you still playing football for Armagh then?"

"Yes, indeed. In fact, at the time, I had just moved up to become captain and we were pressing for the Ulster title. Your mother was just a little'un, and your auntie Dierdre was just born. I saw this advert at the Gaelic grounds for night classes in physical therapy, so I enrolled and within two years was qualified."

"Did ya go full time?"

"No, I kept the insurance going as my first profession and then got a couple of evenings a week at the Mater Hospital. A few years later, as I was easing off the football, I was asked if I could help out with the Armagh team doing physio work."

"Didn't you also coach?"

"Sure did. It was a busy time. However, I wasn't distracted by things like the TV that are commonplace today. So Shane, how was your trip this week over to the physio chap I recommended with the golden touch?"

"It went well. However, the whole experience was a bit weird."

"What do you mean?"

"Well, Mom came over with me. It took a bit of time to

locate the address. It was a small-terraced house on a main road in an area we had never been to before. We knocked and were let in by his assistant. Then we were shown to a narrow staircase by the receptionist where we queued up behind about twenty people."

Joseph scratched his brow and considered. "Yes, I heard that he had a rather small, cozy practice. Not your typical therapy place."

"We waited for about forty minutes on the stairway. The door creaked open, one man exited, and all I heard was a shout of, 'Next.' It was for males only, so I went in. Mom had to stay outside, still squeezed on the stairway."

Shane fidgeted through his long locks as he continued. "Oh. When I squeezed into the room, the size of a small bedroom, there were about seven or eight people sitting on a bench on one side, and the physio examining a patient on a bench on the other side. He said, 'Sit down. I'll see you in line,' so I waited for about another fifty minutes."

"Why was the wait so long?"

"He went to the adjacent room to treat the ladies."

"I see."

"He reemerged later and treated the next guy in line."

A piercing whistle could be heard from the kitchen. Granda went in and soon reappeared with a pot of tea. He then went over to the sideboard and took out a couple of cups. Within a few minutes the tea was poured and being enjoyed. Granda leaned toward Shane.

"OK. Well, what did he say when he examined you?"

"He asked me to take off my clothes down to my pants. He stood me about four feet away and looked at me from all angles."

"So, he was being thorough?"

"Sure was. He then asked if I had had an accident about a year to two years ago. Well at first, I couldn't remember anything. Then a bit like a Eureka moment I exclaimed that something did happen to me."

"What was that?"

"It was that time I fell in the school swimming pool area and got my foot trapped. You remember I had to go to the A&E to get it treated."

"Yes. I remember that."

"Anyway, he said that an accident at about that time threw my back out."

"It's impressive that he could tell that from just one look at you."

"He dug his fingers into my back like they were below the skin and felt all around. He said I strained some muscles in my back that left it out of line and therefore putting strain down through my left leg, in turn pulling on the Achilles tendon. He said he could feel one disc was slightly bulging out but luckily not ruptured"

Joseph pondered this for a few moments. "So, he believes you are getting subsequent tears of the tendon because of the strain through the muscles in your left leg?"

"That's what he said."

"So, what did he recommend?"

"He asked me to slightly bend forward against the bench. He got me in what seemed like a wrestling grip, asked me to relax, and then he jerked hard."

"Did it hurt?"

"Not really, but it was strange. Now I do feel a release in stress in my leg."

"What did he recommend next?"

"Told me I needed to come back for two more sessions over the next two weeks. In between he asked me to apply a special liniment to my back."

"So, then your treatment will be finished before the Belfast Schools Cross-Country Championships?"

"Sure will."

"Well, that's good."

"Yes, I cannot wait to run without the thought in my head that the tendon will snap."

"So, he didn't do anything to your tendon directly?"

"Didn't touch it. He wrote a short note on the back of a cigarette packet and asked me to take it to the receptionist downstairs. Then Mom paid two shillings for a bottle of thick white liniment that I've been applying since."

Granda smiled. "Sounds like you're on the mend. Come back to me after your final treatments and before the championships, and we can talk tactics."

"Of course, Granda. Many thanks."

Shane then went into the kitchen and helped his grandfather prepare his dinner. As Shane was about to leave for home to get ready for his part-time job at the Eagle Inn, Granda went to his coat pocket.

"Here's a florin. Grab a taxi back from the Grosvenor and then a taxi to and from work. This should cover it."

"I can't really accept this, Granda."

"You can. Now be off with you."

BLISTER ON THE MOON

Shane rushed home from his grandfather's house and changed into a shirt and tie and smart dark trousers, ready for his evening's work at the Eagle Inn. He had started his part-time job as a bartender at the pub working for Mr. Quinn about six months earlier. This brought in some much-needed extra cash to support his interests in music and running. He began doing one evening a week and then had progressed to two at the beginning of the year, Fridays and Saturdays, the busiest evenings for the pub. He worked in the more refined part of the Eagle Inn, the lounge bar.

Shane caught a taxi up to the Eagle Road and was dropped off beside the front steps of the pub at six twenty-five just in time for his shift. A set of steps climbed up to the public bar designed more for the working classes with its noise, smoke, hustle, and bustle. An adjacent set of steps descended to the lounge bar, the quieter. more reserved area, often preferred by courting and married couples and white-collar workers. It served more spirits than beers, a corollary to the balance in the public bar. As he entered the lounge, he saw Mr. Quinn looking busy by the counter.

"Hi, Shane. Great to see you. We'll be having our cocktail session between seven and eight o'clock."

"Hi, Mr. Quinn. No worries. I'll get everything set up."

Shane approached the counter, lifted the flap, and went into the storeroom behind the bar. There he put on his Eagle Inn jacket and checked himself in a mirror hanging on the wall to make sure that the hair cream he had applied was keeping his long locks neatly in check. That is me ready now. Better get Mr. Quinn's spirits, liqueurs, and other bits and pieces ready for the cocktail evening event.

The pub was always busy. A lot of other bars in West Belfast had closed. Shane had heard rumors that Mr. Quinn paid protection money to the IRA to support the Irish freedom fight.

But whatever the case, Shane was glad to have his job.

Carrying a packet of a half-dozen eggs he reentered the area in the lounge behind the counter. He greeted his colleague who was wiping down the bar counter.

"Hello, Barney. How's things?"

"Can't complain, Shane. Will you be helping Mr. Quinn out with his cocktails this evening?"

"Sure will."

"Thank God for that. I was worried he'd be asking me. I don't have a clue what all the eggs and milk and liqueurs are for," said Barney wiping his brow.

"Me neither. I just set them up for him. He's very secretive about how he makes the cocktails. Says he'll take his recipes to the grave."

"Aah, part of the mystique. I think that's why he charges the big bucks."

"Yes. You know he charges almost twice as much as a glass of whiskey for a normal cocktail?"

"Go away."

"He does. And he charges a fifty percent premium on that for his signature cocktails," said Shane as he neatly laid out glasses on the bar.

"Wow. What a business. Do the patrons complain at the cost?"

"Not at all. They can't get enough."

Then a shout rang out from a waiter. "Shane. A wee Bush, a gin and tonic, and a baby lemonade."

"Coming Mike."

Shane walked up the bar. He served Mike and then saw the other waiter, Gerry, come his way.

"Hi, Gerry, what d'ya need for your tables?"

"Big order, Shane. Two glasses of lemonade shandies, two pints of Guinness, a whiskey soda, a gin and tonic, a brandy, and a Pernod."

"Will any whiskey do?"

"Yeah, no problem."

"I'll do the one on promotion, Cream of the Barley, then."

"Sounds good, Shane."

"Any orders from the bar?" Shane asked a few patrons sitting there quietly.

"Please top this up, Shane."

"Coming Dr. Crane."

"Anyone else before I get engulfed in the cocktails evening?"

"A wee Bush, Shane."

"Coming up, Peter."

After serving the waiters, both students like him, and the bar counter customers, Shane laid the contents for the cocktails on the back ledge under the bar mirrors and shelves. There was crème de menthe, green chartreuse, Pernod, Drambuie, advocaat, and several other spirits. Seven o'clock was approaching. The lounge was close to full. Then Mr. Quinn appeared, having returned from the upper public bar. "All ready, Shane?"

Shane beckoned over Mr. Quinn to inspect the layout. "I believe so. Anything else you need?"

"Some salt and pepper. And is there any cream?"

"No problem. Will be right up."

Shane delivered the other essential ingredients and then went to the front of the counter to take the orders. There was an orderly line of customers eager to get going. He could hear requests being shouted out.

"A Shamrock special."

"A Babycham surprise."

"A loaded advocaat."

"A Quinn special."

Shane wrote out the initial orders and passed them to Mr. Quinn. "This should get you started, Mr. Quinn."

"Looks good, Shane. It's going to be a bumper night."

"Way to go."

The next hour was permeated with the shaking of a metal cocktail container. The customers watched in awe. One shouted over to Mr. Quinn. "So, it was a bit of a surprise to us, Mr. Quinn, when you entered the All-Ireland Cocktail Shakers final," he said. "When you were trying those cocktails out on us a few months ago, we didn't realize how serious an activity it was for you."

"Wasn't sure myself, Roy," Mr. Quinn said. "It just sorted of developed as I went along."

"So how many were in the final?"

"Gee. There must have been about forty."

"Wow, and you came back with the All-Ireland trophy. Way to go."

"Yes, a pleasant surprise for me also."

Shane kept the orders flowing and did his best to make sure that Mr. Quinn could focus on making the cocktails. However, the patrons were keen to speak with the cocktail champion, and Mr. Quinn would not deny them a response.

"Love seeing the trophy behind the bar," a lady said as she approached the bar.

"Thanks, Allison."

"Glad you've set up a regular weekly cocktail evening. I look forward to getting in here each Friday for seven o'clock. Starts the weekend off well."

"Couldn't agree more."

Shane called out the completed orders. "Here you go, Mr. Albright. This one is yours, Mr. Baker. A Babycham surprise for Mrs. Eastwood."

When the initial rush had quelled, and Mr. Quinn had better time to speak with his customers, he emerged at the front of the counter and mingled with them. Some of the customers had heard about the shootings in Gransha earlier that day and knew that Mr. Quinn had had a close shave.

"We hear you were a hero today, Mr. Quinn," one regular patron said.

Mr. Quinn brushed it off as no big deal. "Well, I wasn't really involved, you know what I mean like?"

"We hear you helped save some casualties."

Mr. Quinn blushed at the compliment. "The commotion occurred further up the hill from me. I took cover until the shooting stopped and then headed back up to see if I could help with the injured. I ran back to my house and rang for the ambulances, and then Mrs. Quinn and I came out with blankets and pillows to help the wounded until the medics arrived."

"You're a hero to us, Mr. Quinn," a couple of patrons said.

He blushed again. Then a toast was raised.

"To Mr. Quinn!"

"Here, here."

Shane kept quiet, not wanting anyone to know he'd been in the vicinity of the gun battle earlier that afternoon. He was thinking that he didn't want his father, who would drink at the Eagle Inn from time to time, to find out he had been that close to danger. He was concerned that his father would be worried and that he may ask him to limit going out of the house. He also thought that he'd be annoyed that he didn't mention this to him. Better that he doesn't find out, Shane thought. Shane's attention then reverted back to delivering the orders. Over the din he could just make out someone saying to a friend, "Protection money has its perks. I bet the gunmen deliberately waited until Mr. Quinn disappeared down the hill and out of sight before opening fire."

As the evening progressed and eight o'clock arrived, Shane started to clear away the cocktail materials. He then returned to the normal duties of a bartender, serving the patrons at the counter and the waiters as needed. A couple of middle-aged businessmen were sitting at the counter and Shane could hear them discussing the escalation of the Troubles. Shane knew them quite well as they were regular patrons. However, he did not know exactly what they did. He remembered that Bernie, another of his bartending colleagues, had once mentioned they owned a business together that was doing very well. He had referred to them as self-made men. They were neatly attired in sports jackets, with shirts and ties. One, whom Shane knew as Conor, had a front tooth missing and often spoke with a sort of lisp. His bespectacled friend Peter was very deliberate in his delivery and distinctive looking with a well-groomed greying goatee beard. Shane felt Peter was more likely to be the main one who drove the business and made sure everything was on the straight and narrow. Both had Green sympathies from what Shane could make out, but he was also aware from some of their previous discussions that they relied on a relatively peaceful Belfast for their business to flourish.

Peter looked up from studying his folded newspaper and turned to his drinking partner. Peering over his glasses, which were part way forward on his nose, he said, "Conor, what's the place coming to with these random shootings? Do people think we live in the Wild West?"

"We're becoming the Wild West Belfast, Peter!" said Conor. "I catch your drift, but you've got to remember what the Falls Road was like a couple of years ago."

"Aye, I remember it well. That Orange crowd coming into West Belfast causing mayhem and burning anything they could see. What possessed them?"

"God knows. However, I believe they felt threatened by the Civil Rights marches. They were concerned about an erosion of their special privileges."

"What special privileges?"

"Probably centuries old ones when Ireland was captured by the English."

"Is it really a big deal?"

"It's always a big deal in this country."

"But where are these special privileges playing out?" asked Peter.

"You can see better opportunities for Protestants today than for Catholics."

"What d'ya mean?"

"How many Catholics are employed in the two biggest businesses in Belfast, the Harland and Wolf Shipyard and the Shorts Aircraft facility?"

"Gosh, never thought of it."

"Next to no one. Discrimination is rife! In fact, the number of Protestants unemployed in Belfast is very low, yet for Catholics it's amongst the highest in Western Europe."

"See what you mean. Well, we are European now. So, this will be sorted out before long. Do we need this mindless violence amongst our people?"

Just then another gentleman came over to the bar from one of the tables. "Shane, could you top this gin up with a bit more tonic? I'll never hear the end of it from Mary if it's not just right for her," he said.

"No problem, Dessie."

Shane took the glass, added more tonic and passed it back.

Then Dessie turned to Conor and Peter. "Couldn't help overhearing your conversation. We must get these English people off our streets and out of our land."

"But if we shoot them on the streets, the British will just send more troops," Peter said, "and then there will be more of them, not less."

He took a sip from his glass and Conor took over. "Dessie has a good point there, Peter. They're invading our country."

"It only seems like yesterday the army arrived to protect the citizens of West Belfast," Peter said.

"I remember well, Peter. All the ladies in the area were bringing out their best China and taking tea and biscuits down to the army blokes where they camped out at the corner of the streets. They were heroes."

"So, what happened to change that?"

"Beats me."

"I'll tell you what happened. They started to search houses in West Belfast," Dessie said. "They weren't quite like the Special Air Service who have a reputation of entering and leaving without a trace. Those fellas left a lot of damage."

"Yes, I believe that's what caused the resentment, and the IRA reemerged partly fueled by that," Conor said.

Then a person sitting quietly reading his paper at the end of the counter joined in. "If the army left, we would quickly be back to the devastation that was happening in the lower Falls a couple of years ago. We seem to quickly forget. Now we have gun battles in the streets and in front of our children. In fact, casualties amongst children are as high as for adults."

"God bless us and save us!" Peter said.

Then Dessie looked over to the gentleman. "I don't think we've met. How would you know what would happen if they left?"

Shane turned to Barney. "This looks like it may get out of hand. Should I go up and get Mr. Quinn back down?"

"Not yet, Shane. I know all these gentlemen. They're all pillars of our society. I believe they'll not escalate the discussion further. Let's wait."

The gentleman at the end of the counter slowly rose to his feet and reached across the bar in front Peter and Conor to offer Dessie his hand. They shook hands.

"No, we haven't met. I'm Paul Crane. I work down in the Royal Victoria."

"Pleased to meet you," Dessie said shaking his hand.

"I know because I operate on the casualties. Before the army arrived, we were working around the clock treating people. We had to pull in all the surgeons in the Royal Victoria and delay less serious operations. In fact, we even had to recruit some of the orthopods from Musgrave Park," Dr. Crane said. "We had new types of injuries, gun shots, severed limbs, severe burns. It was so bad we had to draft in experts to help from the U.S. and Middle East who had experience with these types of injuries. Once the army forces arrived, that subsided. Now we're opening that back up again, and we're seeing the casualties rise."

"Catch your drift," Dessie said.

Then Peter stood up and raised his glass. "Well, I believe that there is one thing we can all agree upon."

"What's that, Peter?" Conor asked.

"There'll be no more tea served to the army on the streets of West Belfast from here on."

"Yeah. Never a truer word," Dr. Crane said.

"Agree," Conor said.

"Here, here," Dessie said.

Shane was so pleased when the conversation petered out. He watched Dessie return to his table, Dr. Crane dive back into his newspaper, and Peter and Conor strike up a conversation on their forthcoming weekend trip to Strangford Lough for a bit of fishing.

Shane and his colleagues finished up at the Eagle Inn at about eleven-fifteen just after Mr. Quinn returned from taking the local general practitioner home in his car.

"Is that you finished for the day, Mr. Quinn?" Barney asked.

"Yes, finished now. Dr. Gillman is the third person I've had to drive home tonight. I got Gerry from the public bar to drive my car behind me each time to bring me back."

"We have to look after our clientele," Shane said.

"Absolutely. They're the reason we're here. They're our North Star. Can't let them be in danger or embarrassed just because they've had a bit too much to drink."

Barney and Shane finished up the cleaning of the bar counters, then went back to the storeroom, took off their Eagle Inn jackets, and hung them up. Mr. Quinn followed them in.

"Another full day in God's Country. Safe home everyone."

"Safe home, Mr. Quinn."

"Would you like a lift, Shane?" asked Barney.

"Much obliged, Barney."

Barney dropped Shane off at the end of his street on the Falls Road on his way back home to the lower Falls near the Clonard Monastery. As Shane was getting out of the car, Barney leaned over to him. "You know I was thinking back to the discussion at the bar. I was lucky a couple of years back. My property was just a couple of streets away from the main destruction that led to the Troubles. I just hope that doesn't return."

"You got it."

Shane got out and walked up the street to his house. He breathed in and cherished the gentleness of the cold air in his lungs and on his skin. It was both invigorating and calming. Belfast was peaceful now.

The following morning, Shane woke at about six thirty as normal. He enjoyed the quietness of early weekend mornings. Tyrone was unlikely to awake for another hour or so and hence Saturday and Sunday mornings were his times for reflection and preparation. He was lying in bed and thinking about what lay ahead of him this day, the one in which he would get for his upcoming birthday a new stereo unit. Yes, that'll be much better for the sound quality of my vinyl LPs, he thought. A couple of years ago he had been pleased to inherit his paternal grandfather's gramophone; however, it did not do his record collection justice. Glad that Da has got that good overtime pay, he thought. I doubt Mom and he would have agreed to the expensive gift without it.

Soon Shane's thoughts drifted to his other passion, running. He picked up and started reading his copy of the *Athletics Weekly*, the gospel for athletes in the British Isles. Every week he would read it from cover to cover, often imagining himself performing the feats of some of his heroes. "Wow, one on Ron Clarke," he said out loud in his excitement. Luckily, he didn't wake Tyrone, who was snoring in the bunk below. "So, Ron Clarke is saying you must look your best to give your best," he said quietly to himself. "I must make sure going forward that all my kit has been ironed and neatly folded. I'm sure Mom would agree."

Shane understood that there was a budget for the purchase of the new stereo unit but was not aware of the limit. He knew that the new record turntables were advertised with different features at a range of prices from twenty-five to fifty pounds. Just hope my parents have budgeted enough, he thought.

Brendan had given Lily the funds, which were now securely in her purse. She would accompany Shane. Brendan was up early to walk Keeper and see them off.

"Good luck, Lily. We're counting on you to get a good deal."

"Watch this space." Lily said.

"And Shane, remember that this is your birthday and your Christmas present!" Brendan said.

"Got it, Da."

Shane and Lily walked down their street to the Falls Road. Shane was sporting his new Gazelles and taking a further opportunity to break them in. He was thinking about how well the new trainers fit and that they should be nicely worn in within a week or two. No more blisters for me. Lily looked up at Shane as they walked. "How are the new trainers, Shane?"

"Smooth as silk, Mom. These are the best."

"Great to go out with my big son twice in one week."

"Thanks for coming along, Mom. And thank you for accompanying me to see the physio earlier this week. I've never been on that side of town before."

"Glad to come along, Shane. I also never really hit that part of town before. better not to have youths going there on their own." Lily then examined her purse. "Just checking that I have everything. All good."

They continued to the corner.

"So, did you put your linament on theis morning?" Lily asked.

"Sure did."

"How's it working?"

"Very well. Great feeling once it's applied."

"So, is that strain still there in the tendon?"

"It's improving. Following the work the physio did and applying the liniment, I can certainly feel less strain in my left hamstring and an ease it my calf muscle and Achilles' tendon."

They progressed to the Falls Road but did not go to a bus stop; rather they stopped and waited on the corner. A key aspect in West Belfast was that the buses were now part of the barricades network. They had been commandeered by the public to make roadblocks that weaved the length of the Falls Road to protect the inhabitants against further brutal attacks.

"Who would have thought that Black London taxis would be part of West Belfast everyday life?" Shane said.

"Yes, no one could have predicted that a couple of years ago. Anyway, thank God. This is the only way we can get around these days."

"And great to see that many of the adults in the neighborhood have a new income."

"Jobs are scarce here. Every cloud has a silver lining."

"Shouldn't be long now. They tend to come along every few minutes."

"Just hope that the next one stops. They often tend to get filled up at the Glen and Andersonstown."

"Well, if it's full, another will come soon."

"Here we go. Looks like this taxi is pulling over. There must be space for us both," Lily said.

"Looks like it."

The taxi pulled to a stop, and Lily and Shane jumped in, taking the last remaining seats.

"A shilling each please," the cab driver said.

"Here's a bob and two tanners," Lily said.

"Many thanks."

"Now for the horizontal rollercoaster down the Falls Road in and out of smoldering barricades," Shane said.

"You got it," the cab driver said.

"Why are the cars and buses in the barricades often set alight?" Shane asked the cab driver.

"Beats me. Can't fathom it."

"Must be the kids doing it for kicks and giggles," a middle-aged female passenger said.

Lily leaned in closer to Shane and progressed conversation in a whisper so as not to disturb the other passengers. "I normally take this route with Tyrone each day to get him to primary school. However, now he's turned eight years of age, he's telling me that he can travel on his own as that's what his classmates do."

"Yes Mom, he may need his independence going forward. I was going on my own from that age. However, things are getting very tense in Belfast these days, so the situation is different. You never know when violence could erupt at short notice." Shane fidgeted remembering his recent gun battle experience in Gransha.

"Yes, I know what you mean. Also, you were going only as far as St. Patrick's in Donegal Street, toward the center of town. The new Edmund Rice school is about half mile up the road from there. It would be a further ten-to-fifteen-minutes' walk. It's that extra part I'm concerned about. I just want to be sure he'll be safe."

"Other kids from his class will be taking that walk, so most likely he'll be fine. Probably better to go with him for a bit longer and see how the walk up is since this new escalation of trouble."

"Good advice, Son."

The taxi passed by the Royal Victoria Hospital and stopped to pick up passengers next to a barricade.

"Would you look at the state of those tires on that car?" Lily said. "They're worn done!"

"No big deal, Mom. That car is now firmly committed to the barricades and in fact is smoldering. Its driving days are over."

As the taxi progressed down the Falls Road, it came to stop. This was beside the public baths. Next door there had been a Mercedes-Benz showroom. Shane thought this was strange, as it was highly unlikely that anyone in the area could afford a Benz. He shook his head and thought what a shame it was that those great cars were now propping up the barricades. Sacrilege. What a waste of excellent cars.

"When I make my millions in music, I'll buy one of those Benz cars," he whispered to Lily. He pointed to the striking frontage of one of the epic cars stacked in the barricade at eye level.

"When you make your millions, Shane, I'll buy a Rolls-Royce," Lily said.

The people sharing the cab could hear this discussion and

burst into laughter.

In the lower part of the Falls Road closer to the city center, there was an even higher concentration of barricades. This is where the houses had been burnt out in 1969. Shane could see the buildings on each side of the road invariably had broken windows surrounded by charred black highlights, the aftermath of the many fires. Many of the buildings had been gutted completely. There were six passengers in the taxicab, including Lily and Shane. The driver had the slide window between him and the passenger side open. The daily news was blaring on his radio. There had been significant disturbances in the Middle East. Gunfights, bombs, and street protests were going on.

The cab driver turned back to his customers, "Aren't you glad you live in a civilized society?"

Shane looked out at the smoldering barricades and charred buildings beside him in the Falls Road and thought, Tell me about it.

Lily and Shane got out of the taxi at its terminus by the old St. Mary's school. The new school had moved to the upper Glen Road.

"Let's take the back roads to Bertolli's. Will be quicker," Lily said.

"Sure thing, Mom. Is the Bertolli Electrical Store the only one to have the new turntables?"

"Your father checked it out with some of his mates at the fire station. He was told that Mr. Bertolli managed to swing getting a large delivery several weeks before further deliveries would come to the city. So, it appears that he is the only vendor at present."

"Wow. He must be well connected."

"Sort of. He was in the same class as me at primary school. He had a certain nature about him even at that age. Better to say that he is a good wheeler-dealer."

On the way, they passed through a narrow street with men's and women's boutiques. This area was Belfast's equivalent of Carnaby Street in London. They stopped to look through the window in a Men's boutique. Both were struck by a jacket at center stage; it was a Kid Curry fur-lined leather jacket.

"Wow!" Lily said, thinking about the western *Alias Smith and Jones* that was broadcast every Monday evening on BBC television. The whole family were fans and would watch the cowboy series together. The jacket was a replica of one worn by one of the main characters of the series, Jed "Kid" Curry.

"Can you see the price, Shane?"

"Uh, it's one-hundred-and-fifty pounds, Mom."

"Gosh, what a price to pay for a coat these days."

They progressed on to Bertolli's Electrical Store.

"Now, Shane, I would like you to have a look and try out all the different systems. Let me know which one suits you best. Once you select your preference and let me know, then please make yourself scarce and leave me to Mr. Bertolli to complete the deal."

"Understood, Mom. You gotta do your thing."

Lily and Shane entered the shop, and Lily went over to the counter to greet Mr. Bertolli as Shane followed behind.

"Hello, Gerry. How's things?"

"Grand, Lily. How are you doing these days?"

"Great, Gerry. Only seems like last week that we were both competing in the Belfast Irish Dancing Schools' finals."

"Those were the days, Lily. Yes, where has the time flown?"

"Time and tide wait for no man."

"True saying. Now what can I do for you, Lily?"

"This young man has a birthday coming up. He would love to own one of your new stereo turntables."

"Oh, this is the runner I've been reading so much about in the *Irish News*."

"Sure is."

"So, Shane, I see the Belfast Schools' Championships are coming up soon. Are you ready for them?"

"I've been recovering from a bad Achilles injury, Mr. Bertolli, but I'll do my best."

"So, are you likely to medal?"

"I hope so if I run my best. The main thing is to help the St. Mary's team to victory."

"Go for it. As an ex-St. Mary's man myself, I will of course be rooting for you," Mr. Bertolli said. "Lily, may I borrow your son and take him through the new range of stereo turntables that have just been delivered from Japan?"

"Be my guest, Gerry. I'll just have a mosey round your shop and see what else you have."

Mr. Bertolli moved to the row of turntables with Shane. "As mentioned, Shane, these models have just come in from Japan. Amazing sound." The new turntables looked very impressive to Shane, who looked up at the row in awe. Mr. Bertolli explained the features of different models and tried some LPs for Shane.

"So, what are the extra features of the top-of-the-range one to the next one down, Mr. Bertolli?"

"With the top-of-the-range model you have an extra-long metal rod that can stack up to five LPs. It's also designed with a slightly higher specification of components that give the crispest sound. Here, let's try them out and see if you can notice the difference."

Mr. Bertolli selected a vinyl and placed it in the second down model. "Now listen," he said.

Although Mr. Bertolli's vinyls were of classical opera and not Shane's main easy listening, Shane was very impressed with the stereo sound. "That one sounded great. I can't imagine you'd get a better sound than that."

"Then you'll be pleasantly surprised."

Mr. Bertolli moved to the top-of-the-range model. "Let me show you how this model works. I'll place three LPs on the metal rod and play a sample from each record."

Shane listened attentively as the first track played. "I see what you mean, Mr. Bertolli. The sound is a bit crisper and deeper."

"OK. Let's drop the next LP. What do you think of it?"

"Yes, I can tell the difference. Amazing."

The top-of-the-range model was the one that Shane was most interested in. He settled on that model. It had the highest sales price of fifty pounds. He went over to his mother. "Mom, this is the model I like best."

"Trust you Shane to choose the most expensive one."

"Great sound. Great value," Mr. Bertolli said.

Lily discreetly beckoned Shane away. He went to the other side of the display but stayed within earshot and listened attentively.

"Now Gerry. How much do you want for this model?" Lily asked.

"Well, it has a sticker price of fifty pounds, but for an old school friend I could bring that down to say forty-five pounds."

"Well, it is for the lad's eighteenth. Why not let's say thirty pounds?"

"Oh. That would be robbery. The best I can do is forty."

"Gerry, you must have about fifty stereo players to sell. I'm willing to take one off your hands straight away. Let's say thirty-five."

Shane was listening and hoping dearly that a deal would be struck. He was worried that Mr. Bertolli would not drop to his mother's asking price.

"Lily, you know things have been tough for businesses in the city center since the Troubles started. Let's stick at forty."

"Gerry, things have been difficult for all of us in Belfast. Thirty-five is a fair deal and a reasonable knockdown. Just think that you can say to your next customers that you were the first to sell one in Belfast on the first day you displayed them. Let's send the boy into the Belfast Championships competing for your alma mater in a positive spirit."

"You have a way with words, Lily. You drive a hard bargain. Alright, seeing that it's his eighteenth, let's do it."

Mr. Bertolli stretched out his hand and Lily shook on it. Shane breathed a sigh of relief. Mr. Bertolli packed up the unit and speakers and put them in two large cloth bags. Shane carried one in each hand. They left the store and walked up the street.

"Mom, you were magnificent! Thanks."

"Only the best for my boy," Lily said with a little smile on her face.

Lily and Shane walked back by the side streets again.

"Mom, may I ask how much money Da gave you to get the stereo unit?"

"Thirty-five pounds."

"So, what would have happened if Mr. Bertolli was not prepared to come down to that?"

"No chance of that, Shane. I read up about the manufacturing cost of these new units and the profits being made. Rest assured that the profit Gerry made was rather attractive to him."

"Wow, I don't think I'd have the guts to negotiate like that."

"Well, when you kids were younger, and your father wasn't getting overtime, I had to negotiate for many things."

"Yes, I remember. When I started at St. Mary's, you bought me that new duffle coat. I remember the sales guy shaking in his boots when you were sorting out the price. I thought he was going to just give you the coat for free if you didn't reach a deal."

"That was a good deal for him also. He just didn't realize it when he was in the middle of the negotiation. Rest assured that he made a good profit on it."

"Wow. I still don't know how you pull it off."

"It's relatively simple. I'll let you in on my secret. You must do your homework first, and then you must put yourself in their shoes. Bottom line is that salespeople want the sale. You just must play that game of chess to figure out where a mutual deal is."

"Better you than me."

"One day, Son."

They caught a taxi by the old St. Mary's school.

"Should be home in about half an hour and then Shane you could try out your new present."

"Is that OK. before my birthday?"

"We'll make an exception this time. Anyway, your father is eager to hear how it sounds."

The taxi made good progress up the Falls Road stopping to pick up new passengers and dropping some off as required. As the cab approached the traffic lights before the Royal Victoria Hospital, an army blockade was in front of them.

"Wonder what this is?" Shane asked.

"The security forces have recently been stopping the taxis about here and quizzing the passengers," a lady sitting opposite him said.

"Yes, they'll just ask for your identification. Some people show driver's licenses, but as most around here do not drive, the majority use library cards," said the cab driver.

"I hear the libraries in the area have had a great surge in interest now that people need identification," Lily said.

The cab driver continued. "Better be aware that the army blockade is more about demonstrating that order is in place so that the news will be positive today. Reporters are usually close by, outside an exclusion zone set up with metal barriers. They'll watch from a short distance and report on the security operations in their press releases. The army often chooses this spot, between Grosvenor Park to the left and the new Sinn Fein office to the right."

"I bet they're also sending a message to the republican groups by camping out on the Sinn Fein headquarters' doorstep," the female passenger said.

"I bet you're correct. Anyway, nothing to be concerned about. The army guys are often quite pleasant."

That was the case this time. There were five passengers plus the driver in the cab. As normal, the driver showed his credentials first. Then in turn the passengers showed theirs. The female passenger was with her teenage daughter, and a middle-aged unshaven man, who smelt as if he had just left a pub, was the final passenger. They showed their credentials and were quizzed, and all was going well. Then Shane showed his identification and was quizzed on what school he went to, what age he was, and strangely what were his hobbies. When he mentioned music, the soldier perked up.

"Who's your favorite artist?" the soldier asked.

"That's easy, Bob Dylan."

"Great choice."

Then it was Lily's turn. She showed her library card identification and answered where she lived.

"What is your age?"

"It's impolite to ask a lady her age," Lily said, with a menacing look on her face.

The soldier politely asked the question again and received the same answer. "Sorry madam, I'm obliged to ask a prescribed set of questions. It's nothing personal."

"It's personal to me. It's impolite to ask a lady her age," Lily said, with a piercing gaze.

Then the soldier popped his bent neck out of the taxi and spoke with one of his superiors outside. Next a corporal bent his neck into the cab. "I'm sorry madam, but we need you to answer the question."

After several attempts and the same response, the whole cab was asked to disembark into the street. The rest of the passengers were not pleased at having to go through this ordeal but had no choice. The mother of the young girl threw a stern glance in Lily's direction.

"For God's sake woman you are going to get us all arrested," the slightly drunk man said stumbling to stand straight on his feet.

However, it was obvious that Lily was not going to be intimidated. They were lined up beside the cab while the corporal tried the question once more, only to get the same reply. It was damp underfoot, and Shane was careful not to place his shiny new Gazelles into any puddles.

"For God's sake, Mom, just give them your age!" Shane whispered.

"How dare you take the Lord's name in vain, Shane! You will go to confession this weekend."

Shane remembered that it had been drilled into him by Lily and Brendan not to argue or disagree with the security forces. He knew that this was because his parents were concerned that things could escalate, and arrests could be made. Now he was witnessing a situation where his mother was the one being resistant to a security force's question. Shane's breath became shallow. He was concerned they were going to be arrested. He could see that the other passengers were agitated. Why is Mom so reluctant to give her age, he thought. It really does seem to be a big deal to her. Shane decided to try to handle the situation and spoke directly to the corporal in a trembling voice. "I know my father was born in 1925, so my mother had to be born close to that."

"Well let's say she's two years younger than her husband. That would make her forty-four years of age," the slightly inebriated passenger said.

Lily jumped in. "Who do you think you are you little gobshite? Columbo?! What gives you the right to guess my age?"

The gentleman meekly shut up.

"Mom, you cannot use words like gobshite," Shane whispered.

Lily looked straight at Shane making him feel uncomfortable at rebuking her. After that the original soldier turned to Lily and said, "For Christ's sake Mrs. McMahon, just give us any age."

"Young man you should wash your mouth out with soap."

"Sorry Mrs. McMahon," he said, sheepishly.

An attending army captain, thirty-something, came across. "My name is Captain John Green. What's the issue here?" he asked in a posh English accent, turning to look round at the press.

"Mrs. McMahon insists she will not answer the question as to how old she is. She says it's not polite to ask a lady her age," the corporal said.

"I would think that the British army would honor the centuries-old etiquette and not force a lady to give her age," Lily said.

"I understand, madam. I can see that you do not want your age mentioned in public." The captain pondered for several seconds while gently rubbing his jaw. "Mrs. McMahon has a good point. Now let's see if we can resolve the problem here." he said. "How about this, Mrs. McMahon? I will ask your son one question and if he gets it right you may all go on your way."

"OK," Lilly said with a puzzled look on her face.

He then deliberated for a few more seconds and turned to Shane. "The private tells me you're into Bob Dylan."

"Absolutely," Shane replied, just so glad that his mother was not being asked her age again.

"OK. Here's your 'starter for ten'," said Captain Green mimicking the host of the popular television show *University Challenge*, Bamber Gascoigne. "At the Isle of Wight festival in 1969, who played lead guitar for Bob Dylan?"

The taxi driver and passengers all looked at Shane with rapt attention and with hopeful expressions on their faces. Shane pondered for a few seconds.

"Robbie Robertson," Shane said.

"Correct," said Captain Green. "Sorry to detain you. Please have a great rest of your day."

With that, all the passengers got back into the taxi. As Shane climbed back in last the captain noticed his new running shoes.

"Nice trainers, Mr. McMahon," he said.

"Thank you," a smiling Shane replied, pleased that his new hip running shoes were getting noticed.

With that the taxi started off. The rest of the trip continued uneventfully further up the Falls Road. Shane was in deep thought, puzzled at why his mother would go to such lengths to guard her age. Why would she put us in so much danger? I'll have a chat with Da and see if he can throw any light on it. He also thought about how restrained the army soldiers had been. He had not expecting that. In fact, he even had admiration for how obliging the captain had been and how he defused a very tricky situation. Intelligent guy, he thought. Really had a good grasp of people's characters.

Shane was eager to get back to the house and hook up his new record player. He sat the cloth bags containing the new stereo in the sitting room and then started to open them. He went to business, and very soon the stereo unit was ready. Shane ran his finger along his record collection trying to decide which would be the first album played on his new record player. He stopped and pulled out a Taste album. This was it. Their lead guitarist, Rory Gallagher, was one of the best blues rock guitarists around, on peer with the one in Cream. He read the list of songs. Shane smiled. What could be more appropriate after the day he had just had than "Blister on the Moon," a song of defiance and freedom? In the spirit of the moment, he beamed it out at high volume.

    Shane moved over to the front windows looking out into the street. The two upper smaller windows were open, and he could feel the freshness of the cool air hit his body as he breathed in. It felt invigorating. He spread out his arms, closed his eyes, and with no thought for his tender Achilles tendon danced energetically to the music. Brendan, Lily, Scarlet, and Tyrone came into the room. Shane was expecting his parents to tell him to turn down the volume. To his pleasant surprise they did not. They just came in and danced with their children. As Shane looked out through the net curtains, he could see that many of the neighbors had come out onto the street and were also dancing.

RELAX AND STRIDE

Shane woke up early on Sunday morning at his usual time about six-thirty, planned his week forward, and then focused on the day ahead. He would also take advantage of the quietness of the early morning to continue reading the *Athletic Weekly*. On this particular Sunday, Shane was thinking as well about an exciting engagement he had before going off for training. He had a lunch engagement at the Milk Bar on the Glen Road with Siobhan. In preparation he got up at about eight o'clock and took a shower. He came downstairs and went to the kitchen. A pot of tea was sitting on the table. He felt it and it was very hot. Just made, he thought. Somebody must be up early. He poured a cup and went to the parlor. Brendan was sitting there reading a paper.

"Wasn't expecting to catch you up so early, Da."

"Well, the early bird catches the worm. Anyway, your ma needs me to mend one of the kitchen chairs, so I'll be getting to it right after my cup of tea."

"Do you have a minute for a question, Da?"

"Anytime. How can I help?"

"Well yesterday Mom and I had a rather tricky episode with an army blockade, down by Grosvenor Park. The army was insistent that Mom give her age, but she wouldn't. It led to a very tense situation. Luckily an army captain was sympathetic and let her off."

"Not surprising."

"Why's that?"

"Well, if I tell you, then you need to swear to me that no soul will ever hear this from you, especially your ma."

"You've got my word, Da."

"Firstly, I'll start off by saying that your ma would never put her family in danger. If the incident had gotten worse, she would've come up with a solution. For example, she most likely would've asked to have a quiet word with the officer in private and then give her age. Secondly, in our generation it's not right for anyone to ask a lady her age. It's the normal etiquette we have been used to."

"Yes, I could sense that."

"You'll find this hard to believe, but your ma is actually five years older than me."

"What? Doesn't look it."

"Do I look that bad?"

"No, you know what I mean, Da."

"Just pulling your leg. In our generation it's not kosher for a lady to be older than her husband. There is a sort of, what shall I say, stigma about it."

"Why?"

"There's the implication that the lady has been left on the shelf and is desperate to get off it. That was not the case, I must state, in your mother's case. I know that she was proposed to twice before I proposed, once when she was twenty-one and once when she was twenty-six."

"And she didn't accept one of them?"

"Obviously not. Bottom line is that she was not in love."

"So, it took your charm, Da, to sway that."

"Dead on. I can definitely say we have always been deeply in love."

"Wow. This makes a lot of sense of how she has reacted over the years to this question. I understand now. Gosh, what a love story. I'm impressed. I'm honored."

"And so am I, Son, every day."

Shane got ready to leave for the nine o'clock morning Mass at Clonard Monastery.

"Must be off now, Da. Enjoy mending that chair."

"See you soon, Son."

Returning at about ten-thirty, Shane met the rest of the family just as they were leaving for their normal eleven o'clock Mass.

"Enjoy Mass. It's a beautiful day to walk down," he said.

"Will do, Son. Enjoy your lunch today," Lily said.

"Have a great meal and look after that young lady," Brendan

said.

"Look after that young laaady," Scarlet and Tyrone said together.

Shane gave them a stern look.

Shane arrived at the gate of the O'Connell residence at exactly twelve o'clock. He could see a mesh curtain rustle in the sitting room. He approached the front door. As he was about to knock, the door opened and a slim, well-dressed middle-aged lady with a smile on her face greeted him.

"Good to meet you, Shane. Would you like to come in? Siobhan will be down in a couple of minutes."

"Mrs. O'Connell, I presume. Pleased to meet you."

"Pleased to meet you too, young man. Now look after Siobhan. Won't you?" she said as Shane entered the hallway.

"I'll take the best of care with her, Mrs. O'Connell."

"Hopefully you won't have to jump over any more hedges."

"Hope not. It looks like someone restored your hedge to its glory."

"Yes, Mr. O'Connell is a dab hand with those sorts of things."

"Grand," Shane said. "Shame about the gun battle on Friday. Has this type of thing happened in Gransha before?" He stood fidgeting, wondering when Siobhan would come down.

"No, son. A complete shock to us all. It was dreadful!"

"I couldn't believe what I saw when I ran round the corner."

"Shocking. What is the world coming to with gun battles on our streets? I'll be glad when all this nonsense comes to a halt, and we can get back to some normality."

"Yeah. Know what you mean. Were any of your neighbors badly hurt?"

"Poor Mrs. Wilson across the way, who was tending to her roses in her front garden, was shot in the side. Y'know the bullet just missed her liver or it've been much worse. Mrs. O'Leary ran to her aid and on the way was shot in the leg. She was lucky too. Heard that it was just half an inch from her femoral artery. They were both very lucky not to be worse off. Mr. & Mrs. Quinn from down the road came with blankets and pillows to help them until ambulances came. Then the two casualties were whisked off to hospital."

"Yes, I saw those ladies from a distance. Was the gentleman washing his car hurt?"

"No, thank god. Mr. O'Reilly escaped OK. He'd just finished washing his prized Ford Zephyr and was in the process of polishing it when a hail of bullets piled through it. He was lucky to have gotten away with his life!"

"Yes, I saw that too. If Mr. O'Reilly needs any help with fixing his car, my Uncle Liam has a garage on Stockman's Lane. I'm sure he'd give him a good price."

"I'll let him know, Son."

Siobhan came downstairs to the hallway. Shane glanced across and was bowled over by how amazing she looked. He greeted her from a short distance but didn't embrace her.

"Thank you, Mother, for looking after Shane until I got ready."

"All part of the service, Dear. Now be off with you both and have a great time."

"Bye, Mrs. O'Connell," said Shane with relief.

Shane and Siobhan departed down the Gransha Park hill to the Glen Road. Five minutes more and they would be at the Milk Bar. Siobhan curled her arm around his and held his hand as they entered the Glen Road. Overcoming his nervousness Shane gently firmed his grasp.

"So, you were buttering up my ma then, Shane?" Siobhan said, egging him on.

"Uuh, just making conversation. Breaking the ice. You know what I
mean like?"

"I do indeed," Siobhan said, prodding Shane's insecurity.

Soon they came to the Milk Bar. They entered and a waiter showed them to a table. As the waiter departed to get the menus, Siobhan leaned over toward Shane.

"So, tell me something you've found out about me, Shane."

"You first."

"OK, no problem. Well, my younger brother Dermot is a couple of years behind you at St. Mary's. He tells me you and your two running mates, Paul, and Tim, I believe, are icons at the school."

"What?! If there are any icons, it would be the Gaelic footballers and the hurlers. They always come first," said Shane. "I suppose we're just flavor of the month because of the schools' cross-country championships coming up."

"Now your turn."

"Well, I know you have a scholarship for engineering at Liverpool University."

"So, you have been checking up on me then," Siobhan said with a grin on her face.

"Not really checking up. My da mentioned that he sometimes bumps into your father at the Eagle Inn. He said that your father is very proud of you."

Siobhan blushed slightly. Then the waiter appeared with the menus.

"Anything you fancy here, Siobhan?"

"Everything! Now, what shall I choose?"

"I'll go for the Belfast Fry," said Shane.

"Hope you burn that all off during your training," Siobhan said. "Now, what shall I go for? The bacon and cheese quiche looks good. I'll go for that."

They placed their orders, and the food arrived shortly afterward.

"Bon appetite," Shane said.

"Absolument."

"Tres bien. Parlez-vous francais?"

"Not at all. Just know a few words."

They tucked into their meals. As they were finishing off their plates, Siobhan looked up at Shane with a serious expression.

"Let's address the elephant in the room, Shane."

"What d'ya mean?"

"What's your position on the Troubles?"

"Wow. Was not expecting that."

"Well, it's important ya know in this country and I'd like to know where you stand on it."

"Understand."

Shane considered this for several seconds and then plucked up the courage to respond. "Aah. Well history would indicate that a united Ireland is a fair and just solution. However, I don't believe that anyone should die for it." Shane then paused for a few seconds to gather his thoughts.

"Go on," Siobhan said.

"How shall I put it? I've strong support for equality and the Civil Rights Movement. All people in Belfast and Northern Ireland have an equal right to their opinions and to live here freely and peacefully. I'm all for inclusion, and that's why I joined the Belfast United Harriers running club, which encourages membership from all sections of the community."

There was a pause for about twenty seconds as Siobhan appeared to be considering his response. Shane was fidgeting uncomfortably in his seat. Have I blown it, he wondered. He sat quietly awaiting a response. The silence was deafening to him but was eventually broken by Siobhan.

"Good answer, Shane. Anything different and I would've been straight out that door!" she said as her heart beat faster, "Now, tell me something about yourself that I don't already know."

"I've applied to Queen's to study music. I'm hoping I'll get the grades. Have always wanted to go to Queen's."

"Good. Go for it. So, do you play any instruments?"

"I play guitar and often compose songs."

"Now that's interesting. Tell me more."

"At the weekends when I have some spare time, I go out to our backyard with an acoustic guitar and work on rhythms and lyrics that come into my head during the week."

"So, when do these themes come into your head?"

"Basically, any time, but mainly when I'm out running, and my mind wanders onto other things. Now about you. Tell me one thing that will surprise me."

"OK, then," Siobhan said stalling for a while and taking the time to get the most appropriate story. "I'm part of an engineering team at St. Dominic's that has entered an Ulster-wide competition to build a battery-powered go-kart. Following the exams in June there will be a race-off up near Aldergrove Airport."

"Wow, I would love to see that. I also mess about with go-karts and old bangers in wasteland behind my Uncle Liam's garage in Stockman's Lane. He taught me how to race them."

"Great. Well, you better come along and see how we get on."

"Count on it."

There was a short silence, and then Shane continued, "So why Liverpool University?"

"There was an opportunity to get a sponsorship through university and work experience as well. That effectively guarantees you employment going forward. And to be honest I couldn't see a bright future here in Belfast with the Troubles progressing."

"Yes, see what you mean."

"I wasn't sure that I'd be accepted. It was a pleasant surprise."

"A great achievement."

"So, what did your folks say about you being caught in the gun battle in Gransha?"

"Nada, nothing."

"Not a word. Why not?"

"I didn't tell them."

"That's strange. Why not?"

"Well, for a couple of reasons. If they were aware I was that close to danger, they'd continually worry when I go outside."

"And the other reason?"

"I may be asked to restrict myself going outside."

"I see. Fair point. Unfortunately, I didn't have that option. My mother witnessed the gun battle from her bedroom window."

"Oh, I see."

"Also, she saw that heroic thing you did in getting ahold of me and ensuring that we jumped to a safe location."

"Wow, I didn't see that as heroic at the time. It was a must-do."

"Well, she was impressed. She said to me that she has only seen Steve McQueen and you do such a thing."

"Wow, being referred to in the same sentence as Steve McQueen. I'll take that as a compliment gracefully and cherish it!"

Siobhan leaned over toward Shane. "What's your favorite type of music?"

"Deep blues, and blues rock."

"A bit heavy for me. I prefer traditional Irish music and folk rock."

"Have you heard of Horslips? No albums out yet, but they're an up-and-coming Celtic rock band."

"Have I not? I hear they do a great live gig. I'm going to see them at Ulster Hall next Saturday evening."

"Go away. So am I. My eighteenth is coming up and my uncle Liam bought me a ticket for the concert."

"What a coincidence. My eighteenth birthday is also coming up soon, and my parents bought me a ticket. I'll be there with some of my school friends."

"Well, let's meet up at some stage during the concert."

"Deal."

They were finishing off their coffees when there was a minor commotion at the next table. There were two elderly ladies sitting at the table with a young waiter standing beside.

"I'll take the bill, Josie."

"No, I'll take the bill, Betty."

Then Josie grabbed the bill off Betty. Betty grabbed it back. "No, I'll pay the bill."

Then Josie grabbed the bill back. "No, I'll pay the bill, Betty."

This went on for a while. The bill ripped apart. The young

waiter was not sure what to do and went to get the manager. Shane and Siobhan were both trying hard to restrain laughter. The manager came to the table. He had two bills with him. He said in an authoritative voice, "Well Ladies, I hope you enjoyed your lunch. I have split the
bill into two equal amounts and suggest you each take one."

This seemed to do the trick. Peace broke out. Shane turned to Siobhan. "Then how will we pay our bill?" he asked.

"We'll go Dutch."

"But I thought I had to make it up to you for manhandling you and hurling you over a hedge?"

"Well, I need to pay my bit for the pleasure of having one hundred and thirty pounds of pure Irish beef covering and protecting me during a gun battle."

"Well actually, one hundred and thirty-five pounds."

"Then all the more value for me!"

Shane came home following his enjoyable lunch and got ready for the afternoon training at Queen's University. He then thought about how Tom Clyne, an Andersonstown businessman, had formed a cross-community running club, Belfast United Harriers, to remove sectarian barriers despite a lot of local opposition. Brave man bringing communities together in this environment, Shane thought. Great to be part of it. He's also managed to wrangle getting us permission to use the Queen's University facilities on Sundays at the Dub Lane. Paul, Tim, and Shane had joined the club. All local West Belfast team members would meet by Casement Park, the major Gaelic football and hurling ground, to be driven over.

Tom always asked the lads to meet on the corner opposite Casement Park at the end of a row of shops. This made it easier for him and the other carpool drivers to swing by and pick them up. Shane, Paul, and Tim turned up before any of their running colleagues at three o'clock on the dot. All three were about the same height at approximately six feet. Paul had shoulder length wavy auburn hair, whereas Tim had long straight fair hair that extended a couple of inches over his shoulders. Like Shane they both wore headbands in the colors of St. Mary's when they were going running. Paul looked up above at the red brick wall at the end of the shops. Something was different.

"What's this above us?" Paul asked. Shane and Tim looked up.

"Let's go over to the other side of the street to get a good look," Shane said. The trio crossed the road and looked up in amazement.

"Seems to be one of those murals that are popping up all over the place," Tim said.

"Yes, they're a recent theme in Belfast. The press loves to see them and often sends pictures of them across the globe," Shane said.

"So, what's this mural all about?" Paul asked.

"There's a patrol of grey-haired and balding elderly soldiers carrying rifles," Shane said.

"Oh, I see it," said Tim, nodding his head. "This is a throwback to the characters in *Dad's Army*. See the slogan at the top, 'No Tea for Dad's Army'?"

"Oh yes, I can see now. I like that show. All those bumbling old veterans set up during the second world war to protect Britain from a German invasion. You've got to laugh," Paul said.

"Yes, hilarious. My family never misses an episode," Tim said.

"Hey, I think whoever did this went the extra nine yards to make the soldiers look just like *Dad's Army* characters. Look at that one. Image of Captain Mainwaring," Shane said.

"Yes, see that. And the one on the other side looks like Private Frazer," Paul said.

"And the one in the middle like Lance Corporal Jones," Tim said.

Then they all mimicked the catch phrase of Corporal Jones as they danced around in circles. "Don't panic! Don't panic! Don't panic!" They fell about in laughter.

As the laughter eased, Paul continued in a sober mood. "So,

the British Army is being mocked. They're going to love that! What bright spark thought that one up?"

"Actually, it's a work of art. It could be a Cunningham, it's so good!" Shane said.

"What's a Cunningham?" Tim asked.

"Terry Cunningham is an up-and-coming artist in Belfast who's chronicling the Troubles on canvas. His art is attracting a lot of attention."

"Ooh!" Paul and Tim said, in a mocking way.

"So, you're now an expert in art, Shane?" Paul said.

"Not exactly. I saw a program on him on TV the other night. Anyway, it's not a Cunningham. He only paints on canvas as far as I know. Belfast must be spawning more top-quality artists."

"Sounds a bit artsy, fartsy to me," Paul said, causing everyone to laugh.

"Shall we head back over to our meeting point?" Tim asked.

"Prefer to stay here," Paul said. "Don't want to be standing underneath it if an army patrol comes along."

"Good point," Shane and Tim said together.

Just then, John McGee came around the corner and up to his three friends. He was a younger athlete, about sixteen years of age and a talented runner with great potential. At six-foot two he stood a couple of inches taller than the three senior athletes. His jet-black long curls hung down onto his shoulders as usual, but today his head was heavily bandaged.

"What happened to you?" Paul asked, with a look of amazement.

"I was supporting the demonstrations against the troops in Ballymurphy last night. One of the bricks I threw ricocheted off a large wheel of a Saracen and came back and whacked me on the head!"

Tim and Paul started to snicker. Shane nudged them and motioned to keep quiet.

"I was lying there bleeding on the ground and the motherfucker soldiers advanced past me. They just ignored me lying there bleeding out!"

"Hey John. I'd ask for a refund from that elocution teacher of yours," Tim said.

"What?"

"Never mind."

"The bastards, they didn't even stop to see if I was OK!"

Tim made a sign to Paul and Shane circling his finger close to his temple, signaling what an idiot John was. Then Paul moved to John and stared him eye to eye in a serious manner.

"You were lucky they didn't stop and beat the shit out of you. You're not going to have a successful running career if you carry on like this!"

Soon three cars arrived. The lads had been waiting for over fifteen minutes. Mr. Clyne was at the driver's seat of the first car. Tim leaned in through the open window and spoke across the passenger in the front seat to Tom Clyne. "Late from your time-management course again, Mr. Clyne?"

"Get in, wooden tops," Mr. Clyne said dangling his hands out, mimicking puppets from the popular kiddies' television program.

Tim looked over in the direction of Paul and Shane and winked. Everyone was amused that Tim managed to get a dig in on Mr. Clyne's tardiness. Tim and Paul got into the car with Mr. Clyne, while Shane and John took the second one and squeezed in the back beside a guy who had been picked up earlier. Others who had arrived took the third car. The vehicles took off for the university training grounds at Dub Lane.

The university grounds were like a Shangri-la within a war zone. Shane always felt a sense of freedom running in the grounds and down along the towpath by the river Lagan. The most experienced lads went out for a fifteen-mile run, and the others including John McGee for about ten miles. They started out together as usual and quickly formed into groups.

"Six-and-a-quarter-mile pace here," Paul said. "Unless you want a quicker pace and head off with the senior group."

"With you," Shane said.

"Me too," Tim said.

Then Pete McGuirk from St. Malachy's Grammar School and Phil Laverty from Annadale Grammar School joined in with them. Pete was about five foot ten and had short cropped dark brown hair. Shane knew he would be a key rival at the upcoming championships. Phil was a lanky guy, standing six-foot-four. He too would be a contender, however, Shane was confident he would beat him so long as his tendon didn't flare up. Always good to have Phil in the race, Shane thought. He starts off fast and then suffers a bit for it. Shane, who always preferred to start off conservatively, would often catch him within half a mile and then tuck in behind for a while, as Phil shielded him from the wind. The groups settled into a steady cadence, and friendly banter commenced as normal.

"So, guys, is anybody going to try and take our crown at the weekend?" Pete asked, referring to his St. Malachy's team.

"We're going to have a crack at you. We'll most likely be only able to get one or two runners in the top ten, but we should pack the rest strongly," Phil said, on behalf of Annadale.

"Well, we at St. Mary's hope to give both your teams a run for your money," Paul said.

"We hope to get three runners in the top ten," Pete said.

"We should do as well," Tim said. "We hope to be ahead of you with our top three."

"Maybe, but our St. Malachy's team is likely to pack the rest better than you. Our team is full of seasoned runners. Sure, aren't you using hurlers and Gaelic footballers to make up your numbers?"

"That's our trump card," Shane said. "It's true that we'll close in with hurlers and footballers, but they're all top notch in their sport and preparing seriously for the cross-country run. They train five to six times a week. They'll be ready."

"Game on!"

"I believe we've flogged this subject to death," Paul said. "Let's leave it now for the battlefield."

Tim eased over to run beside Shane. "So, I hear you had a heavenly date today, Shane."

"What? How'd ya know that?"

"A little dicky bird told me."

"Is nothing sacred anymore? Beats me how word gets around."

"Not only that, but we also know who she is."

"No way!"

"So, are you going to tell us all about it?"

"Absolutely not!"

Everyone fell about laughing as they worked to keep moving forward on their run. Shane was wondering if they really did know whom his date was with. However, he was not prepared to discuss it further.

"So was this your first time out socially since that embarrassing episode with your ma?" Tim asked.

"What? What d'ya mean?"

"Oh, he means the experience at the cinema in early December," Paul said.

"Oh that. I was trying to forget that."

"What happened at the cinema?" Pete asked.

"Long story," Paul said.

"Well, we have a long run for this long story. We're all ears," Phil said.

"You remember the cross-country club race at Beaver Park in early December?" Paul asked.

"Oh. Yes."

"Well bright spark Tim here mentioned to Shane and me on the way back that the Dustin Hoffman movie *Midnight Cowboy* was playing at the ABC and that because it was X-rated, they had put on an X-rated support which just happened to be a soft-porn movie," Paul said.

"So of course, we couldn't let Tim go on his own, so we said we'd come," Shane said.

"Of course."

Tim picked up the story. "We got into the ABC even though

we were all under age. The place was just about a quarter full, so we had a good choice of seats. We went down the center aisle about halfway and then midway along a row which we had all to ourselves. We were just discussing what we were about to see, when I turned around, looked back up and saw three middle-aged ladies sitting in the back row. I looked again as one looked like Shane's ma. So, I nudged him and whispered to him that I thought his ma behind us in the back row."

The guys burst into laughter, then Shane continued the story. "I said to Tim that he had to be joking. He assured me he was not. So, I turned around gingerly and sure enough my mother was sitting there between two of her friends."

"Why were your mother and her friends at an X-rated movie?" Phil asked.

"Well, every year for the Christmas Tree ceremony at the City Hall in early December my ma meets two of her old school chums. They go to the ceremony, check out the city lights, and then often finish off with a meal. This year they decided to take in a movie afterwards. They saw that a cowboy movie was on, so they went to the ABC."

"Jeez!"

"So, I told the guys to crouch down in their seats as it was unlikely we would have been seen. We did that. Soon the lights dimmed, and then the support movie started," Paul said.

"I was sitting there praying to God that none of the actors or actresses would take off their clothes. At first it was encouraging as the main character was in a subway train in London and everyone was fully clothed," Shane said. "However, when this character blinked, he could see everyone naked. Well-bosomed attractive females in full display; the lot. I then prayed to God that my mother hadn't seen me."

"So, what happened?
Tim picked up the story from here. "The movie finished, and the lights went back on. The ice-cream ladies went down to the front of the auditorium just in front of the screen as normal and stood at the end of each aisle. Shane's ma got up and went

down past our aisle and bought three ice creams. You know, the oblong-shaped ice creams in paper with the oblong-shaped cones. Obviously, we thought these were for her and her two friends."

"We were confident she hadn't seen us. She came back up the aisle. Then she stopped by our row and came across to us. She asked if we enjoyed the movie and handed us the ice creams," Paul said.

"What did you say?"

"Tim and I thanked her. I don't think Shane said anything. He was looking pale. She then went off and back to her friends."

"As *Midnight Cowboy* was about to start, I looked back, and they were gone," Shane said.

"What did you do when you got home?"

"I knew I had to say something to my ma. So, I saw her alone in the kitchen and asked her what she was doing at the cinema. She said that after their meal she and her two friends thought it was a good idea to go and see a cowboy movie. I said to her, 'But it wasn't a cowboy movie,' to which she replied, 'Well, we didn't realize this at the time.' Anyway, my ma then asked me what we were doing there. I just said the same thing, that we wanted to see the acclaimed movie, but that we didn't realize what the support movie was about."

"What did she say to that?"

"She turned to me and said, 'Do you think I came down the Lagan in bubble.' Then with a smirk on her face she said that would be the last we would talk of it."

"Wow. Glad it wasn't my mother," said Tim. "She would have beaten the bejesus out of me."

"Well guys. Thank you for the therapy session. I'm over it now and up and running and going out socially again."

"You got it. As your mother said Shane, this will be the last time we speak of it."

"Can I have that in writing?" Shane said with a glint of irony.

The guys continued with their run and progressed to other

topics. In just over an hour and a half, they came back to luxury showers at the Dub Lane facility. Tom Clyne had a reputation for staying in the showers much longer than everyone else. He would invariably still be in the showers when the other groups got back some thirty minutes later. The group often joked that the shower was his main objective and not the training part. When the lads arrived back, the coaches were as expected in the showers. There was a long bay of showers. The guys came into the shower room and grabbed a bay each. Shane was next to Paul.

"So, you should be OK for the big race in a couple of weeks' time."

"Hopefully. I see the specialist guy I've been going to on Wednesday, so I'll see what he says. If all is good, then I can join you for the fartlek session on Thursday."

"Sounds like a plan."

After a bit more friendly banter, this time at Mr. Clyne's expense, it was a drive back, and for Shane a couple of hours studying before bedtime.

Shane met the specialist the following Wednesday. He decided to keep the support tape on so the specialist could see how he had been managing the ankle.

"Looks like you had some good treatment there," said the physio to Shane, with a group of about seven male patients looking on. "Who strapped you up?"

"My grandfather. He used to work as a physio."

"He knows his stuff. Did a good job. I assume he had you on hot and cold."

"Sure did. He said to come off it today."

"Makes sense. What's his name?"

"Joseph McKeown."

"The Joe McKeown who physio'd for the Armagh Gaelic team?"

"Yeah. Do ya know him?"

"Haven't met him but heard of him. In fact, when I was

training for my physio exams, I studied one of his pamphlets. Helped me enormously. Please send him my best regards. Maybe one day he and I could meet up for a beer."

"Sure. I'll let him know."

"OK. Let's have a look at the tendon."

Shane held the foot up, and the physio bent down and examined the heel.

"I'm going to press around it. Tell me if any area hurts." The physio prodded around the tendon. "No pain?"

"No. Not so far."

"Well, your grandfather's treatment did the trick. Looks like you had a small tear with a bit of inflammation. But it seems to have healed now. All looks good."

"Oh. Grand."

"I'll fix a restricting tape onto it. Keep it on till you see me next week. Try not to get it wet. No need for hot and cold now."

"Great!"

"OK. Now let's get to your real problem. Take you shirt off so I can look at your back."

The physio examined Shane's back and got him to maneuver into weird angles as he checked things out.

"Disc looks to be back in place. That's most important. Still a bit of work to do on alignment."

He then grabbed Shane once again and yanked him at certain points.

"Yes, that looks better. One more session should do it. See you next Wednesday."

As Shane was leaving, the physio shouted after him, "Keep applying the liniment."

"Will do."

The next evening Shane went out for a fartlek session on his own. Paul had a family function and had to pull out of their planned training session. Shane was thinking about his tendon as he upped the pace of his initial warm-up. He had planned to sandwich a four-mile fartlek stint in-between two

two-mile steady sections. The warm-up went fine. He pushed hard in stretches of four hundred yards down to sprints of fifty yards. The Achilles was holding up well. On his warm-down he thought back to when he was a young lad, about eight years of age, when he would often play about running races on the street against his friend Ron. Being taller and almost a year older, Ron would always win. Shane was improving but could not see much hope. He explained this to Ron who decided to let him into his secret.

"I'm not beating you because I'm older and taller. I'm persevering despite hurting badly to win, and not showing you my pain," Ron said.

This was succinct and Shane thought about it. "So, what I need to do is to keep going longer despite hurting badly?" he asked.

"That is the long and short of it. Most people give up when they are hurting. Winners go the extra nine yards. Remember that your competitor is also hurting, and it really comes down to who has the will to win the most."

This was a message that Shane carried through to his successful performances in the early stages of his school running career. When he was competing in under-fourteen 800-meter and 1500-meter track races or in three-mile road races, he would force himself to hang on a bit longer. This often delivered the desired result. Winning seemed easy to me then, he thought. How has that mentality deserted me? He realized that nowadays his mind focused more on his injuries during races than on pushing forward when he could. This was distracting him from a pure focus on winning or achieving his best performance on the day. He realized these doubts that had crept in never gave him a fair crack of the whip to show his true talent. Now that my Achilles is on the mend I can get back to that winning mentality. I'll apply this at the Belfast Champs.

The following Saturday, Shane enjoyed a very rewarding eighteenth birthday, made even more exciting by going to the

Ulster Hall and meeting up again with Siobhan. Shane as agreed bumped into Siobhan and her friends at the end of the show.

"An electric performance as expected," Shane said.

"Yes, fabulous," the girls said.

Siobhan's friends then said they were off to buy some tee-shirts, largely as an excuse to let Siobhan have some time on her own with Shane.

"Following the Belfast Champs next Saturday there will be a disco at St. Mary's in the evening. Would you like to come along with me?" Shane asked.

"Only if your team wins, Shane. I will not spend an evening with a bunch of 'Sarky Sues' crying into their beers."

"Got it. I'll tell the lads then that we must win just in case they had any misconceptions. I'll meet you at your house at say seven o'clock and we can walk up then."

Siobhan smiled in agreement. Her friends then returned wearing Horslips tee-shirts.

"Well, we better be off home," Siobhan said.

She moved over to Shane, stared into his eyes, and in front of her chums gave Shane a kiss on the cheek, much to his surprise. Then Siobhan disappeared off with her friends. Shane stood on the spot bewildered and took a few minutes to regain his composure. Then he too headed off home.

Later the following week, on the Thursday evening before the Belfast School Cross-Country Championships, Shane once again visited his grandfather. As normal, Granda made a pot of tea and the two sat down at the dinette table.

"What did the physio say, Shane?"

"He was very impressed with your work, Granda. He said it was spot on."

"Grand," Joseph said slightly blushing.

"He said he used one of your physio pamphlets when he was studying for his own physio qualifications."

"Wow. That little paper. Glad it came in handy."

"Here's his phone number. He'd like you to call him and

suggested you both might meet up for a beer one day."

"I may just do that."

"On Wednesday I went for my last session. He had applied a tape the previous week a bit like yours which he asked me to wear up to then. He told me to do some hard runs with it on to test the tendon. He checked my foot again on Wednesday and gave the all clear. I no longer need the tape."

"Grand. Now, what about your back?"

"He worked on it both Wednesdays. He said the disc is back in position and that I now have proper alignment. I'm good to go!"

"Great!"

"So now for another topic, I was toying this thought over since we last met, Shane. Seems to me that you need a goal to get you back to your best."

Shane had heard many stories of his Granda's great sporting exploits from Lily. Joseph McKeown had been an elite Gaelic football player and captained his county, Armagh, to win the Ulster Championships. Lily often explained to Shane how he had overcome adversity and injuries to reach his peak. Shane knew he understood the mentality required to get to the top and was an excellent strategist. Shane was also thinking about his last few races where he bottled out of pushing hard at the right time. He knew he needed something to perk up his confidence and drive him back to the performances he used to deliver. "How's that, Granda?" Shane asked attentively.

"What is it that you want to achieve?"

Shane thought for a while, rubbing his chin. "I want to run in the World Cross-Country Championships for Northern Ireland. However, it's gotten back to me that many people at the club don't think I can make it."

"Do you believe you can make it, Shane?"

"I'm finding it hard to see how I can beat the elite athletes who are currently on the team."

"There is one person I know you can beat, Shane."

"What do ya mean, Granda?"

"You can beat yourself!"

"What? Please explain."

"Do you feel you can give the extra nine yards to beat your last performance?"

"Yes, I can do that."

"Then focus on beating yourself. Always set the standard against yourself. Push to just give that better performance each time in training and racing. Can you do that?"

"Sure, I can".

"Then focus on that and do that and beating the elite athletes will take care of itself!"

Shane was surprised at his Granda's direct approach but motivated by this advice. He decided then and there that he would set himself targets accordingly.

The Belfast Schools Cross-Country Championships took place at the Bog Meadows on the Andersonstown Road. Because of the location, adjacent to Milltown Cemetery where violence often broke out, there was a strong army presence as the school buses arrived. The elite athletes from St. Mary's warmed up together. They were nervous in advance of the race, but that was important to get the adrenalin flowing. Before a race Paul was always focused, staring ahead as if oblivious to others. Tim would be joking around, his way of releasing tension. Shane knew he needed to step up and ensure team spirit and unity. He made a point of getting the full team together, nine runners in all, for a team huddle just before the gun went.

"Now remember, six to score but the remaining three of us can push back other teams' runners and help the cause. At the end we are all a team and there are nine medals if we pull this off. Now three cheers for St. Mary's!"

They let out three big cheers and declared themselves ready. The competing teams could see this. Shane could see from some of their faces that this show of strength and confidence set their competitors back a bit. We now have the upper hand, he thought.

The race commenced. Paul, Shane, and Tim went to the front and pressed the pace. This was part of their race strategy. Pete McGuirk and Greg Hollow from St. Malachy's kept on their shoulders, as did Phil Laverty and Mike Barr from Annadale. There were three laps. As Shane came round to complete the first lap, he could see his parents and siblings cheering him on, a bit further along was his uncle Liam, and then to his surprise Siobhan and her parents. This gave him extra motivation. The pace picked up on the second lap as Paul, Tim, and Shane to plan worked together to drop off the others. Shane was feeling the pace but remembered his granda's advice and worked hard to beat himself. As they entered the final lap, it was just the three of them together at the front.

Paul pushed harder. Shane's legs were burning, and it was getting difficult to hang on. He thought back to his childhood friend Ron's advice and stayed longer than comfortable at the front with Paul and Tim. He held on as long as he could but then had no option but to fall back a bit. Tim looks to be suffering as well, he thought to himself. If I recover to a comfortable cadence, I may be able to pick him off. Shane focused strongly on this strategy, slowing a bit to a comfortable pace but keeping close enough to the two in front in case one dropped back. He could see Tim trying to stick with Paul but then dropped back rapidly as if he had "blown." Shane soon caught him. Now he had a dilemma. He would normally push past a rival quickly before they got a second wind. However, he was worried that Tim might drop back further and be passed by the St. Malachy's and Annadale rivals, which would hurt the team's chances. He looked back and could see Pete and Phil running together some twenty yards behind. He knew Tim and he had to stay together. Although it was a risk that Tim could recover to beat him, he couldn't afford for him to falter further. He caught up with Tim. "Can you hang with me?" Shane asked.

"Will try," Tim said with a gasp.

"Almost there. We need the first three for the team."

"Count on me."

Soon they both eased into a comfortable stride pattern. Halfway around the lap Shane could see Tom Clyne on the sidelines and heard him yell, "Relax and stride. You've got this."

Tim was showing a resurgence but was still breathing heavily. Shane nodded over to Tom as they passed to let him know they would hold the course. Shane and Tim entered the final straight together with about one hundred and fifty yards to go. Shane was thinking of his grandfather's advice to give that extra bit to beat himself. He was doing this in training and now had to transfer this to racing. He took a deep breath and pressed hard even though he was suffering with a burning feeling in his chest and pain in his muscles. He summoned up the will and sprinted off leaving Tim in his wake.

When the race finished, all three St. Mary's elite runners medaled, with Paul as expected winning and Shane just heading Tim for second place. Now they moved to cheer on their colleagues. The team event was very tight between them and St. Malachy's. Joe O'Loughlin, who was more known for his Gaelic footballing prowess, put on a final sprint to pass four runners in the straight as he was cheered on by his three colleagues. He came in twenty-eighth and was the sixth and final St. Mary's scorer. St. Mary's just managed to beat St. Malachy's to the team gold medal by one point. Joe was the hero.

The St. Mary's Christian Brothers had granted the cross-country team the school assembly hall for a disco that evening. The runners and many friends met up for a wild and rewarding event. There must have been about one hundred youths present. Siobhan accompanied Shane. The music and craic were great. Shane was thinking that this was and felt like victory. As a senior member of the victorious team, Shane plucked up the courage to do his best to get around and speak with as many of those who turned up as possible. He introduced Siobhan to Joe O'Loughlin, "This is the hero of the hour. He's the captain of our Gaelic football team."

"Pleased to meet you, Joe. I was down at the Bog Meadows

today and saw you sprint down that final straight," Siobhan said.

"Well, I could hardly do anything else with Shane, Paul, and Tim waiting for me in the crowd in the final run in and shouting to me that my finish was critical. I had to leave it all out there."

"You certainly did. That was an impressive sprint."

"Yes, surprised me as well. However, it was easier than I thought it would be. I was feeling exhilarated by the thought we could win if I picked up a few spots."

"It made all the difference. Pipping that St. Malachy's runner on the line pushed the victory from them to us," Shane said.

"It was the least I could do for you guys. It was great to be part of the success."

John McGee came across and whispered into Shane's ear. "May I have a moment of your time, Shane?"

"I always have time for you, John. Siobhan, would you excuse me for a few minutes?"

"No problem. This is your gig, and you need to mingle."

Shane walked off to a quieter spot with John.

"I know this isn't the correct time. However, I'd appreciate a chat with you Shane when you have some time next week. Things are getting worse at home, and I'd appreciate your advice," John said.

"Sure thing, John. I have time later in the week as I ease down for the Ulster Schools' finals. How about Thursday evening?"

"Yes, that works fine."

"I was planning on doing a ten-mile easy run at say about six-and-a-half-mile pace. I could run up to your house, and you could join from there, and then we could loop back to your place before I head for home. That would then be about a six-mile steady-paced run for you. Would that work?"

"Yes, fits well."

"Then I'll call by your place at about six-thirty, and we can have a good talk while we run."

"Sounds good. Thanks Shane."

Shane made his way back to the bar where he had left Siobhan. He noticed her speaking with his wild cousin, Dan, from the Ardoyne area. He had come over for the celebration. His mother had arranged for him to stay at his Auntie Lily's in the Falls that night. Wild he was, with a six foot two frame and larger than life. As Shane approached, he noticed Dan holding Siobhan with an arm around her in a sort of friendly way. Then his hands started to wander.

"Would you please decouple yourself from my girlfriend?" Shane said to Dan in a cordial manner.

"So, one lunch and concert Shane and suddenly now I'm your girlfriend!" Siobhan said with a wicked grin.

"Sorry I didn't mean to assume..."

"As the man said please leave his girlfriend alone," Siobhan said to Dan as she eased him away.

Everyone laughed, and Dan headed off in the direction of the dancefloor. "She's a right one, Shane," Dan shouted back.

Shane could see Dan hurling himself toward a ring of attractive young ladies dancing around their handbags as Black Sabbath's "Paranoia" boomed out. Soon the next song started, a softer track from the local hero with the dolce tones, Van Morrison. It was "Brown Eyed Girl." Shane turned to Siobhan. "They're playing our song," he said, in a corny fashion.

"You now owe me another trip to the Milk Bar for that lame cliché."

With that they migrated to the dancefloor and danced the night away.

There was a heavy schedule of cross-country fixtures coming and Shane had generally prepared his training runs to accommodate this. Monday came along, and Paul and Shane were training together and talking as they were coming toward the end of their workout. They had completed the fartlek part of the run with just a couple of miles to go.

"So, it'll be important to ease down towards the end of the

week, Paul. Want to be fresh for the race and I want to protect my Achilles."

"Dead on, Shane. Definitely ease down on Thursday and Friday. You're running with John on Thursday, isn't that right?"

"Yeah. That'll just be an easy run."

"I'm tied up on Thursday evening, however, I could join you for say a steady five mile run on Friday."

"Deal. Say, five-thirty?"

"Works for me. I'll run over to yours."

"Also, we need to get the team pumped up on Saturday, especially as we have a few novices."

"Well, they're seasoned Gaelic footballers, so well-conditioned. However, know what you mean. You're the people person, Shane. That'll be in your court."

"Got it. I'll come up with something to fire them up."

To be able to get good distances in around Belfast, they had to run through different sectarian areas. They entered an estate considered mainly Protestant and took a side street through.

"Just a couple of miles to go, Shane. How're you feeling?"

"Feeling great. I'm running on air following the Belfast Champs at the weekend. Achilles is a bit tender but standing up well."

"Can't wait for Saturday."

As they were coming through the estate gun shots rang out. Both came to a halt. Then Shane noticed that Paul had been hit. He was bleeding out badly. Shane could see blood seeping from his tracksuit top near his side and left arm. Then Paul eased down onto one knee. Shane crouched down beside him.

"How badly are you hurt?" Shane asked in shock.

"I felt two piercing cuts, one in the left arm, and one through the right side of my stomach."

"Lie down and relax. I'll get help."

What should I do, Shane thought. Oh yes. Must stop the bleeding immediately and then go for help. Must prioritize the stomach wound. He took off his track suit top and pressed it against the stomach wound. "Hold this tightly to the wound."

OK. Now the arm. He removed his headband and tied it around Paul's arm above the wound pulling it tight to restrict the blood. "This should ease the bleeding."

Shane heard a noise and looked up. To his horror he saw three masked gunmen running toward them. Oh my God! Shane thought. Then a cold sweat broke over his whole body, and he started to shake at the shocking realization that they had been the target of the attack. Although he could not fathom why, he realized that worse was likely to come. He could take no evasive action. He stayed firmly fixed to the spot applying pressure to Paul's stomach wound. The gunmen approached. One came across towards them and aimed his rifle in the direction of Shane and Paul. Shane heard the rifle cock and then the petrifying bellow, "Take that you Prod bastards!"

TEARING US APART

Shane stared into a gun barrel as one of the gunmen stood above him. "We're Catholics. We're just out for a run!"

The other gunmen had stopped in their tracks several yards back. "How do we know you're not lying?" one of them shouted over.

"We run for St. Mary's Christian Brothers Grammar School in the Glen Road," Shane said trembling.

Then one of the gunmen said to the others, "They're telling the truth. They were part of the team that just won the Belfast Schools Champs. I saw their photos in the *Irish News*."

The three gunmen stepped away, but Shane could still just make out what they were saying. "We were sent out here to do a job, and we can't do that properly. God knows how I'll explain this one."

"Can we not move to another street and complete the mission?"

"No, the place will soon be crawling with the forces. Must head off now."

The three gunmen started to run off. Shane shouted after them, "Can one of you ring for an ambulance? I must keep pressure on the wound."

There was a phone box at the end of the road. To Shane's relief one of the gunmen did enter it and made the call. Twenty minutes later an ambulance arrived.

Shane accompanied Paul to the Royal Victoria Hospital. Paul was taken in for emergency surgery. An hour or so later Paul's parents arrived. Shane was standing by the reception desk. He waved over to Paul's parents and joined them. "So sorry about what happened to Paul."

Mrs. Nairn visibly upset and still in shock replied, "You have nothing to apologize for Shane. You saved his life."

"Well, he won't be able to win the Ulster Schools

Championships now."

"There are more important things in life. I'm so glad that he's alive. Just need the news from surgery. George, when did the surgeon say he'd be out?"

George decided to check with the front desk. "They say not for another forty-five minutes Joan. Would you like to come down to the café for a cup of tea?"

"Yes. Let's do that. Shane, would you like to come along?"

Just then Shane saw his Uncle Liam arrive through the entrance slide doors. "I see that my uncle has just arrived. I'll hang on here for a few minutes, and we'll join you soon."

As Mr. and Mrs. Nairn headed off to the café, Liam came over. "Lily and Brendan asked me to drive down to the hospital immediately while they got ready and grabbed a taxi. They'll be here soon. I offered to loop in and pick them up, but they insisted I go ahead straight away. Got to do what big sis says."

"Yeah, I understand, Uncle Liam. Thank you for coming."

Shane's Uncle Liam was the only one in the family who had a car, a Ford Vauxhall Viva. He was often called upon in needed situations for lifts. When Brendan and Lily arrived, they together with Liam and Shane met up with Paul's parents in the hospital café.

"No word from the doctors yet?" Lily asked.

"Hopefully soon."

Paul's parents were distraught. His mother continued to sob. About an hour later they were called to the reception outside the operating theater. The operation had been a success. Mrs. Nairn burst into tears of relief.

"Paul is out of the danger list but has lost a lot of blood," the surgeon said. "I suggest you go home and come back tomorrow."

"Can we see him?" George asked.

"If you're up to it. I just want to prepare you; he's still under the effects of the anesthetic so he's not conscious."

"I just want to see my boy," Mr. Nairn said with a quivering and painful voice.

"Please follow me."

Liam spoke with Lily, Brendan, and Shane for a few minutes and then drove them back home. The euphoria of the few days earlier had turned into despair. As he departed, Shane muttered to himself, "Welcome to Belfast."

The following morning Paul's parents were due to visit the hospital. Shane decided to ring through to them after lunchtime to find out how Paul was doing. Mr. Nairn answered the phone.

"Hello, Mr. Nairn. Shane here."

"Hi Shane. We got great news this morning that Paul is off the danger list."

"Oh. Great!"

"The surgeon said he should make a full recovery, and he was confident that Paul should be able to get back to top-class running."

"That's great news!" Shane said. "Just wondering when I may be able to visit him."

"The doc said only immediate family should visit today, but tomorrow is fine for other visitors."

Brendan was a firefighter and was the hands-on leader to a team of eight. He was often away for a few days at a time, invariably tackling the fallout of bomb blasts. Many businesses were being bombed. The family was used to these absences. Brendan would not discuss difficult cases but would often have a chat with Lily on the less troublesome ones and explain where he had been. The kids sometimes were within earshot and would be keen to hear how their father braved the dangers and helped rescue people and put out the fires. On that Wednesday evening Brendan returned from an overnight stay away and was telling Lily and the kids about a fire he tackled. Shane returned from visiting Paul and sat down with the family to listen.

"I was called out to Holywood in the early hours of the morning. There was a fire in one of Harry Dee's pubs."

"Where's Holywood?" Tyrone asked.

"Holywood is just outside Belfast. On the coast on the way

to the seaside at Bangor."

"Do we pass it on the train when we go to the seaside, Da?"

"I believe we do, Tyrone."

"Who's Harry Dee?" Scarlet asked.

"He's one of the area's top businessmen. He has a string of pubs across the counties Antrim and Down."

"Oh, yeah. I've seen him," Shane said. "He sometimes comes up to the Eagle Inn and meets Mr. Quinn.

"Yes," Brendan said. "All the pub owners and managers in the Belfast region tend to have an alliance. It works through the Bartenders' Guild, I think. They even have a golf league that John Quinn plays in."

"Oh, yes. I've heard of that," Lily said. "There was a program on it last week on TV."

"Da, did you see John Wayne in Hollywood?" Tyrone asked.

Tyrone was well versed in Hollywood heroes as Lily often talked about the movie stars. Brendan smiled and put Tyrone on his knee. "This is a different Hollywood. It's special to Northern Ireland. It's so special that it has its own unique spelling. It only needs one 'L' whereas the one in America has two."

"So, do we have movie stars as well?"

"No, instead we have good pubs, beaches, and golf courses."

"Oh, I see," Tyrone said. "Disappointing Da, but I'm glad that Ireland also had a Hollywood."

Shane knew his parents were very concerned by his dice with death. He put on a brave face but was not hiding his distress well. He was aware that his parents would have discussed this several times and that his mother would have asked his father to have a heart to heart with him. He could see that Brendan was working up to speaking to him on this tricky topic.

"Shane, do you have a bit of time to accompany Keeper and me on a short walk?" Brendan asked.

"Of course, Da. Where are you taking Keeper?"

"Oh, just up the road to the Falls Park. Although it's dark, the lane up to the grass bowling green area is lit up."

"Sure thing. I'll get my jacket."

"Dinner will be ready in an hour," Lily said.

"No problem. That works well. We'll be back by then," Brendan said.

Brendan grabbed Keeper's lead, and they departed. As they reached the Falls Road and moved up toward the park, Brendan started the conversation Shane knew he would.

"You know in this new Belfast we must live with and deal with terror every day."

"Yeah, I know very well, Da."

"How are you bearing up after Monday evening?"

"Doing my best, Da. But I wonder how much longer I can keep this going here."

"I understand, Son. Does that mean you are considering leaving?"

"Not really. I very much want to go to Queen's University. However, I get the creeps when I think how those guns were pointed right at us."

"I don't blame you. It's a hard thing to deal with."

Soon they reached the Falls Park and progressed up the main avenue to the grass bowling pavilion. There was a bench there, so they sat down. Keeper obliged by lying down underneath it and staying quiet. Brendan and Shane breathed in the serenity.

"It's hard to believe after such a devastating episode that this land we live in can be so peaceful at times," Brendan said.

"That's a beauty that's always been here," Shane said.

"Let me explain how I handle things, Shane. Maybe it can be of some help?"

"Thanks, Da. Go ahead."

"D'ya remember when we returned from our vacation in Carnlough a couple of years ago just after the devastation in the lower Falls Road commenced?"

"How could I forget? I remember it well. In fact, I've an indelible memory of looking out from the raised walkway at the central train station over Belfast, toward the city center, and then along Divis Street and the lower Falls Road. I could see that the sky was red, fed by flames from beneath as Belfast burned. It reminded me of my impression of Rome burning from my history lessons."

"Yes, it sure did. Well, you may remember me asking taxi drivers to take us back home."

"Yes, I do. If I remember correctly most refused."

"That's right. Everyone was afraid of going up the Falls Road because of the danger and concern that their taxis would be taken for the barricades."

"Eventually, you got one who said he would take us."

"That's right. However, he said we couldn't get up the lower Falls and that we needed to route through a dangerous Protestant area, the Shankill Road. This is not somewhere Catholics would go by choice."

"That's right. I remember we went up there and people were outside, standing on the streets. However, they didn't stop us, and we meandered along some side streets and alleyways before emerging out on the Falls Road by Andrews Flour Mill."

"Yeah, and I can tell you that this was one of the scariest times of my life. Your mother and I weren't sure we would all get through that area safely. The last thing we wanted was to put you and your sister and brother into danger."

"I remember you both letting out great sighs of relief as we emerged by the flour mill."

"That's correct. That day stays with me. It makes me shudder to think of it. It's something I must come to terms with. I find that it gets easier with time. You'll find the same."

"I understand, Da. I never thought you'd be disturbed by anything."

"We're all disturbed. The key is how we handle it. We must be strong. That helps greatly."

"Yes, I get it. Thanks, Da."

"Now Shane, please speak with me at any time if you have concerns. The Troubles in the province will come to an end at some stage. We'll get to the end of this. The key is to manage these situations and not let them destroy your life."

"Got it, Da."

"Well, must be getting back now. Don't want to be late for dinner or I'll have a greater authority to answer to."

Shane ran over to Ballymurphy on the following evening and met up with John McGee outside his house at six-thirty as planned. They progressed down Monagh Road to Kennedy Way on route to Lady Dixon Park on the upper Malone Road.

"Shocking what happened to Paul and you on that run!" John said.

"Yes, really disturbing. Could have been worse. We're both still alive, which is the main thing."

"How's Paul doing?"

"He's on the mend but has a long way to go. I was down with him yesterday and he was sitting up and in good form. In fact, the surgeon said he should get back to running by the end of the year. I'll head back on Friday afternoon and have a more detailed chat with him. I didn't want to overdo it yesterday."

"Great to hear. Please pass on my best wishes to him when you visit on Friday and tell him I'll visit early next week."

"Sure thing."

"Are you still OK speaking with me on my issue? Seems minor in comparison."

"No worries, John. Let's get out of Andy Town before we get into it."

The lads focused on their run without further discussion until they cleared Andersonstown and were approaching the Malone Road. Then Shane asked, "How can I be of help, John?"

"I'm thinking of giving up school and running."

"Aah! What's brought that on?"

"Things aren't good at home. Ma's nerves are gone, and she's hitting the bottle badly. The kids are not getting fed properly and not being looked after well."

"OK. Let's take this one step at a time, John. How old are your twin sisters and your younger brother?"

"The girls have just turned nine years old, and Sean is seven."

"Your mother, isn't she the top ballroom dancer?"

"Yes, was. Her partner has always been my da, but since Da had a collapse and angina diagnosed they haven't been going to dancing. He can only move at a slow pace, and Ma spends most of the day in a soft chair, watching TV, smoking, and getting drunk. The kids are missing out."

Shane considered this carefully. "OK. I get it. Let me ask you a few questions."

"Be my guest."

"Didn't you do well in your O-levels last year at St. Joseph's?"

"Yes, well in some."

"But enough to get you to A-levels?"

"Yes. I excelled in languages so am now studying French, Spanish, German, and Gaelic, of course."

"Wow, four A-levels. Do you enjoy taking these subjects?"

"Absolutely I do."

"Well, you're just one year from taking your A-level exams, so it would be a shame to drop out now. Education is the best thing we have going for ourselves in West Belfast. It's our ticket out if we choose to take it!"

"Suppose so."

"Why consider giving up running?"

"Well, it would give me the time to look after the younger ones. I would get a job and be able to afford to feed and clothe them properly."

"Fair point. However, do you enjoy running?"

"Love it."

"Last month you broke one-fifty for the indoor 800 meters in the meet in Glasgow. I'm aware of only one other Irish junior who has done that time. When the outdoor season comes along, you're likely to get international honors."

"Suppose so."

"Well, why throw that away? Let's see what your other

options are. Does your elder brother bring in money to the family?"

"I believe that Colm gives Ma some, but most of it's going to booze and ciggies."

Shane pondered on this for several seconds. "OK. here's an idea. Would Colm be open to giving you, say, a quid or so each week?"

"Yes, I think I could swing that."

"Then ask him. With the money go to Smith's the grocer, Hourihane the butcher, and McCallum at the bakery. I know they've been sympathetic to families in need. I'm sure they'll give you a good deal. It may be yesterday's bread or vegetables and some offcuts of meat, but they'll be very nutritious. Then say, for example, twice a week, make the family a good meal."

"OK. I can do that."

"Great. So, stay the course in your studies and keep the running going."

"Will do, Shane. Many thanks."

The two of them pressed on around Lady Dixon Park and then made their way back through Andersonstown to Ballymurphy. The time seemed to whizz by as they talked. Shane parted company with John at the base of his street and then kept on the Monagh Road, followed by Springfield Road, which led to the Falls Road and home. He thought about the plight that John was in. There but for the grace of God go I. Hope John will work on that advice.

On Thursday evening Brendan brought back fish-and-chips for the family. Shane had just finished his run and showered. Everyone sat down at the table in the kitchen. Brendan dished out the meals, neatly wrapped in newspaper.

"This one's for you Tyrone. Here's yours Scarlet with mushy peas. A fish supper for Shane, and for Mom, a deep-fried halibut."

"Thanks, Dad," said the kids.

"Thanks, Bren. Always great to have the family together for a carryout," Lily said.

They all tucked into their meals and were partway through when the phone rang.

"I'll get it. Hope it's not your work, Bren," Lily said.

She disappeared into the hallway and arrived back less than a minute later. Her look toward Brendan said it all. Brendan rose and went to the hallway to take the call. He then returned to the kitchen.

"So much for the best laid plans. Must go now. There's been a major accident on the Queen's Bridge in the city center."

"Understand. Travel safe, Bren."

"Good luck, Da," the kids said.

"I'll be home as soon as I can."

Brendan departed and walked down the street to the Falls Road where he caught a taxi to the city center.

After being dropped off at the old St. Mary's school, Brendan took the short walk in the crisp evening air to the Queen's Bridge. As he approached, he breathed in the fresh air knowing this would be his last calming moment for a while. He had taken trips at short notice such as this one before and most led to a grueling job in hand. He embraced this responsibility conscientiously. He braced himself and approached the Queen's Bridge. He stopped abruptly as he surveyed what was in front of him. Brendan was taken aback by the number of fire engines and army Saracens on the bridge. He moved closer and could see two cars smashed, coupled together, and merged around a large metal lamppost, that had bent over but was still attached to the bridge. It was leaning toward the river at an angle of about forty-five degrees. He realized this was not going to be an easy operation. He prepared himself for a few seconds and then moved quickly to his team which was in position by the carnage. He went to his next in command. "Report please, Geoff."

"Doesn't look good, Bren. Four student females in one car wrapped around the lamppost. Two seriously hurt, and the other two with non-life-threatening injuries."

"What's the deal with the other car?"

"Apparently a sectarian group in the car opened fire on the army convoy as they drove by and got more than they bargained for in return. A Saracen was close by, caught up with them, and moved to force them to the side of the road as the gun battle continued. The car was slightly pinned and moved onto the bridge. The car with the students was coming the other way, and they collided. Because the Saracen was abutted to the first car, the one with the students got trapped between that car and the bridge wall. As they continued, the cars got forged together, and the students' car wrapped around the lamppost."

"Jeez! Status on the sectarian group in the other car?"

"There were four in total. Three shot and killed outright. The other with minor injuries. We extracted him, and he's been taken to the hospital."

Brendan moved with Geoff over to the mangled cars. "I see now," he said. "You can't decouple the cars for fear the remaining one will fall into the river."

"You got it."

"Status on the young ladies?"

"One accidently shot through the arm, but otherwise OK. A second with bad injuries due to the crash but should survive. The driver and back passenger on that side seriously hurt with crush injuries."

"Got it. So, we can't remove the two closest to us as that would reduce the weight stabilizing the car?"

"Yeah."

"Therefore, we'll need to stabilize the car by other means before we can extract the occupants. OK. I'll speak with the army captain and get help to obtain the materials we need."

Brendan left and explained everything to the attending senior army personnel. Several soldiers were sent to get wire cables and additional equipment. Brendan then spoke with the ambulance crew.

"Hello gentlemen. Here's the deal. We'll need to stabilize the cars before we extract any occupants. We should have that completed in the next hour. However, I'm concerned about two of the occupants. They may need medical help now. Can you come and assess?"

"Understand," the chief paramedic said. "Joe and Harry, can you come over please?"

The head medic explained to his men and the two paramedics went with Brendan and checked the young ladies. As they approached, one of the injured ladies cried out, "Help me. Please get me out of here!"

A paramedic in a calming voice replied. "We'll do that as soon as possible. May I ask your name?"

"Anne."

"Well, Anne. My colleague and I will check out you and your friends now and treat you initially before we remove you. This is most important. We will need you to stay calm."

"We'll do our best," she said and then cried out in pain.

The medics moved into action. Just as they grabbed the essential materials from their bags and were coming back, Brendan could feel a pull on his jacket. He was shaken initially by this but turned around gently. He saw the seriously hurt driver tugging at him. He looked into the car and could see that her legs were badly broken and bleeding out. She had multiple injuries. She was struggling to catch her breath, but was able to whisper, "I don't want to die. Please get me out of here."

"We're here to help. Please stay calm. We're moving as fast as we can."

The materials and tools that Brendan and his team needed were delivered within twenty minutes. His team went diligently to work securing the cables to stable anchor points on the opposite side of the bridge and to both mangled cars. Meanwhile the medics were working as best they could on the young ladies. They were removed within the next forty-five minutes. Sadly, one had died. The others were taken in ambulances on the short distance to the City Hospital. The chief medic updated Brendan and the army corporal with the news. With trepidation Brendan asked, "Which of the young ladies didn't make it?

"The driver," the chief medic said.

Brendan was gutted. He thanked the medics and the army corporal for the great work done to save as many people as possible. He then grouped his team in a huddle and thanked them. After that, it was back to the fire station, just half a mile away for a full debrief and write-up.

At eleven o'clock that night Brendan arrived back home with his head bowed and the trickle of a tear rolling down his face. Lily was there to meet him. She went over and hugged him.

"We lost one," he said.

This was not the first time that Brendan had returned in such a state. Lily did not ask any questions, rather she gently eased him onto the sofa and put her arms around him.

"Just a young girl. A student at Queen's. She wanted to live."

"Now, there Bren. I know you did your best."

"Could easily have been one of our kids. She was about the same age as Shane. How can we look after our children in this place now?"

"This is our home, Bren. This is their home. This'll not last forever."

"Can't see an end to it. Do you think we should move to the South or England?"

"They don't really want us, Bren. The South says it's our problem, not theirs. England says we're the enemy. We'd be discriminated against in both places. In any case you'd be bored. Just think of all the good you're doing here."

"I just want my family to be safe. I just want our kids to be safe. I fear for Shane, as he now becomes an adult. What future has he got here?"

"I know how you feel Bren. Keep the faith. Things will work out. You'll see."

The shocking story of the shooting of Paul had spread throughout Belfast and, of course, through St. Mary's school. Shane attended the school assembly each morning where prayers were said for a speedy recovery for Paul. Shane visited him again on Friday afternoon. At the time he arrived, he was the only visitor. "How are you feeling today?"

"Strangely very good. It must be the meds they have me on. I'm really pleased the surgeon said the operation was a complete success and that I should get back to full fitness and running at my best by the end of the year."

"Yes, it's a good sign you're sitting up and thinking of getting back to running."

"Absolutely. How's the team doing? Is it ready to go for it tomorrow?"

"We're all prepared. Just missing our star man."

"Sorry to let the team down."

"Hey man, the team is running for you."

"I'll be rooting for you all. Just hope the team qualifies for the All-Ireland Championships."

"We'll leave it all out there, Paul. No problem."

The following day the Ulster Schools Cross-Country Championships took place in Barnett's Park, near Shaw's Bridge, by the river Lagan. Shane reckoned that if the runners who had scored in the Belfast Schools performed at the same level and if their sixth scorer could get into the top seventy, they would qualify. The race started. Shane stuck in close to Tim toward the front. Near the end of the first of three one-and-a-half-mile laps, Tim and Shane were in a breakaway group with Pete from St. Malachy's, two guys from a school in Derry, and one from Fermanagh. Shane had settled in and was feeling comfortable. He could hear the shouts from supporters in the crowd. At the end of the lap, he passed his family. A roar went up from them. "Go for it, Shane!"

Fifty yards further on, Siobhan, her brother, and her parents were waving Shane on. Then he saw his godparents, Liam and his wife, Clodagh. He was most buoyed by the fact that Clodagh, a relative recluse, had come out to support him. He was moving well but his thoughts drifted to the shooting. He was thinking that Paul should have been in this race and if so, would have been pushing from the front.

The race progressed. It seemed to fly by. Suddenly in the distance Shane could hear a bell ringing and an official shouting, "Last lap." He could hear shouts of encouragement.

"Go Shane!"

"The team needs you, Shane. Go for it!"

The shouts seemed distant to him. Then there was a loud cry. "Bollocks, Shane. Wake up!"

Shane recognized this voice. It was Tom Clyne. The searing bellow woke Shane out of his daze. He looked ahead. The group he had been with was now some hundred yards in front of him, ascending a steep hill. In between, about fifteen runners had passed Shane, and he was now down in the twenties. He could see Tim pushing at the front. That's where I should be, he thought with frustration. He gritted his teeth and pushed hard. He passed runner after runner. Following a final blast down the finishing straight he came home seventh. Oh Jeez, what have I done? I've let the team down, he thought.

St. Mary's put up a gallant effort, but without Paul and a below-par performance from Shane, they came in eighth and just missed qualifying for the All-Ireland finals. However, Tim medaled in second and Shane qualified for the All-Ireland finals as a fastest loser. A runner from a school in Derry came in ahead of Tim. Shane met up with Tim and did a warm-down.

"Well done, Tim. Second place. Great!"

"Thanks Shane. Impressive to see that finish of yours."

"Should have done better. Let the team down."

"You're a stalwart! A few points wouldn't have made a difference. If Paul would have been in the race, then Mickey's eighty-third place would be substituted with most likely a first. The extra eighty odd points would have placed us second behind Derry. Just bad luck what happened to Paul and you."

"Thanks, friend."

As they came back toward the start, a scout from the American university Villanova came across and spoke with them both.

"Sorry to hear what happened to Paul, and to you Shane," He said. "I'm Father Maguire. The university would like to offer you both scholarships. We also have one set aside for Paul for his recovery."

"Thank you, Father," Shane said.

"Yes, please send the offers in, Father," Tim said. "We've been talking about going to Villanova."

Shane visited his grandfather once again the day after the Ulster Schools Championships. Joseph approached and without saying anything hugged him as he came through the front door. Then as normal he put on the kettle. "Are you happy with your performance yesterday?" he asked.

"Wasn't all there, Granda. It was a half-decent performance, but I'm disappointed. I couldn't keep my focus. Kept thinking back to the shooting. Feel like I let the team down."

"You've come through a lot in the last week. Just let it go."

"Thanks, Granda. You always seem to understand."

"Shame about Paul. How's he doing?"

"He's coming along fine, Granda. He's even talking about getting back to running late summer."

"Let's hope he's right. So, are you ready for the All-Ireland finals?"

"Yes, I'm slowly getting over the shock of the shooting. My head is starting to get back in the right place. I'll get in a couple of good sessions early in the week and then wind down for the race."

"Yes, good to be hungry on race day. Please pass on my best wishes to Paul when you next see him. Ask him not to be a stranger when he recovers."

"Will do Granda. I'll make sure to bring him over when he's up and about again."

On school days Lily would rise early and put a fire of sticks and coal together in the living room. Then she would wake the children and get them ready for school. The kids made sure that the transistor radio was on and tuned to Radio 1. "Tonee Blackburrrnn" was a jingle that would often ring out. The jingle kicked off the *Radio 1 Breakfast Show* hosted by Tony Blackburn at seven o'clock on weekday mornings. This was prime time for families getting ready for the day. He played popular music from artists such as T-Rex, Slade, Bowie, and Deep Purple. He'd refer to their chart positions and pave the way for Thursday nights when *Top of the Pops*, an institution, would broadcast on television with the full chart. In those especially cold winter days, Tony Blackburn was a positive voice that raised people up.

One cold morning in the week before Shane's All-Ireland race the kids were huddled around the fireplace getting warm. Lily came in with porridge and handed each a bowl.

"Mom, why do we call you Mom rather than Ma or Mammy?" Tyrone asked. "Nobody else in my class calls their mother, Mom."

"That's because Mom is special," Shane said.

"It's about your American connection. Isn't it, Mom?" Scarlet asked.

"That's right. Your Grandfather McKeown's elder brother, Francis, emigrated to America, to Philadelphia in fact. When your Granny McKeown was expecting me, Francis' wife Ethel was also expecting. Their daughter Josephine and I were born on the same day."

"So did you and Josephine keep in touch?" Scarlet asked.

"Yes. We became pen pals. Josie would keep me updated on all things American and me her on all things Irish."

Then Lily continued. "She would advise me of all the new movies. Also, she'd discuss the new fashions. From time to time we'd exchange gifts. That's why I have so many hip American sweaters and she has some cool Aran pullovers."

"So why do you use Mom?" Tyrone asked.

"We agreed to embrace each other's culture and terminology. That's why I prefer to use Mom."

"Mom, no one else in my class is called Tyrone, yet there

are three Jim's, two Michael's and two Peter's. Did my name come from America?"

"Yes, it did. It's the Christian name of my favorite Hollywood actor, Tyrone Power."

"Didn't my name also come from Hollywood?" Scarlet asked.

"Yes, it's from my favorite movie, *Gone with the Wind*. It's the Christian name of the main character, Scarlet O'Hara."

"Did Shane's name come from America?" Tyrone asked.

"Yes and no. Shane is actually named after my maternal grandfather, Shane Crilly. I was very close to my grandfather. He died a few months before Shane was born, so I gave him that name."

"But isn't there a Hollywood character called Shane?" Shane asked.

"Yes, absolutely. He's the lead character in the famous cowboy movie *Shane*. He was played by Alan Ladd. However, that movie was released several years after you were born."

"Nevertheless, I bet you're glad I have the name of a Hollywood character?"

"Dead on," Lily said.

"So, Mom, I know you know all the presidents of America in order. Did that come from your link with Josie?" Shane asked.

"Sure did, Son. And Josie knows a lot of facts about Ireland."

"

"Well, that's easier for presidents as there has only been one to date in Ireland, Éamon de Valera."

"Good catch, Shane. And do you know where he was born?"

"Don't know."

"America. New York in fact. So, the connection gets better."

"Who is your favorite American president, Mom?" Tyrone asked.

"No competition there; Jack Kennedy of course. His ancestors hailed from Ireland."

"Is that why we have a road called Kennedy Way?" Scarlet asked.

"Sure is."

"And isn't it most apt with your American passion that it's close to us in West Belfast," Shane said.

"You got it," Lily said.

That was Lily's last words on the subject. Then they all finished their porridge and got ready for school.

The day before the All-Ireland finals Shane and Tim were driven the several hours to Tuam in Galway by a member of the schoolteacher-parents association. The gentleman had a tape deck in his car, a recent phenomenon. They listened excitedly to his vast array of albums including *Bridge Over Trouble Water*, *Deep Purple in Rock,* and various B.B. King, Fleetwood Mac, and Taste albums.

The Ireland Schools' Senior final was uneventful. The Free State, as Lily referred to it, had some top-quality runners. Tim and Shane had come into the final straight together with two hundred meters to go. I must dig deep, Shane thought. He tried to. What's up. Nothing is there, he thought as he saw Tim pull away from him. In fact, as he accelerated to the line, he passed the runner from Derry who had edged him to the gold medal in the Ulster final. Tim finished in sixth place, with Shane close behind in eighth. Disappointing performance, Shane thought. Wasn't all there. Not my best performance. Can't get my head fully focused on racing at present.

"Have to say that we both had a good end to the season," Tim said, as they warmed down together running a further lap of the course.

"Yes, suppose so," Shane said. "I do believe though that a fully fit Paul would've won this race."

"Agree. However, he's alive and on the mend."

"I think we'll see him back at his best next season."

"Yeah. Better get ready for that. He'll be gunning for us."

"Look forward to it."

THREE-POINT TURN

Scarlet was standing impatiently beside her mother. Tyrone watched studiously from ground level at their mother applying cyclical foot pressure to the cast-iron treadle on her Singer sewing machine, as he played on the floor with his Meccano set.

"Scarlet. Number eight is now carefully sewn on," Lily said. "Go try it on."

"Thank you, Mom. Looks great. Will do."

She picked up the new white-collared blue cotton football shirt and bounded up the stairs to her bedroom. A few minutes later Scarlet reappeared in the parlor, kitted out in Everton soccer team colors.

"What do you think, Mom?"

"Yes. That should do the trick. It's very important to look smart and elegant when playing football."

"Do you think the boys will notice?"

"I'm sure they will."

"Will Ciarán O'Loughlin notice?"

"He'd be a fool if he doesn't. You look great," Lily said. "Isn't his big brother, Joe, now a key player on the Antrim Minor Gaelic Football team?"

"Yes, he got into the team earlier in the season and is now the captain. They say he'll progress to the senior team soon."

"OK. Scarlet. Go out now and bowl those guys over!"

Lily placed the wooden cover on the Singer machine and then departed up to her bedroom to return some of the spools she had used.

"Scarlet, why do we support Everton?" Tyrone said.

"Because Shane supports Everton."

"Oh. OK." Tyrone pondered for several seconds. "So why does Shane support Everton?"

"It goes back to when you were just a toddler. Our Uncle Joseph, Da's eldest brother, passed away in the summer of 1966. Mom insisted that Shane accompany Da to the funeral in

Liverpool. That's where Everton plays."

"Oh. Why was our uncle in Liverpool?"

"He was a builder and worked on the new Catholic Cathedral."

"Wow. That sounds exciting!"

"Yes, he would often tell Shane and I stories when he came back to Belfast."

"So how did he die?"

"He was hit by a car. In fact, it was a hit-and-run accident. The police never found who had done it."

"Oh. That's so sad."

"Da was devastated as he was very close to Joseph."

"So why did Shane pick Everton and not Liverpool to support? A lot of my classmates support Liverpool."

"The day after the funeral, Shane walked down to the end of the street from the bed-and-breakfast they were staying in and saw some kids crowded around a curly blond headed man. It was Alex Young who was one of the heroes of the FA Cup victory a few months before. Shane queued up and got his autograph."

"Wow. I'm glad I support Everton. So why do ya have a number eight sewed to the back of your Everton shirt?"

"That's because my favorite player is Alan Ball, and he wears the number eight. He was a key player when Everton won the league last summer."

"Oh. Can I get a shirt with number eight on it as well?"

"You'll have to ask Mom."

Scarlet departed to the street to play in a football match. Ad hoc games regularly occurred in their street, mainly in summer evenings and on the weekends. As she emerged one of the boys said,

"Great. Here comes Scarlet. That'll help the Gaels win."

Shane was among the players assembled and could see that this buoyed Scarlet. He knew that she was a well-respected player with great skill.. Now that the cross-country season was a few weeks' back, Shane had eased his running training back to less than fifty miles a week, focused further on studying for the forthcoming A-level exams, and felt free to join in other sports. He was always keen to participate in the street's football games. He beckoned Scarlet over. "So, Scarlet can you play upfront again. I'll be in midfield. When you see me get the ball, drop your marker and I'll feed the ball to you."

"Will do Big Bro."

The competition was always between the Gaels and the Champions. Those who knew how to speak Gaelic were on the Gaels team. Many families in West Belfast knew Gaelic and practiced it. The McMahons were one of those families. Shane and Scarlet would often converse in Gaelic and therefore represented the Gaels. The Champions were named after a popular television program, in which the main characters had special powers. Anyone passing a soccer game in the street was free to jump in and participate.

As the game finished, several boys came up to Scarlet, "Well done, Scarlet. A hat trick! Love your Everton shirt."

"Thank you, Guys," said Scarlet with a pleased look on her face.

Then Ciarán came across. Scarlet's heart beat a little faster. "Well done, Scarlet. You helped our team to victory. Just one point. In future try just to tackle the opposition. My ankle is hurting badly from the one where you took out three players. Unfortunately, I was in the middle of that group."

"Nothing that a cold-water soak won't sort out, Ciarán. It will teach you to look out for me in the future!"

Later that day Shane grabbed his Martin acoustic guitar and went out to the back yard. The immediate area outside and adjacent to the kitchen was a small courtyard, paved with flagstones. Shane went to the wooden rocking chair that he had brought out a bit earlier. He had also brought out a small pine side table and a guitar stand. He put a pad and pen on the table and started tuning his guitar. He could hear the kitchen window creak open. He knew Lily liked to listen in when he was composing, while she was preparing dinner. As he tuned the guitar, he could hear the upstairs window of the back bedroom of the neighbor's house open a bit. This was the bedroom of Heide, the next-door neighbor's twelve-year-old daughter. He also knew that Heide would often listen in. He didn't mind and kept a focus to make the session good, especially as he had a secret audience.

"OK. Let's get some music for the lyrics I wrote on the weekend," Shane muttered to himself. He tried a few options and then settled on a theme that he liked best. He quickly wrote down the music. Another ten minutes and I should have this wrapped up, he thought. He practiced away and felt he had it licked. He then played and sang the full song. As he played, Lily came out with a folding chair and quietly sat down beside him. Once he had finished, he asked, "What do you think, Mom?"

"Sounds great Shane. How long have you been working on this song?"

"I had some lyrics in my head that I toyed with while out on runs over the last couple of weeks, and then I laid them down in my notebook on Sunday morning. When I was out running this week, I had beats and rhythms running through my head. I worked with them for the first time just now."

"Wow. Well done. Can't believe you could write a song so quickly."

"Once you get in a flow, it just all comes. Then I just have to play around a bit to see what works."

"Great. Now how is my big lad otherwise?"

"I'm fine, Mom. Took me a bit of time to get over the shock of the shooting. However, Paul is doing fine and I'm in one piece, so I have come to feel that I've been lucky."

"Just worried you can get over it OK. Traumatic experiences are not easy to shake."

"Yes, agree. It doesn't completely leave you, but I now find that I can get on with life."

"Great! Only seems like yesterday that I was cradling you in my arms. Soon you'll be off to university."

"Well, not going far, Mom. And I'll still be living here."

"I know. I suppose it has just dawned on me that you're becoming a young man now. You'll be up and gone before long."

"Suppose so, Mom. But you'll always be in my life."

"Thanks Son. Now, must be getting back to dinner. Your father will be home soon."

They both stood up and embraced each other, their bond as strong as ever.

One Friday morning in April Lily shouted to Shane that there was a phone call for him. Shane came down the stairs to take it. Pete McGuirk from St. Malachy's was on the line. Pete was a member of the Belfast United Harriers and one of the runners whom Shane trained with some weekends. Races were invariably held on Saturdays. When there was an open weekend, the runners would often get together for long runs on both the Saturday and Sunday. Shane thought he might be calling to arrange a run.

"A few of the guys were recommending going out to see the Irish Cup final tomorrow, Shane. We have six tickets for Windsor Park behind one of the goals. Should be good. Tim is coming to the game."

"So, no long run tomorrow then, Pete?"

"We were planning on a shorter ten-mile run in the morning at the Dub, then some lunch, and then down to Windsor Park. The lad I was telling you about from our year in St. Malachy's, Martin O'Neill, is playing. He's quite a sensation, and this may be one of his last matches here before going over to England to play."

"Yes, I remember you telling me about him, Pete. Somebody referred to him as the new George Best, but if he's even half as good, he would be worth seeing. Count me in."

The group got together the next morning for a run and then lunch at a pub by the university. They then dropped their running bags off at Shane's house which was closest and made their way to Windsor Park. The game kicked off and was as exciting as they had hoped for.

"Wow. Martin O'Neill certainly delivered," Shane said.

"Yes, two goals," Pete said.

"Great game to watch," Tim said.

"Derry City didn't know what hit them. They won't want to play Distillery again in a hurry," Shane said.

"Well depends on whether Martin O'Neill is playing for them next season. It's unlikely because of the interest from over the water," Pete said.

The lads set out for a quick drink in a local pub to celebrate before heading home.

"So which clubs are interested in Martin O'Neill?" asked Shane when they settled down in the pub.

"I heard Nottingham Forest were interested, and I believe Everton are in the hunt," Pete said.

"Let's hope that it'll be Everton" Shane said. "We need someone exciting to play alongside Alan Ball, so we win the league again next year."

The local evening news, which followed the national news, was a major must-see for viewers in the province. Politicians from the various parties together with civil rights leaders would often be invited to debate salient issues. One program that attracted a lot of attention was chaired locally by a Belfast-born journalist, Gordon Burns. He was elegant but inciteful in his interviewing technique. Politicians were often more concerned about facing him than their counterparts from the other political parties. Despite that, he was a debonaire and handsome character who one thought was more likely to be the next James Bond than a political presenter. One evening in April Shane came down from studying in his bedroom to catch the news. In the parlor there were seven young ladies from the same class as Scarlet, together with Lily and Scarlet fixated on the program. There was little room for Shane, so he stood up at the back against the door and watched from that vantage point.

"So, are you all interested in politics?"

One of the young ladies replied as if the script had been previously prepared, "Yes, we need to study the news for a school project."

It was obvious to Shane that the ladies were more infatuated with watching Gordon Burns than taking in the full news details. Houses around the province had similar experiences. When the local program finished, the girls rose to depart. Shane looked in Scarlet's direction and shrugged in a puzzled demeanor.

"We're all studying the news for a most important school project, Shane," Scarlet said.

"Yes, I get it. Hope you all got the key details."

As the group rose and departed, Shane thought to himself, I'm sure Scarlet's class doesn't take political studies. Gordon Burns must be a very important influence for them.

Exam time was fast approaching. Lily's sister, Deirdre, had arranged for Dan, who was in the same year at St. Mary's as Shane, to come over and stay with them. This way he would to be close to the school to sit the examinations. It seemed that every youth in the area was now focused on exams. Shane was thinking to himself one evening as he was studying that the evenings were a bit quieter outside, apart from the normal din of helicopters circling the area every night nonstop. Of course, there is always the din metal trash can lids banging on the ground a couple of times each evening, he thought, but I hardly notice that now. Yes, when they see an army patrol entering the area the locals feel that they must warn those engaged in paramilitary activities so that they may escape the vicinity and hide. The things that really do disturb my concentration are the gun battles in the vicinity; however, they are only once or twice a week. The occasional bomb blast really shakes things up, he thought. Luckily, they are often over a mile away, but they do shake the place. However, for Belfast standards the evenings are quieter than usual. Nevertheless, no more peace now that Dan is coming over, he thought.

Following dinner, the family would often watch TV. *Alias Smith and Jones*, of course, and *The Old Grey Whistle Test* were regulars. *Top of the Pops* was a stalwart. Then there were some FA Cup soccer games televised live, and on Saturday nights, *Match of the Day* with highlights of English Football League games. Strangely everyone in Belfast seemed to support an English Football League team. Dan was a Manchester United fan, as were most school kids. Other popular teams were Tottenham Hotspur and Liverpool. Unlike some of the teams that had dynamic nicknames such as the Wolves, the Cockerels, or the Rams, Shane's team Everton had a more benign nickname, the Toffees. This was a legacy of toffee shops that had been in the vicinity of Everton's football ground, Goodison Park.

One evening toward the end of April while taking a break from his studies for a cup of tea, Shane was thinking about the FA Cup final. This is going to be right in the middle of the exams in early May, but we can't miss it. I'll arrange for a few of the guys to come over to watch at our place.

Several youths plus Tyrone and Scarlet crammed into the parlor for the FA Cup final. Unfortunately, the black-and-white television was playing up with reception. The house did not have an aerial on the roof, as some did for better reception. Usually there was no problem with the two-pronged aerial sitting on the top of the TV. Of course, on final day, just twenty minutes before kickoff, it played up delivering a poor signal. Scarlet jumped to the rescue and held the arial higher. John McGee shouted out, "That looks great!"

"What? It's still fuzzy," a couple of the guys said.

"I'm not talking about the screen. I'm talking about your sister, Shane!"

Now this made Scarlet's day. She blushed. Following that She was prepared to stand there for the next two hours if need be. The following commands came thick and fast.

"Up a bit." "Sideways a bit. "Down a bit."

Eventually a spot was found where the picture was perfect. Then the study books came out and were stacked on top of a coffee table until the arial delivering a perfect picture could be rested, and of course Scarlet could sit down.

"Hope Liverpool wins. The Irish player, Steve Heighway, is one of their best players," Pete said.

"I prefer Arsenal," Dan said. "They're going for the double. Hasn't been done for nearly ten years."

"Who did it last?" one of the guys asked.

"Tottenham in sixty-two," one responded.

The game started. Everyone was shouting at the TV in excitement. Eventually Arsenal won out with a cracking Charlie George goal.

After the game, everyone exited to the street and started up a football game between the Gaels and the Champions. Shane's guests plus Dan, of course, were honorary participants for the Gaels. Soon Siobhan entered the street, and Shane waved her over to play. He had arranged to meet her that evening and asked her to wear her trainers. She came over to Shane. "So now I understand why you asked me to wear my trainers, Shane. You needed someone for your team who could actually play football!"

"What? You know how to play football?"

"Look and learn."

Gamely Siobhan got stuck in and was quickly seen to be quite a skillful player. As Scarlet also had good skill, the two of them passed the ball to each other. This frustrated the guys as they found it difficult to win it back. The game lasted for almost an hour. It continued until the winning team had scored ten goals. By that time there were twenty people on each side as more passersby joined in the fun. Siobhan and Scarlet each scored four goals as the Gaels were victorious again.

The next morning Shane was lying in his bunk thinking about Siobhan. Love her spirit, he thought. Love her cheekiness. Excited about the way she got stuck in to the football game. Excited about her. Will have to take full advantage of being with her during the next few months before she heads off to Liverpool. After the exams we should be able to get out more together. Just need to figure where is safe to go to. Can't believe that I feel like this about someone. Can't get her out of my head.

Later that day Shane met with Siobhan at her house at about lunchtime following Mass.

"How about a walk down to the Falls Park?" he asked.

"Beautiful day for it. Let's go for it."

They set off down the hill on Gransha Park to the Glen Road and then moved along the road, past the army barracks and Milltown cemetery on the opposite side of the road and entered the park. It was a sunny day and beams of light were piercing through the tree cover as they walked up the main lane in the park.

"Great to spend precious time with you, Shane."

"Yeah. Look forward to our times together."

"We need to prepare for me moving away to Liverpool."

"Let's take it one step at a time."

"Why have you done this to me, Shane?"

"What? Done what?"

"Made me fall in love with you."

"I'm in love with you too. It's a good thing."

"It hurts."

"It hurts me as well."

"I had all my plans laid out and then you came along."

"Good thing I did at the time."

"I know. But now I'm going away. What do we do?"

"We stay in love, and we'll get through."

She stopped in her tracks, turned to Shane, and kissed him.

The presence of Dan during the exam period created a buzz. He was a larger-than-life character. As well as being tall he had handsome looks and the gift of the gab. He could charm any unsuspecting damsel. Dan stayed at the McMahon's for about four weeks. He came over about three weeks before the exams started for studying and stayed through the exams. Lily had arranged for him to use the sitting room to study. In Belfast, sitting rooms were well-presented rooms that practically were seldom used except for special occasions, for example, when guests turned up. On many of the evenings since Dan arrived, talk and laughter could be heard from the sitting room. One evening Shane came down from studying in his bedroom to watch an episode of *The Man from U.N.C.L.E*. Dan came out from the sitting room accompanied by three attractive seniors from St. Bernadette's Girls Grammar School and joined Shane and the rest of the family in the parlor to watch the show.

"Just a few friends who've come round to do a study session Auntie Lily," Dan said.

"OK, Son. Great to see that devotion to your studies."

Dan took a lounge chair and squeezed in with one of the young women. Shane squeezed in between two of these young ladies on the large sofa. He was not complaining. He did wonder, however, if Dan had ever done any studying. He pondered that Dan could be singularly responsible for the worst A-level results for many a year at St. Bernadette's.

The exams were over in late May. Dan returned home to the Ardoyne. Now came the freedom for all not having to study, but the anxiety of waiting for the results, which would not arrive until early July. During this time Shane had booked his driving test. His Uncle Liam's car servicing garage was in lower Stockman's Lane and backed out onto an old, deserted tarmac-laid wasteland area. This was an area of about an acre and was excellent for practicing driving. Liam was also a budding racer and often built and raced go-karts. When Shane would come over, he would often help with making engine mountings in Liam's foundry, fitting engine components, and testing out the go-karts. Liam also raced some saloon cars, and there were several bangers that Shane learned to drive in. He became quite an expert driver. Between his tutelage from Liam and watching *Bullitt* at least four times, he could whizz around any difficult course. He was expert at sliding around corners and doing wheelies.

Liam was preparing Shane for his driving test.

"The key now is to slow down, stay calm, and make sure you perform everything deliberately and calmly," Liam said.

"I understand, Uncle Liam."

"Please remember to unlearn all the things I taught you about go-kart racing. Let's save that for after you get your license."

"Got it."

"You need to perfect three-point turns, emergency stops, and hill starts. When executing them, the name of the game is to demonstrate control. In fact, because of the ramps on most of the roads to calm the traffic, it is unlikely you'll be able to get above third gear."

"No problem. I'll be ready Uncle Liam."

Liam and Shane had worked on his driving skills throughout the winter, and both agreed he was now ready. Liam would often take Shane onto the main roads in his car to give him practice for his test. These were reasonably quiet roads so that Shane would build up his confidence.

One evening Liam asked Shane to drive up above Cave Hill and then on toward the Aldergrove International Airport with him.

"But, Uncle Liam, it'll be dark before we return."

"That's the point, Shane. We need to get you some night driving."

As dusk fell, they progressed above the top of the Cave Hill and then on several miles to just before Aldergrove Airport. Liam knew of some open land where Shane could practice his three-point turns and emergency stops.

"Now is a great opportunity to practice all the party pieces for the test," Liam said when they arrived.

"OK. Here we go," Shane said.

Shane went through the required maneuvers perfectly. On the way back there were a couple of hills where they stopped and practiced hill starts. Then night fell, which was a different experience for Shane. Although he didn't need the night driving for his test, it would be important for general driving once he passed his test. On the way back in a darkening early evening, they pulled onto the shoulder of the road and looked down on Belfast.

"This is another reason I brought you up here, Shane. You'll ever see a more serene and peaceful sight."

As the lights lit up down below, Shane was in awe. He realized that Belfast was a very attractive city as the lights turned on in the dark. He could see that it became even more appealing as more and more lights were progressively illuminated in the darkness.

"There is a majesty about this," Liam said.

"Wow. It's an incredible sight. It shows a different side of Belfast with solitude and grace as the city goes to sleep."

It was a poignant moment for Shane experiencing a peace often no longer witnessed in the city.

Driving exam day arrived on a Friday afternoon in early June. It was a beautiful and sunny. Shane took a taxi down to the lower Falls Road where the test center was located. He met with the driving examiner. At just over six foot tall, Shane towered above this short, stout middle-aged man, who gave his name simply as Mr. Laughlin. He did not smile and just fired out orders without any softer side. Shane thought to himself, Just like being back in class. As they got into the Ford Fiesta car, Shane was given a sharp brief. "You must wear a seat belt. Please deploy it now. For safety reasons I will not use my seat belt."

"The test will take about forty-five minutes. You must perform blemish-free a three-point turn, a hill start, and an emergency stop. For the latter you will hear a loud knock and then you must stop abruptly. Do you understand?"

"Yes. Got it."

"Before we start driving, I will ask you some highway code questions. You must pass at least eight out of ten."

"No problem. I'm ready when you are."

Shane delivered the first eight correctly. Mr. Laughlin stopped at that point and then the driving test commenced.

"Now we will be going up the Whiterock Road, so start off by heading up the Falls."

"Excuse me Mr. Laughlin. Is it a good idea to go up the Whiterock? It's quite volatile."

"Look sonny, are you trying to tell me how to do my job? The Whiterock has good hills, so it will be a thorough test."

"Understood."

So up to the Whiterock it was. As the car approached the Whiterock, Shane signaled in advance and assuredly turned the corner. So far so good, he thought to himself.

"Now go about six hundred yards and turn right into the first road."

Shane executed perfectly. The road he turned on was flat, providing a good place for a three-point turn.

"Drive up past the first lamppost. Then when you're ready and when the road is free from any traffic, execute the three-point turn."

"Got it."

Shane carefully progressed past the lamppost, signaled, and turned to the right toward the opposite curb. He kept saying to himself that the key to a successful three-point turn was not to hit the curb. Focus, focus. It must be executed on the road. Shane progressed carefully and with good control at the slow speed and then came to a successful stop a couple of yards before the curb. He looked in his mirror, signaled and started to gently reverse. Then all hell broke loose! Further along the road, about one hundred and fifty yards away, Shane noticed a car speeding down toward him. It was out of control and followed closely by a couple of army jeeps and then a couple of Saracens. All five vehicles were coming straight at the test car, while it was still located in the middle of the road.

"Holy shit!" Mr. Laughlin said.

"Hold on," Shane said.

Shane reversed sharply back and hit the lamppost. He then

changed to first gear and shot forward while completing the three-point turn. He mounted the opposite footpath and drove along the street on the footpath inside the lampposts. He could see in his mirror that bricks and petrol bombs were being hurled at the army jeeps and Saracens. A mob had entered the street from the surrounding houses. There was an alleyway to the right that Shane decided to aim for, now with the stick shift in fourth gear going at sixty miles per hour. As he progressed, the car passed them on the road as he looked across. The kids in the car were not much older than Tyrone, ten years old at best! Shane brought the test car back to the road and sped toward a ramp in front.

"Slowdown!" Mr. Laughlin yelled. The car bounced into the air and landed with a bang. "You just sped over a *sleeping policeman!*"

Shane then came to the alleyway and did a McQueen-like skid around and exactly aligned the car up the alleyway. He drove as fast as the Fiesta could muster. He realized that the key now was to get to safety. As he headed down the alleyway, masked youths with bricks and petrol bombs appeared in the distance. He knew he couldn't continue. Bricks were being hurled toward the car, with a couple landing on the car's hood. He had noticed another alleyway at right angles about thirty yards back. He slammed on the brakes and as quickly as possible put the stick shift into reverse.

At this stage Mr. Laughlin was being thrown around badly and was almost on Shane's lap. He quickly moved to engage his seat belt as Shane reversed with speed and turned left into the other alley. As Mr. Laughlin settled back into his seat, Shane came to the end of the alley at the main Whiterock Road. It was madness. The road was filled with bricks, trash can lids, and burning gas bottle remnants. Shane realized there was no escape through the Whiterock, and a mob was following behind in the alley. The rioters were out to hijack cars and cause as much disturbance as possible. There was another alley directly opposite on the other side of the road. Shane looked right and left and then kicked hard on the accelerator and made a beeline for it. He just got there in time as a Saracen came down the Whiterock and took off the Fiesta's rear bumper. Nevertheless, Shane kept the car on course and headed down the alley.

The name of the game now for Shane was to get as far up toward the Falls Park as possible through the back streets and then loop back to the Falls Road. To do this he had to take another sharp turn right out of the alley. He did this and turned up a hill that was surprisingly quiet.

"I can take the driving from here, Mr. McMahon. Let's swop seats," Mr. Laughlin said.

Shane brought the car to a smooth halt on the side of the road. Just then he could see out of his mirror the mob spilling out onto this road. Mr. Laughlin went to unlock his seat belt.

"Hold tight, Mr. Laughlin! We've got company. Buckle up, we need to move fast!"

This took Mr. Laughlin by surprise, but he quickly complied. Shane maneuvered the stick shift into first gear, progressed smoothly through the gears, and in top gear accelerated as fast as he could.

As he was not sure if the lower Falls Road would be safe, Shane implemented his strategy of progressing toward the Falls Park. He headed up past Milltown Cemetery to the Andersonstown Road, turned left down Stockman's Lane and then over toward Balmoral Avenue. The roads were safe there, and Shane was able to slow the car down and progress at a careful normal speed. From there he made his way down Balmoral Avenue to the city center. As he approached the test center, he looked in his mirror, applied the turn signal, and smoothly drove the car in and parked in full alignment in the parking spot assigned.

Shane thought about how lucky they were to escape the danger in the Whiterock. Then he thought back to his driving test and was resigned to the reality that he had not passed, despite the extenuating circumstances. He was feeling sick within. He had worked so hard to pass his driving exam. Once he had his driver's license this would permit him an additional freedom in a country where freedom was rapidly eroding. He had been so looking forward to drives on his own and maybe obtaining a cheap but reliable car from his Uncle Liam to get to Queen's University each day in the fall. He was also most concerned about the damage to the examiner's car.

"Sorry about the damage to the car," Shane said.

Mr. Laughlin looked shaken up and in shock. "Don't be concerned about that. The insurance will take care of it. You were right about the Whiterock. Sorry to put you through that ordeal. This was, of course, an unusual driving test experience. However, I've seen enough of your driving skills and acknowledge that you've had significant defensive driving experience."

Shane was surprised at these warm comments.

"On that basis I'm going to pass you." He handed a pass slip to a startled Shane.

"Thank you, Mr. Laughlin. Much appreciated."

With the pass certificate in hand, Shane walked out of the test center and headed for the lower Falls to take a taxi home.

Because of the disturbance further up the Falls Road by Whiterock, the taxi driver took a detour. Apart from that, it was an uneventful ride back. When Shane got home, Liam was there with his parents.

"How was the test?" Liam asked.

"Grand." He showed them the pass certificate. "However, it wasn't a typical test." Shane then explained what had transpired.

"Jeez. So glad you got out of there unscathed," Brendan said. "Hate to think what may have happened"

"Yeah. Scary! So lucky to get away."

Then Liam said, "What did the examiner say to you when you finished? Any feedback on your driving?"

"Our preparation worked very well, Uncle Liam. He said I had good defensive driving skills. On that basis, he said he felt he'd seen enough, that there was no need for a further test, and then handed me the pass slip."

Lily broke out a small bottle of champagne that she had kept for this occasion. "This calls for a celebratory drink."

"All's well that ends well," Liam said.

One Wednesday evening in mid-June, Dan came over from Ardoyne to visit Shane.

"Let's go down to the pub nearby on the Falls Road for a drink," he said.

Shane now felt a freedom that came with the completion of the exams. "Why not? No more exams to prepare for so let's go!"

Dan was a hive of activity. That evening in the pub he chatted up many young lasses. As closing time approached, Shane saw Dan checking out two male youths about the same age as them toward the other end of the bar.

"What's the deal there, Dan?"

"I've noticed them a few times looking in our direction. I sense something's brewing."

Shane looked across and saw the youths get up and leave. Dan said to Shane, "We may walk into an incident outside. Stay beside me, remain calm, focused, and determined, and follow my lead."

"Got it. Just what I needed for a peaceful evening out."

Dan and Shane got up and moved to the exit swing doors.

"Ready Shane?"

"Ready as I'll ever be."

They exited the pub. As they walked across the forecourt, the two youths approached them and stood off about five yards, blocking their path. They were tall, each at least six foot three, and looked menacing.

THE LONELINESS OF THE LONG-DISTANCE RUNNER

Outside the pub, the leader of the two youths called over, "So, I saw you chatting up the young ladies."

"What of it?" Dan asked.

"Well, one of them is my girl."

"Which one was that?"

"The tall blonde."

"Oh, that one. Wow she's hot. Congratulations!"

"I don't like anyone chatting up my girl."

"Well, she didn't seem to mind it."

At this point the aggressive youth got a bit hot under the collar and was restrained by his friend. Then Dan blurted out, "So, I guess you're here now to teach me a lesson."

"That's the long and short of it."

"Well, Top Cat in that case let me explain how this is going to play out. When you go for me, I'll hold you off. I won't aim a punch at you, just defend myself. Eventually, you'll tire out. While this is going on, my friend here will go over to your friend, Benny the Ball, there and beat the crap out of him. Then I'll invite him over here to do the same to you. The reason why I won't lay a punch on you is that I'm a black belt in karate, and if I was to injure you my license may be revoked, and we wouldn't want that to happen, would we? On the other hand, my friend here doesn't have a license but does have the training and skills."

At that Benny the Ball was suddenly looking uncomfortable. Shane kept a firm stare. Top Cat had a wry and uncomfortable grin on his face.

"So, you're impersonating a karate black belt now?" he said.

"How badly do you want to find out? I would recommend that you and your friend do an impersonation of Tommy Smith and John Carlos in the Olympics and sprint off while you can still move!"

They stared at each other as in a Sergio Leone spaghetti western. Then Top Cat and Benny the Ball stepped back a few steps and hightailed it around the corner.

"Hopefully, that will be the last we see of them," Dan said to Shane.

"Thank you for the development opportunity, Cous," Shane said, in typical *Butch Cassidy and the Sundance Kid* fashion.

Dan and Shane made their way back to the McMahon residence. Shane was thinking to himself, good job those guys backed off. They don't realize how lucky they are. This was not because Shane was an expert in karate; he wasn't. Rather it was because Dan truly was a level-three black belt in karate, and an emerging talent in Belfast.

The following Saturday morning, Lily called up the stairs to her children, "E for B! Breakfast." Not getting a reaction, she shouted once again. "E for B and Georgie Best!"

Tyrone, Shane, and Scarlet eventually surfaced. "E for B" stood for "Eggs for Breakfast," a television campaign to promote the use of local eggs supported by the soccer legend George Best. Northern Ireland had its fair share of stars, and they didn't come bigger than George Best. He was considered to be among the best soccer players of his generation, if not the best of all time. Shane looked forward to George Best coming back home to Belfast. In addition to the normal soccer game, George would often do adverts for key Northern Ireland businesses. The McMahons loved to watch any adverts with their local hero. Tyrone and Shane insisted on Cookstown sausages because they were "the Best family sausages." Lily always rose early in the mornings to make sure her children had a hearty meal to start their day. On weekdays it was invariably porridge, but at weekends the Belfast Fry was the popular choice.

Another local hero was a well-renowned comedian, Tommy Coyne. During the last couple of years he had regularly been seen on variety shows on British and Irish television. During the previous summer he had a well lauded 1970 holiday season at the Blackpool resort area in England. Following this he was invited to take part in a newly created television show *The Comedians* which was now airing on the British ITV channel. To the surprise of Shane and his senior colleague Bernie, who were working behind the bar in the lounge of the Eagle Inn early one Saturday evening in June, in popped Tommy Coyne. Tommy often did charity work for the Christian Brothers and had just met with a senior Brothers' committee at St. Mary's Christian Brothers Grammar School, about half a mile further up the Glen Road, to discuss a parent's evening gala. He had been taken there in a taxi and had arranged for a taxi to pick him up from the Eagle Inn.

When Tommy arrived, the lounge at the inn was reasonably quiet. Bernie and Shane were working in the lounge bar. Bernie despite his unassuming character struck up conversation with Tommy when he first arrived.

"Hello, Mr. Coyne. Great to see you. What brings you to our humble place?" Bernie asked.

Tommy looked up at the six-foot-four figure who had greeted him, who projected a commanding presence. "Hi there. Just been up the road at the Irish Christian Brothers House in the St. Mary's School grounds. Y'know, I feel an enormous gratitude to the Brothers for how they educated and developed me. I like to help them out when I can," Tommy said. He then ordered a drink from Shane and continued, "Friends mentioned that they really enjoyed the ambience of the Eagle Inn and that I should check it out. I thought I'd give it a go this trip. The place looks great!"

"Thank you, Mr. Coyne. Much appreciated."

"Oh, just call me Tommy."

"Welcome Tommy."

"I didn't go to St. Mary's even though that is where I usually meet with the Brothers, rather I went to St. Patrick's Christian Brothers' Primary School."

Just then Shane's other colleague, Barney, arrived to take over duties from Bernie. He quickly picked up on the discussion. "Oh, Shane went to St. Patrick's as well," Barnie said.

Shane was taken aback with embarrassment at having been dragged into the conversation and nearly dropped the glass he was polishing.

"Wow! So, you're also a kindred spirit from St. Pat's? Who taught you there?" Tommy asked.

Shane provided a few names, one of whom had also taught Tommy and had been a key mentor to him. This perked Tommy up even more. He was now his buddy.

Shane became the recipient of a signed bar coaster from Tommy which acknowledged their education from the Irish Christian Brothers at St. Patrick's. Within thirty minutes of his arrival, as word got around the area, the pub became packed. Tommy was in his best public image delivering one-liners and bowling the patrons over with laughter. After Tommy had been in the pub only one hour, a driver came in and told him his taxi was outside, and off he went. Shane was pleasantly surprised at how down to earth and genuine this star was. It seemed to him that Tommy was comfortable amongst "his people". When he got home, he proudly showed his signed bar coaster to his parents, and both were amazed that he had been speaking with a Belfast icon.

Shane continued training largely on his own. He found this tough as the training sessions needed a lot of willpower and commitment. It was much easier when he had company. Normally that would be Paul. He would make a point of traveling to the Dub Lane Sports Center in the Queen's University grounds on Sundays to train with the Belfast United Harriers distance runners. However, he was looking for more involvement to take the pressure off solo training. Queen's University had another sports center on the Embankment in the university campus, so Shane would travel there once a week and meet up with whichever runners turned up. The sports center was a state-of-the-art facility built as part of the Ulster 1970 Exhibition. As Annadale Grammar School was on the Embankment and less than a mile away, some of the runners he competed against during the winter months would turn up. Shane would often go out for interval or fartlek runs with the groups that would be there.

One day as he finished, he and a few of the guys went into the large gymnasium. They stopped short when they saw that two Commonwealth Games gold medalists were training there. One was Mary Peters who had won the Pentathlon and Shot Put and the other, Mike Bull who was the Pole Vault champion. One of the guys knew Mike Bull, so he invited the group over to say "hello." Shane was in awe and shocked that he was actually shaking hands with and speaking to a gold medalist. Mike explained that he was in his final preparation for the summer European Games in Helsinki. Shane managed to pluck up the courage to join in the conversation.

"How do you manage to keep your studies going with suc intensive training?" Shane asked.

"I believe in the balance of a healthy mind and a healthy body. Both complement each other well," Mike said.

"Makes sense. Many thanks." Shane liked this concept and was comfortable that he had, without purposely considering it, been doing the same.

An athletics coach came across and spoke with the guys. In discussion he mentioned that Mary Peters was not intending on competing in Helsinki at the European Games. Rather, she was deep in her preparation for the Olympics in Munich, Germany, the following year. He mentioned that she felt this gave her the best chance of succeeding at the Olympics. Shane at first couldn't understand why a top-class athlete would miss the chance of another gold medal to prepare for one at a later date. Athletes were invariably one bad injury away from ending their careers, so most focused on competing in whatever big competitions came along. However, when he considered it later, he realized this was a master plan. It was a strategy that he would adopt albeit at a different level to ensure that he peaked at the right time. He made sure to record any strategies he wanted to follow in his running log. This also contained all details of his daily training sessions.

Siobhan came across to the McMahon's for a meal one June evening. Lily made sure that one of her special toad-in-the-hole meals was prepared. Everyone enjoyed their dinner and then moved to the parlor for a cup of tea.

"Shane tells me you're competing in a racing event next weekend," Brendan said to Siobhan.

"That's right, Brendan. Next Saturday with a start at noon, up by the open area next to Aldergrove Airport. We had to design an electric-powered go-kart and get it made. On Saturday we take it for a race-off."

"Are you all prepared?"

"Yes, I'm in a team of four girls competing for St. Dominic's."

"Go get one for the ladies, Siobhan," Lily said.

"Hope to."

"I believe my brother Liam will be going up with Shane to see how you get on," Lily said.

"I look forward to meeting Liam. He did a nice job fixing Mr. O'Reilly's car. He lives across the road from us."

"Yes. Siobhan's mother asked me if I knew a good garage, and I recommended Uncle Liam's."

"Well done, Son. Liam's always most conscientious about his work."

The following Saturday morning Liam stopped by at ten-thirty to collect Shane. They arrived at the site of the race thirty minutes later, in time to walk around and see all the entries. Soon after they parked their car and entered, Liam got distracted by some of the go-karts and stopped to check them out.

"I'll go up to see how Siobhan is doing, Uncle Liam. I'll pop back for you in a few minutes. Take your time."

"Go for it, Shane. I'll be here."

Shane arrived at the St. Dominic's pit area. Siobhan's team's go-kart was in full display propped up on a set of ramps. Shane went over and introduced himself to the ladies in the pit area.

"Hello. I've come to support Siobhan. Do you know where she is?"

"Oh. You must be Shane? Welcome. She's here."

"Where?"

One of the team responded, pointing to the underneath of the go-kart. "There."

Slightly puzzled Shane bent down, and surely Siobhan was there in overalls doing final checks on the vehicle. She emerged and rubbed her hand across her forehead, leaving a streak of black grease.

"Glad you could make it Shane. We seem to be ready."

Shane looked at her, hair disheveled, grease on her face, and thought, wow, she looks great. "Wouldn't miss it for the world."

"So where is that uncle mechanic of yours?"

"He's here somewhere. Got waylaid looking at one of the other karts. Hold on for a few moments and I'll go and grab him."

"No problem."

Shane backtracked to the vicinity of the entrance where he had left Liam. There was no sign of him. He asked a couple of guys working on their karts who said that someone of his description was checking out a few karts and then headed off along the path. Shane realized that he must have moved closer to the St. Dominic's pit. He thanked them and walked back to speak with Siobhan. When he got back, there was no sign of her. Her three teammates were still standing around. They signaled, "Down there."

"Under the cart again," Shane said to himself. He started to bend down and began saying, "Couldn't find my uncle . . ."

"Oh. Hi, Shane," Liam said lying supine beneath the car alongside Siobhan. "So, if we tighten this lever a bit, the spring will be stronger and the chain will resist slipping as you increase speed," Liam said.

"Thank you, Liam," Siobhan said.

They both pulled themselves out from under the car.

"So, you've now met my uncle, Siobhan."

"Sure have. He's been a great help."

Shane looked over puzzled to Liam, who in turn innocently shrugged his shoulders. Just then the Tannoy system could be heard. The countdown to the race had started, and all nonracers had to leave the area.

"There'll be twelve laps, each about three-quarters of a mile. The teams must rotate drivers every three laps so that all four team members compete. I'll be on the last leg," Siobhan said to Shane and Liam.

"Surely, some of the cars' batteries will run out before the end of the race," Liam said.

"Yes, we hope so. In fact, we're counting on it. We designed ours to last for about thirteen laps from when we start, so we should be good. However, we know some other teams are taking chances and cutting it tight, so watch out for retirements on the last couple of laps."

The race started. St. Dominic's was tracking in about fifteenth to twentieth place out of thirty entrants for the early legs. Shane and Liam watched closely from the pit area. The St. Dominic's team was slick at the changeovers and gently moved up the field. Siobhan swapped into the kart for the last three laps. Shane moved to about half a mile from the finish line to see her come round each of her three laps. Liam moved to the finish line to cheer them on as the kart came past on each lap. Siobhan took to the track in tenth place. In her first lap she got up to seventh. On the penultimate lap three karts ran out of juice and retired. She was about one hundred yards down on the leader, with two karts in between, and poised to move into the medals. With one lap to go she moved into third place. With half a mile to go, Shane saw her pass the second kart, which was grinding to a halt.

"Go Penelope Pitstop!" the driver shouted over to her.

"I'll give you Penelope Pitstop, you male chauvinist pig!" Siobhan shouted back.

Shane killed himself laughing at this. He started outside the ropes running at the same pace as the go-kart to keep cheering and see Siobhan home. She was sixty yards behind the leader with a quarter of a mile to go, with no real challengers close behind. She pushed hard on the throttle knowing that she had enough battery power to get home but was not making progress. The leader entered the home straight, some two hundred yards long, still with a healthy lead and with victory in sight. However, about forty yards from the line the kart stopped, and Siobhan moved past to victory.

As she crossed the line, her teammates came over to congratulate her. A newspaper photographer took a team photograph, and Siobhan as captain was interviewed for the *Belfast Telegraph*. Shane and Liam came over and congratulated her.

"Well done. Looks like you'll hit the papers," Shane said.

"Thanks Shane. It'll be a change reading about my exploits rather than yours."

"I look forward to reading the article. When did he say it'll be published?"

"He reckoned on Monday."

"Great."

Shane arranged to meet Siobhan for lunch the next day. Then he and Liam quietly departed to leave Siobhan to her friends and the glory.

It was approaching mid-June and the exam results were a couple of week from being posted out. Shane passed the time with regular visits with Siobhan, two nights per week work at the Eagle Inn, and of course running. The nights were quite bright, so he would often train a bit later in the evening as dusk approached. Because Paul was still in hospital, most of Shane's mid-week runs were on his own. Nevertheless, he was improving greatly and showing this in a limited series of road races. One late Wednesday evening Shane set out for a brisk ten-mile run. He had several levels of clothing together with a woolen hat and gloves because it was unusually cold. It was a foggy evening, so he also wore a neck warmer up over his nose covering most of his face. This will stop the fog getting into my lungs, he reasoned. With the fog and pending dusk approaching, visibility was poor. He decided to take a route up by Casement Park and then pass through Andersonstown and make his way up to the Glen Road. As he approached Casement Park, he turned right by the Dad's Army mural and headed up the poorly lit lane. Behind the shops there was waste ground. He could hear a commotion and looked over in the dusk to see three masked youths standing over a helpless person with one holding a gun in his direction. He was stopped in his tracks, shocked.

"Shoot," one of the youths said.

He could make out the man on the ground was an army official, and then realized from a glint of moonlight through the adjacent trees that it was Captain Green! Shane murmured to himself without realizing that he was slightly audible, "Holy shit! Jeez! What do I do?" He moved around in short circles behind the corner of the wall. I can't just stand by and let them just murder this person.

The evening fog was so thick that it had precipitated onto his woolen hat forming droplets that began to drip gently onto his dark blue Adidas tracksuit. He could hear each drip as if the sound was amplified. He was trembling as he considered all options quickly. Then a voice shouted out, "Who's there?"

Shane was taken aback. He now realized he had been speaking out loud to himself. The call came again.

"Who's there?"

Shane cleared his throat, braced himself, and kicked into action with little thought for his own safety. He approached the youths and then spoke in Gaelic, as he had heard a lot of paramilitary groups used Gaelic to communicate. This will assure them that I am one of them, he thought.

"I've come over from the park. The adjutant said we must do this quietly and sent me over to take control," he said.

One of the gunmen blurted out in English, "Who the hell are you?"

Then a calmer gunman replied in Gaelic that they had been

ordered to do the execution. Shane affirmed while maintaining his Gaelic tongue, "The orders have changed. And don't address a superior officer like that!"

"Sorry Sir," the guys replied together.

Shane commanded them to head over to Casement Park, go into the lower level in the west side, and ask for the adjutant at the bar.

"You'll be given new orders there."

"Yes Sir," they replied in Gaelic.

As they were about to leave, Shane stopped one of them. "Hand me your knife."

"Here ye go."

"I'll get it back to you later."

"No problem."

Shane approached the hapless army officer lying prone on the ground. He could see that Captain Green was gagged, with his hands bound behind his back and his legs tied together. He was crying out while wriggling on the ground as if attempting to break free from his shackles. He had been badly beaten, but there were no signs of broken limbs. He was shrieking in fear. Shane approached him. "Stay still, I'm not going to hurt you. I'm going to cut the binds. So please stay still."

The captain let out a loud gasp of relief.

"Are you able to run?" Shane asked as he cut the ropes.

"I believe so."

"I guess we have a maximum of five minutes before the gunmen and their leaders realize they've been duped. Let's go. Keep close to me."

"Thank you."

Off they ran uphill through the estate. Shane knew he had to keep Captain Green's mind focused on the job at hand, which was getting back to the nearest barracks. It was important that he didn't dwell on his injuries. The nearest station was at the bottom of Andersonstown Road, where it intersected with the bottom of the Glen Road and the top of the Falls Road by

Milltown Cemetery. It was less than a mile from where they were, but the straight route would be obvious, and they would be easily caught up if a chasing gang was in a car. Shane considered that they needed to take a scenic route back, most likely up by the Glen Road, and then come off onto the nearby fields so that they would not be intercepted on the main road. He was also concerned by the network within the area. Once it was realized that the soldier had escaped, calls would go round to the landlines in houses and other supporters would come out on the hunt. They had to head up the estate within the next few minutes and hope that no one would see them, come off into alleyways, and make their way to the Glen Road. Shane kept Captain Green engaged in conversation.

"Have you ever done any distance running?" Shane asked.

"Yes, I was a member of Birchfield Harriers and competed in road races."

Great! Shane thought. This is most helpful. A proper runner. "You don't sound like a Brummie."

"I do come from Bur-ming-gum," the captain said, reverting to a deep Brummie accent.

Shane remembered that "Bur-ming-gum" was the local pronunciation for "Birmingham." He knew that Ian Stewart was the European and Commonwealth 5,000-meter champion and one of the main contenders for the Olympic title at that distance the next year.

"Birchfield is the club that Ian Stewart runs for. Do you know him?"

"Yes, I've trained with Ian and his brother, Peter."

"Way to go!"

The duo kept going.

"I suppose you're wondering how I was captured by the IRA?" the captain said.

"Had crossed my mind. However, no time to dwell on that. We must focus to get us both away safely."

They made good progress in the dusk. As they topped the hill and entered the alleyway to the right, Shane looked back and could see a group of men running in their direction. He wasn't sure if they could see them as they ran into the alley. The captain stopped him. "You still have the knife. Quickly, throw it further up the road."

Shane didn't need to ask why. He understood. Hopefully the group chasing us will think we went further up the road, he thought. They might go that way or maybe split up. He moved quickly and threw it some fifteen yards further up the road while keeping out of sight behind the hedge that bordered the alleyway. The chasers were just a couple of minutes behind. After a couple of hundred yards in the direction they were moving, Shane could see a couple of people in the distance coming out of back gates. He nudged the captain.

"These may be spotters so better not to take the chance. We need to move off the alley. Let me help you over this fence. We'll pass through the gardens from here on."

"Got it. No problem."

He helped the captain over a fence, and then followed him over. They then ran across lawns, climbed more fences, and jumped over hedges in people's back gardens. Once or twice, they had to stop, crouch down, and keep very quiet as people came along the adjacent alley. Certainly, on one occasion Shane could hear Gaelic being spoken and understood that they were in fact out looking for the soldier and a mystery helper. Concerned with the time they were losing to the main search party from Casement Park, he made sure they got going again quietly. They came to a garden and heard a soft growl. A German Shepherd was in the back garden.

"Leave this to me," said Captain Green.

"Don't hurt it," Shane said.

"Don't intend to."

Before the dog broke into a louder bark, the captain befriended it and stroked it gently. Meanwhile, Shane scaled the adjacent wall of some eight feet. The captain told the dog to sit, which it did, and came across, grabbed the hand from Shane leaning down from the top of the wall, and eased himself up. The dog remained quiet.

"Dodged that one," the captain said.

After another couple of gardens, they were confronted in a backyard by two Jack Russell Terriers. These dogs were not prepared to keep quiet.

"Jeez. They'll know we've gone this way. Must hurry now!" Shane said.

They made their way to the fields, with Shane occasionally supporting the captain by the shoulder as he was limping badly. Traversing the fields was a good move as no one could easily come out of a house and block their path.

They ascended to the Glen Road through the back of a larger house. As they quietly eased their way along the side of the large house, they were taken aback as they passed a window by two large Dobermans that barked loudly and kept bumping the window. They stopped briefly as they looked through the window.

"Time to move," Shane said.

They came to the front of the property, which had a large six-foot wall backed by a hedge that extended over it. They crouched down in the shadow of the wall. Shane peeked out onto the road.

"The road is heavily lit with bright streetlights. When we move, we'll need to cross quickly."

"Ten-four."

Shane led. Captain Green followed and noticed Shane's distinctive Adidas running shoes. They were a pre-release sample pair of the SL-72 model that was designed for the forthcoming 1972 Olympics Games. Tom Clyne, with his connections, was able to get the best equipment for his athletes well before they were released to the market. As his custom, Shane had placed the handwritten inscription, "Go Pre" on the outside middle white stripe of each shoe.

"Nice running shoes," Captain Green said, "Seen some like

them before on someone somewhere. Can't remember where."

"All the rage now," Shane said.

Shane supported Captain Green as they crossed the road and moved to a dark wasteland behind a row of shops on the other side. Shane then led the captain to a stream at the end of Arizona Street, a cul-de-sac with a bakery at the end. This gave access to the stream down a short slope.

"Stay here by this sign for a few seconds while I check the best way through."

"*Oven Fresh to You* logo on the sign. What type of building is this?"

"It's the largest bakery in Belfast. It supplies many bakery shops in Belfast."

"Is anyone likely to be inside?"

"Luckily not at this time. The night shift starts in about a couple of hours' time."

Shane dropped down a bank and after several seconds reemerged.

"Yes, I remember now. The stream runs through a concrete pipe under the bakery. This is our best way through. Come. I'll help you down the bank."

Shane grabbed the captain's arm, and they both eased down the short bank. They then had to crouch down into a large five-foot-diameter concrete pipe that directed the stream under the bakery. Shane asked Captain Green to proceed while he checked behind them. He couldn't see anyone yet coming down Arizona Street. He followed the captain into the concrete pipe and caught up with him. The pipe ran the length of the bakery and was about forty yards long. It was plain sailing from there down the side of the stream to the Falls Park.

As they progressed, Captain Green enquired of Shane, "Have we met before?"

"I don't think so." Shane had kept his neck warmer over most of his face so he couldn't be recognized. He wanted to make sure that no one knew who he was for his own safety.

"Your voice sounds familiar," Captain Green said.

"Well, you Brits with your posh English accents believe that us Irish all sound the same anyway!"

"Fair dues."

The park was close to the barracks. The key then was to get across the main road without being seen. Captain Green was struggling with his injuries but persevered. He could not keep the pace that Shane needed, and the gang was gaining. Shane looked behind.

"I can just see them coming out of the pipe under the bakery. Need to keep moving. Almost there."

When they had arrived at the end of the park, Shane looked back and estimated that the chasers were only about two hundred yards behind. The barracks soon came into sight with just the road separating them from the main gates.

"I can't lose time crossing the road. Better that you go on your own," Shane said.

"Will you be able to avoid this mob?"

"This is my town. Rest assured they'll not catch me."

"Thank you. Much indebted." The captain moved to cross the road but then turned around. "Why would you take such a risk to help me?"

"We're all God's people."

Shane waited in the shade while the captain crossed. As he approached the barracks' gates, he saw several soldiers with rifles exit and help him inside. Then he saw Captain Green turn around. Shane's moonlit shadow disappeared into the darkness.

Shane reckoned that now he had about a one-hundred-yard jump on his pursuers. However, he had to backtrack some twenty yards into the park to take the route he needed, so he was anxious to get going. As the pursuers would progress toward this point, he calculated that he would have at best a sixty-yard lead. He couldn't afford for the paramilitaries to catch and identify him. He needed to make haste.

ANGELS WITH DIRTY FACES

Shane had run practically every inch of the park in training and was confident he could avert the pursuers. He headed off toward the outdoor swimming pool area and skirted around it. Then he disappeared into tracks in the woods, which he could easily navigate in the moonlight. Unfortunately, the moonlight also aided his chasers as they could see where he was going, albeit if just a silhouette. The tracks led him toward the Whiterock Road. As he exited the woods with the persistent gang still in chase, he thanked God once again for the sight before him. The road was filled with rioters, many wearing dark blue tracksuits like his, throwing bricks and petrol bombs. The army was thirty yards down the hill with plastic shields and a water cannon behind.

Thank God for the reliable Whiterock, he thought as he moved ahead. With that he pushed into the crowd in the middle of the street some twenty yards down the gradual hill and was lost in plain sight. The chasing pack following him emerged from the woods. Shane could see them searching for him in vain. After a few minutes, he slowly made his way to the other side of the road and pressed through people into an alley. As he entered, he heard the thumping and ricochet of a large object. It was a plastic bullet, valuable currency in Belfast. American journalists would give twenty pounds for one of them, he thought. He picked up his souvenir and quietly made his was down toward the Clonard Monastery, and then reversed up another street and returned home. He was able to show a fifteen-mile effort that evening for his planned ten-mile run. This sat well in his training diary.

For the next few days, the abduction and rescue of an unnamed army official was headline news. The BBC radio news carried the story.

Good afternoon. Here is the Friday five o'clock news. Sources close to paramilitary forces let it be known to the press that the IRA has opened an investigation to find out who had rescued an army official on Wednesday evening who had been captured by an IRA cell earlier in the day. They stress that it's not going to be tolerated within the freedom fight. There is speculation that he was an informer within their ranks or a security forces undercover infiltrator.

Shane was listening to the news. Good, he thought. No mention that the helper could have been an innocent bystander. So, I should be safe. Shane asked himself if he was having any lingering effects of this trauma. He thought about it over the next few days and realized that he was quite matter of fact about it. He would not let it haunt him the way the near miss with the gunmen several weeks earlier that left Paul in hospital did. He reconciled to himself that he had done the right thing, felt comfortable in his skin, and had no regrets. He was determined to move on with his life.

As June move forward, Shane looked out each Friday for the postman to deliver his copy of *Athletics Weekly*, and as normal read it from cover to cover. He was particularly interested in the articles on training techniques and running strategies, as he continued to plan how he would excel at cross-country the following season. He maintained his running diary and now included a section on his training strategies.

Shane enjoyed his evening work in the Eagle Inn. On some Sunday mornings as he lay in his bunk, he would think of some of the characters that he served in the pub. Many of the stories they brought with them were very entertaining. He thought about one elderly gentleman who would come in about seven-thirty on Saturday evenings, most likely after he had his evening dinner at home. In fact, he had been in the lounge bar the previous evening. He was Polish and had been a refugee during the Second World War. He was known as Mr. Pareki. Word had it that he came to the British Isles during "the War" and served as a pilot in the RAF, fighting in the Battle of Britain. He spoke broken English with a strong Polish accent of course. He would always sit up at the counter, and Shane would invariably be the bartender to serve him.

Mr. Pareki arrived as usual on that Saturday evening. He started the conversation with an introduction he had often used before, "I have just come in this evening to have a quick drink for medicinal purposes."

"What may I offer you, Mr. Pareki?" Shane said.

"A half pint of Guinness and a crème-de-menthe chaser, young man."

Many say that Guinness is good for you with all its vitamins, but Shane was never convinced this also pertained to the crème de menthe. Mr. Pareki slowly enjoyed his drinks while continuing conversation. When his glasses were empty, he ordered a repeat. At about eight-forty-five his granddaughter Sofia came to collect him. They lived in Gransha Drive, so Shane believed that Sofia was always dispatched from the house at eight-thirty to get him. Sofia was about fifteen years old and in the same year as Scarlet at St. Bernadette's Grammar School, so Shane knew her quite well. In her broad Belfast accent, she said, "Time to go, Granda!"

"But I've just gotten here, Girl!"

Shane was impressed with the way Sofia handled the situation. She waited while he deliberately resisted for a bit and then stated, "Well, if you don't come now, I'll go and get Ma!"

Her mother was Mr. Pareki's daughter, and he had to toe the line with her for many years since his wife passed away.

"OK, girl. Coming now."

As he left, he give Shane a wink and delivered words that Shane had heard from him before,

"Women. You can't live with them, and you can't live without them."

Shane also enjoyed the company of two other regulars. They were middle-aged, and he just knew them as Blaine and Gary.

They dressed business casual, so Shane assumed they may have been office workers. They most likely worked together and came in on the way back from work. These gentlemen went straight for the spirits. Cream of the Barley whisky was their drink of choice. Shane thought back to one evening in particular. They had arrived at about six-thirty on a Friday evening a few weeks back . Their conversation had started off quite sensibly, with discussion on the world news. As they plied in more drinks, the conversation subjects lost their accuracy. They had been discussing the topical subject of the Moon landing achieved by Neil Armstrong and company. This was a very popular discussion point globally as the world had watched with excitement the first moon landing in 1969. They discussed this accurately during their first round of drinks. After three or four rounds, they came back to the subject of space travel.

"NASA is sending a rocket to Mars," Blaine said.

"Neil Armstrong will be on the rocket and the first person to land on Mars," Gary said.

"They are planning to send him there and back next year."

Shane was working behind the lounge bar with Bernie that night. Bernie waved Shane over. "Is it true that a rocket could get to Mars and back in a year?" Bernie whispered.

"Don't think so," Shane said. "I saw a program last week on space travel and the subject was brought up. I'm sure they said it would take about a year to get there and another to get back, and no one yet is sure if a rocket could land on Mars."

"Yes, that's what I thought," Bernie said. "Must be the drink talking."

"By the way," Shane said, "I understand that Neil Armstrong may now have retired from space travel. I believe he'll be an ambassador for NASA going forward. So, if the U.S. decides to explore Mars, it'll be with a new leader."

"Yes, makes sense. They probably don't want a mishap with one of the most famous people of the twentieth century."

"Yeah. Don't want him to do a Major Tom. Anyway, they'd probably start that mission with an unmanned spaceship. I think it'd be a long time before a person is sent to Mars."

"Yeah. Agree."

Shane was both amused and a bit saddened by the exaggeration of his customers due to the drink. They were the nicest of people and he had great respect for Blaine and Gary.

There were two guys in their early thirties who would come in on a Friday evening and stay for a couple of hours. They would arrive about eight o'clock just as the cocktail hour was wrapping up. Shane believed they were brothers. Their names were Johnny and Kev. He wasn't sure if they were white- or blue-collar workers. They were always betting with each other and would also spend some time doing the football pools. Shane was often concerned that they would miss sending in the pools on time as they had to be submitted by ten o'clock the next morning. They usually had several rounds of drink and sometimes left the completed pools coupon on the counter. Shane would have to go chasing after them when this happened. They would bet on anything, sometimes on horse races or song contests. In addition, they would often debate on issues such as who was the best center forward in the English League, for example, Joe Royle or Peter Osgood. He would be careful not to get involved in their conversations. One evening earlier in the month the subject turned to music. They were having a big debate on which was the best Beatles album.

"It has to be *Abbey Road*, Johnny," Kev said.

"No, it has to be the *White Album*, Kev," Johnny said.

This went on for some time.

"Hi Shane, Mr. Quinn told us you're an expert in music," Kev said.

"He said you're going to Queen's University to study music," Johnny said.

"Oh, yes. I'm very passionate about music," Shane said.

"We could do with your help," Kev said. "You're the expert, Shane."

"I wouldn't say I'm an expert."

"Yes, we were told you're modest about it," Johnny said.

"Anyway, we need your help to resolve a difference in opinion," Kev said. "What is the best Beatles album?"

Shane was reluctant to get involved. However, in their eyes he was a world authority. So, he felt he better participate in this case.

"That's an easy one," he said.

Now this response caught their attention. At the best of times, it is often difficult to know if a Belfast person is truly listening; however, these two gentlemen were fixed like pointer dogs, focused on the next words that would come out of Shane's mouth. They waited in eager anticipation. There was a deliberate slight delay by Shane to enhance the tension.

"*The Beatles Greatest Hits!*" he said.

"Wow. I never thought of that," Johnny said.

"He's got a good point there," Kev said in agreement.

With that the debate was settled. Shane returned to his glass cleaning duties while pondering, did the Beatles ever release a Greatest Hits Album?

Each evening come nine o'clock most of the customers would migrate to the television sets in the lounge and public bars to watch the BBC nightly news. Invariably the main topic would be the Troubles in Northern Ireland. For about twenty minutes there would be a hush as the customers listened attentively to the news. Shane would also take an interest. Northern Ireland was currently the focal point of the world.

On Saturday evenings at about ten o'clock, two gentlemen would come in. Both would be well dressed in a suit and tie. They looked like businessmen. Shane's colleague, Barney, would often say to Shane,

"Here come the insurance men."

They would go to Mr. Quinn's office. One would stand outside, facing down the bar, while the other would enter the office. Mr. Quinn would always be in his office on Saturday nights at this time. After no more than a minute, the second gentleman would exit the office and often be seen putting a stuffed brown paper envelope in his inner coat pocket.

"The protection money has been paid!" Barney once said to Shane.

Shane and Siobhan met up as much as they could before Siobhan needed to travel over to Liverpool for the university term. However, up to this stage Shane had not taken Siobhan with him to visit his granda. Joseph McKeown had heard about this young lady and was wondering when he would get the chance to meet her. In typical Belfast fashion he did not speak directly to Shane on this. Rather, he mentioned to his daughter, Lily, so that she would have a quiet word with Shane. Lily duly obliged, and Shane arranged to bring Siobhan for a visit to Grosvenor Park to visit his Granda McKeown for breakfast one Saturday morning.

Joseph McKeown was a wily character with great charm and humor. He was quick to the door when the bell rang that Saturday morning and welcomed Shane and Siobhan into his house. "Great to meet you, Siobhan. So, you're the young lady that Shane has been hiding from me?"

Siobhan in normal confident form then said to Shane, "So why have you been hiding me from your grandfather, Shane?"

Shane knew that she loved pulling his leg. He pretended to ignore this comment. This made Joseph and Siobhan laugh.

"So, I hear you're a dab hand at go-kart racing?" Granda said.

"Well, my team pulled together and won the Ulster School's battery-powered competition. It was an amazing experience."

"I heard you were the one who pushed through on the last couple of laps."

"Yes, that was our strategy. We were banking on a few of the teams using too much of their batteries early on, and that's the way it played out."

"Congratulations!"

"Shall I put the tea on, Granda?" Shane said.

"Please do, Son. That'll give Siobhan and me a little time for a chat."

Granda's terraced house had a small dining area and an even smaller kitchen behind a curtain. The area wasn't large enough to swing a cat, but Granda had it tidily laid out to make cooking as easy as possible. Apart from a small cellar where the perishables were kept, most food was in the dining area in a standalone frosted-glass-fronted cabinet. Shane grabbed the tea tin from the cabinet, disappeared into the scullery and pulled the curtain behind him.

Granda had a talent for breaking the ice and getting the conversation going. In the five minutes during which Shane was making the tea, he had established that Siobhan's mother had twin brothers, named Harry and Joe.

"Oh, that'll be the McCartney twins."

"How do you know that?"

"Sure, didn't I coach the twins when they played for St. John's in the Springfield? They were very good Gaelic football players and were in the Minor team that won several trophies."

"Wow. I didn't know that. I must discuss that with my mother."

Then Granda went to the cabinet and took out three dishes and three spoons. He turned back to Siobhan.

"Do you like cereal?"

"Certainly, I do."

"Any particular type?"

"Surprise me."

"Then I'll do Shane's favorite for the three of us."

Granda took out a packet of All-Bran and layered each dish with some. He then added a layer of raisins followed by some Corn Flakes. Then he added some hazelnuts followed by Special K. Siobhan had a puzzled look on her face.

"What do you call that?" she asked.

"It's a serial. I'll tell you next week!"

With that Siobhan and Granda burst out laughing, just as Shane reappeared from the scullery with the tea. Shane was surprised and was wondering what the fun was about. Siobhan explained and went on to mention his grandfather's connection with her mother's twin brothers. Shane had a puzzled look on his face. "I didn't know you had twin uncles, Siobhan." Then he gave a knowing glance to his grandfather. "In five minutes, Granda, you seem to know more about Siobhan and her family than I do!"

After a most enjoyable hour's stay, Shane and Siobhan left to walk back to the McMahon house. As they progressed back up the Falls Road, they heard a large bang.

"It's a bomb," Siobhan said.

"Where did the bang come from?"

"Further up the Falls but quite close."

Shane looked forward. A few hundred yards in front of them he could see smoke rising into the air over a wall and the trees behind. This was the site of an old tuberculosis hospital now used as a senior peoples' hostel. It had large grounds surrounded by a ten-foot-tall stone wall. However, where the wall joined the Falls Road there was a hole big enough for people to climb through. This hole had been there for some years, and children would often go through and play there among the trees in the grounds. As Shane and Siobhan approached, they saw two youths exiting through the hole in the wall and running toward them covered in blood with their jackets in tatters and smoking. Both were screaming. Shane and Siobhan ran up to them, and each caught one and helped them to sit on the curb. Shane and Siobhan took off their coats and wrapped them around them, padding them down to choke the smoke. Both were badly wounded with blood on their faces and hands, but all limbs were intact. They could hear the sirens of ambulances in the distance coming up the road behind them from the Royal Victoria Hospital.

"Was anyone else with you?" Siobhan asked.

"A friend of ours is still in there," one said trembling and stuttering.

People from the surrounding houses people crowded

around. "Rang for an ambulance a few minutes back," one said.

Several minutes later two ambulances came, and the medics took control and attended to them. Shane spoke to the ambulance crew. "We believe there's a third victim still in the hostel grounds."

The leader of a crew of four paramedics thanked Shane.

"Joey and Fergal, you two head into the grounds and locate the other victim," the lead medic said.

"Ten-four."

The two medics made a beeline for the hole in the wall. About twenty yards into the grounds, they discovered the third youth lying there groaning. Luckily, he was in one piece but was bleeding badly. They placed him gently on a stretcher and carried him out of the hospital grounds through the hole in the wall. Before long the medics had all three of the wounded loaded into the ambulances. It would be a short trip back to the Royal Victoria Hospital.

People lingered behind and were talking about what had happened. Some knew who the youths were. Shane and Siobhan stayed to listen.

"These lads often take their guitars and play songs for the patients in the hostel," one lady said.

"They were unfortunately in the wrong place at the wrong time and tripped the bomb," another lady said.

Shane and Siobhan came up to the McMahon household just as the radio was reporting the incident. Lily was sitting in the parlor with full attention on the radio. Shane and Siobhan sat down beside her on the sofa.

> Good morning. A bomb detonated in a hostel for senior living on the Falls Road this morning. Three youths accidentally tripped the bomb and are being treated for injuries at the Royal Victoria Hospital. None of the injuries is life-threatening. The IRA quickly moved to claim responsibility. However, they made it clear that the target of the attack was the British Forces, not the youths.
>
> The previous evening the IRA had planted bombs in several parts of the city. They had telephoned the security forces using their known code

and informed them that bombs were planted in certain areas but did not give the exact locations. The night before one group of soldiers looking for a specific bomb of a similar size tripped it and all six were killed. Other bombs were successfully located and defused. For some reason the one in the hostel was missed.

When the youths were crossing through a shortcut through the wall into the grounds to go to the main entrance, they accidentally tripped the bomb.

"So relieved you weren't caught up in this," Lily said to Shane and Siobhan.

"Actually, we were, Mom, but only later on when the victims needed help," Shane said.

"We waited until the ambulances arrived and took the casualties. Then we made our way on back," Siobhan said.

"Jesus, Mary, and Joseph!"

Soon after, the news revealed the names of the victims. One was Ciarán O'Loughlin, the McMahon's neighbor's son. Shane had taught him to play guitar. There was a flurry in the street when this was announced. There was a knock on the door. Mrs. O'Loughlin was there. Lily answered and immediately gave her a big hug. Shane and Siobhan look on from down the hallway.

"Please come in Ursula. So sorry to hear about Ciarán."

"Thanks Lily. Mustn't stay long. Not long heard myself. I need to go to the Royal. Can Scarlet come over and mind the younger ones?"

"Coming," Scarlet said.

"We'll come over as well," Siobhan said. "I'll just ring my mother and let her know I'll be a bit later than expected."

Lily walked Ursula down to the end of the road to catch a taxi.

"Would you like me to come with you, Ursula?"

"I'll be fine, Lily."

"Will Dave be there?"

"Yes, he's on his way with from Corrigan Park. He's been up there watching Joseph play. Joseph asked to be substituted and is on his way with him. They said they'd take a taxi straight from there. They may be down already."

"Just let me know if you need anything, Ursula. Best of luck."

The following day three saloon cars in tandem came up the street. The McMahons looked across from behind their curtains. Shane could see paramilitaries sporting dark green berets getting out of two of the vehicles at the front and the back. They then positioned themselves to keep watch. From the third saloon car in the middle emerged a well-known face. Shane recognized him as the head of the IRA in Belfast. He lived in the Gransha estate and tended to keep a low profile. He was accompanied by his wife. She was also well known to Shane, and from all reports he had heard she was a very considerate and kind lady. They went into the O'Loughlin's residence. Shane could see the tension on the faces of his parents, with a paramilitary force standing just yards away. After just five minutes, the head of the IRA and his wife returned to their car, and they left.

"They're going now," Lily said.

"Yes, they can't afford to stay here long, especially in a cul-de-sac," Brendan said.

Then some neighbors went round to the O'Loughlin house. When they emerged, they discussed the details with other neighbors including the McMahons, who by then had come out onto the street.

"Apparently, the deputation's purpose was to apologize to the family for the damage caused to their son," the McMahons' next-door neighbor Hilda said.

"Luckily none of Ciarán's injuries are life threatening nor permanently debilitating, or they may have gotten a different reception," Lily said.

Shane learned later that it transpired that Ciarán had to have an operation to replace both ear drums. He heard on the news that Ciarán and his friends had been very fortunate not to have had worse injuries for two reasons. Firstly, the wind was blowing away from them, and secondly the bomb was planted at the base of a tree, which took most of the force. These two aspects saved their lives.

That same evening two men arrived at an IRA safehouse. Their names were Seamus Rooney and Jimmy McGee. Jimmy was about fifty years of age and was responsible for the four IRA cells in West Belfast. Seamus reported to him and was the leader of the cell that planted the bombs. Jimmy's boss was an adjutant responsible for military operations. They were summoned by the adjutant.

"Now, let me do the talking, Seamus."

"I hear he's fuming. It's my fault. I'll take the blame, Jimmy."

"Not really your fault, Seamus. Some eejits at central office fucked up."

They knocked at the door. A bodyguard opened it. Inside there were two more bodyguards. They were all at least six foot four and two-hundred-and-twenty pounds. They were not smiling. "Sit here," one of them said.

Seamus and Jimmy sat down. Sweat was trickling down Jimmy's face. Seamus could see this and knew that Jimmy was worried. I don't think they'll kill us, he thought. Maybe we'll be given a beating.
Hopefully it'll just be a telling off. They sat there for ten minutes. Two well-dressed men then exited. One looked at Seamus and Jimmy with a piercing gaze as they moved briskly to the door.

"Is that the political leader?" Seamus whispered.

"Yes, he's the head Sinn Fein."

"Jesus. This is serious. Who's the other guy?"

"A personal bodyguard."

One of the other bodyguards followed them out.

"Looks like he has two bodyguards."

"Yeah. He'd normally have two at least."

They continued to sit there for another two or three minutes. Then a gentleman dressed in a suit came out. "He's ready to see you now."

Jimmy and Seamus rose from their chairs. Jimmy turned to Seamus and whispered, "He'll only speak in Gaelic. Hope yours is up to scratch."

"No problem," Seamus responded in Gaelic.

They entered and the other man followed.

"Sit here, gentlemen," a middle-aged greying gentleman said in Gaelic as he peered over his glasses.

Jimmy was sweating even more, but Seamus remained reasonably calm. The guy who had fetched them sat in a chair at the back of the room.

"How can we help you, Sir?" said Jimmy.

"Looks like a cluster fuck," said the adjutant.

"Yes, trying to find out why the information didn't get through on the hostel bomb," said Jimmy.

"I'll tell you. Somebody fucked up!"

Jimmy and Seamus sat quietly. The adjutant then addressed Seamus. "Did you give the information to our central division correctly?"

"Sure did, Sir," said Seamus.

The adjutant stared at him, summing him up. Seamus remained calm.

"Do you realize that I had to go and apologize to the boys' parents. Spent all day getting around to all three."

"Sorry, Sir," said Jimmy.

"Why are you saying sorry?" the adjutant said. "You've just told me it wasn't your fault."

Jimmy remained quiet.

"Just had the political guys onto me. Apparently, this bomb has scuppered some initiative they've been working on. Got a lot of earache."

"Sorry, Sir," said Jimmy.

"Cut the apologies," said the adjutant. He then once again turned to Seamus. "Now do we know to whom in central you spoke?"

"Just a code, Sir. 'Charolais'."

"OK. The two of you may go now."

Jimmy and Seamus rose and were escorted out by the other gentleman. They departed without a further word.

When they were on their own Seamus asked Jimmy, "Who was the guy who sat at the back of the room?"

"Don't know his name, but he's the adjutant's counsel. The boss confers with him on important issues. They're probably discussing about us now."

"Wow. He looked like a cool customer," said Seamus as they got back into their car.

"Yes, got a good poker face," said Jimmy. "Jesus, imagine what that meeting would've been like if we had've done something wrong."

"Wouldn't want to."

One morning in late June Tyrone took delivery of a package from the postman addressed to Shane and placed it on the sideboard in the hallway beside the phone. He sought Shane out. He was in their bedroom.

"I'm not expecting a parcel. Wonder what that could be?" Shane said.

"Don't know."

Shane went downstairs and picked up the package. "Seems to be from England. It has a Sheffield postmark."

He took it into the kitchen where he opened it. There was a thank you card and a box of Thornton's chocolates. It was from John McGee. The message read,

> Thank you, Shane, for the advice. Just ran my first international race for the Ireland junior team against England, an 800-meter outdoor race in Sheffield. Came in second to an English guy, and I broke one-forty-eight, setting a personal best. Couldn't think of a suitable present for you, so I got one for your ma instead. Make sure she gives you at least one chocolate. I hear they are the best in Europe.

Coincidentally, Lily entered the kitchen. "Lovely chocolates, Shane. Who are they for?"

"They're for you, Mom."

"For me? Who from?"

"From John McGee. He just ran his first race for Ireland and sent me a thank you for some advice I had given him. He felt you should benefit also."

"What a lovely boy. Please tell him thank you. Perhaps I should make one of my shepherd's pies and take it round to his family. Do you think he'd like that?"

"I'm certain he would, Mom."

Shane made regular visits to the Royal Victoria Hospital to check up on Paul. When he visited Paul one evening toward the end of June he could see that he was recovering well. However, a return home was some time off as he still needed constant attention. Shane and Paul would reminisce on some of the good battles they had at cross-country and on the track.

"I remember the time, Shane, when a couple of years ago you would often beat me in the races with a fast finish," Paul said.

"Working hard to get back to that, Paul."

"Not if I can help it. Those short races worked well for you. However, now you must pull that sprint out after working hard for twice the distance."

"I'm up to the challenge now that I am getting clear of that Achilles injury. When you're fully fit, we can have a fair go at it."

"Dead on."

"Shane, I've decided to skip my exams this year because of the injuries. I'll retake my final year."

"Oh. Sorry to hear that, Paul. But it makes sense. What about the scholarship?"

"My parents contacted Villanova University. They offered to defer the scholarship to next year."

"Sounds good, Paul."

Paul then discussed training plans with Shane for the fall when he should be ready to run again. Both agreed that they would focus on qualifying at the junior level for the World Cross-Country Championships. That would be their number one priority.

"Tim should qualify as well," Paul said.

"Yes, see no reason why not, so long as his schedule allows him to come across the Atlantic for the Northern Ireland Championships," Shane said.

"Yes, he'll need to run in that to guarantee selection."

The exam results were due. Shane was on tenterhooks. He had been checking the post for the past couple of days. Some of his school mates had already received their grades. One morning in early July Scarlet appeared from the hallway carrying a brown envelope. Shane was sitting at the table with Lily and Tyrone. Brendan was just rising from bed after a late night of work. Shane had his back to Scarlet. Then Scarlet proclaimed aloud. "Look what I have. Appears to be an official communication. Probably exam results."

Shane jumped up from his chair. "What! It'll be for me. Give it here."

Scarlet deliberated and teased. "All in good time."

Then Shane rushed toward her. She held the letter up high to stall Shane just that little bit longer and extend the tension. Shane eventually grabbed the letter. Then he sat down. He looked at the envelope, but he was so nervous he had difficulty opening it.

"Give it here," Lily said.

She opened it. Lily kept the drama going as she slowly and deliberately read the letter to herself, muttering. It was obvious that Scarlet inherited her mother's ability for teasing. Then she read it again to herself, muttering. Shane was chumping at the bit.

"Are As and Bs any good?" Lily asked.

Shane came across to her. "What As and Bs? Are you serious, Mom?" he said with a combination of anxiety and excitement.

"Yes, I'm sure, Son."

As hoped for, Shane received the grades that would allow him to follow his dream and go the Queen's University in Belfast to major in Music. The McMahon family celebrated that evening.

Lily made her special Irish stew. In Shane's opinion nobody made Irish stew like Lily. Siobhan came to take advantage of Lily's cooking and celebrate. Shane was at the front door to meet her and brought her into the parlor where all the family was.

"So how did you do with your exams, Siobhan? Did you get As and Bs like Shane?" Lily asked.

Shane felt embarrassed. Siobhan could see this and decided to tease a bit.

"So, Shane, you got As and Bs? Well done," she said. Then she continued with a smile. "No, Mrs. McMahon. I just got As."

Shane stood up, aghast. "Wow, all As in mathematics, physics, chemistry, and further mathematics? No one usually gets that. Fantastic!"

"Well done, to you both," Brendan said.

All applauded Shane and Siobhan. Tyrone then dressed their dog, Keeper, in celebratory ribbons. Keeper was not best pleased but enjoyed the fun. They all sat down for the best Irish stew in town.

While the family dinner was enjoyed, Siobhan asked, "Why's your dog called Keeper?"

"That's a long story. It goes back to when Scarlet and Shane returned one day with this stray dog," Lily said.

"We asked Mom and Da if we could mind the dog while we put up posters on the lampposts and telegraph poles in the neighborhood, to see if we could find the rightful owner. Luckily, they said yes," Scarlet said.

"We were very careful to point out that they could do this so long as they took him to the dog pound if the owner could not be located within the next week," Brendan said.

"Several days later we had no responses to the posters, so Scarlet came to me and asked if I thought we could convince Mom and Da to allow us to keep him. I said let's give it a try," Shane said.

"So, we came to Mom and Da in the parlor and pleaded with them to let us keep the dog, but they were at first reluctant. Da asked for a good reason to keep him," Scarlet said.

Then Tyrone joined the conversation. "I said to Da that he is a special pedigree mongrel dog. Da laughed, and then he said let's sleep on it and we'll have an answer in the morning."

"So, what happened next?" Siobhan asked.

"I was heading up the stairs when I heard Scarlet speaking to the dog. She was in the parlor telling him that he had to impress me. She didn't realize that I was within earshot. The parlor door was slightly open, so I listened closely. She said to him to make sure to win me over. She told him that she'll teach him some tricks, and she spent time doing this. Finally, she told him to make sure he carried these out in the morning when I got up," Brendan said.

Lilly picked up the story. "Brendan came down the following morning before the kids got up. I was in the kitchen. I could see the dog do all these tricks and Brendan was stunned!"

"I came over to Lilly and asked her if she'd mind if we said yes to the kids, and she agreed. When the kids emerged, we got them together and I said to them that if we could rely on them to conscientiously look after the dog and take it on regular walks, it was a keeper."

"I leaped with joy, went over, and hugged Da. Then Tyrone asked what we should call him," Scarlet said.

"I told them that their father has just given him the name, Keeper," said Lily, "Then all I could hear was Tyrone dancing around singing, 'We have a pedigree mongrel dog called Keeper'!"

Siobhan looked down at Keeper who was in turn looking up from under the table at her with appealing eyes.

"Makes perfect sense. He's certainly a keeper."

During the summer months Shane kept working on Friday and Saturday evenings at the Eagle Inn. He noticed that there was a different clientele in the inn. He saw certain groups, akin to gangs, drinking together. Others would walk around with an air, as if they owned the place. It was evident to Shane that the paramilitaries were using the pub for some of their meetings.

One senior ranking person, a middle-aged female, Maria Dern, appeared to be the leader. She was known to be one of the main radicals in the IRA. When she came by, Shane could see people turn away so as not to look her in the eye. She must have a stern reputation, Shane thought. One evening Shane was aware of a tension in the air. When he took some glasses upstairs to the public bar he saw groups at two different tables in the upstairs public bar shouting insults across the room to each other. Maria was in one of the groups. He had heard on the news that the IRA was splintering and a harder line group, the Provisionals, had formed. The original IRA was now named the Officials. Although they were part of the same team, he could see that issues were brewing over strategy. This led to scuffles. The Eagle Inn had seen a few in the previous couple of months but nothing too serious.

On this evening, tempers were getting out of hand. Shane saw one of the guys brandishing a gun under the table he was at. Shane mentioned this to his colleague Bernie who was working behind the lounge bar when he returned back down. They could hear the commotion from the floor below as shouts rang out. Both looked at each other. Then Shane could hear people screaming and shots being fired.

"Quickly, crouch down behind the bar counter," Bernie said to Shane.

Bernie then went around to the customers in the lounge and recommended they exit the pub. They left quietly and in orderly fashion with Bernie escorting them out. After that he joined Shane.

"Don't know if you were aware, but Mr. Quinn had arranged for the wooden bar areas to be reinforced with metal. He always likes taking such precautions. We should be safe here," Bernie said to Shane.

"No, I hadn't heard. Great that he had the foresight. Let's crouch down further."

The gun fight came down to the lounge bar as one group chased another. The reinforcement of the bar was the savior of Shane and Bernie as shots continued to pour out from rival factions. After about five minutes, they could hear people leave and the room went quiet. Upstairs was quiet too.

"Let's just stay down for a few minutes more to be sure," Bernie said.

Soon they felt confident to emerge from behind the counter. Shane could see at least four people down, two motionless, and the others injured, reeling in pain on the ground.

"My God, Bernie, I think a couple of them are dead."

"I'll deal with this Shane. Better for you to go in home."

Shane was trembling.

"Will you be OK, Shane?"

"Just shaken, Bernie. I'll be fine."

Shane took Bernie's advice and headed off home while Bernie rang for an ambulance.

SARACEN CITY

The Eagle Inn had witnessed a few paramilitary disputes, but no one was prepared for the shocking experience of a gun battle. Fortunately they were the exception and the only one that Shane had witnessed in the pub. Most days the inn was a peaceful haven from the hustle and bustle that was gaining momentum in the area. However, one Saturday evening there was a significant change to the norm. As mentioned, late on Saturday evenings, at about ten o'clock the insurance men would come in. The visitations of the Official IRA representatives, conducted more like business encounters, did little to distract the patrons.

On this evening at approximately nine o'clock, Shane saw two hooded gunmen displaying sidearms arrive. He was working with Bernie, so nudged him. "What's going on here?"

"Oh my God. Look," said Bernie. "They're coming over in Mr. Quinn's direction."

Mr. Quinn who was speaking with a couple of customers saw them and walked over to them. Within seconds one of the gunmen shoved Mr. Quinn to the ground. The patrons and the other barmen gasped in horror. One of the gunmen let off a shot toward the roof. "Stay put and stay quiet, and no one will get hurt."

The gunmen dragged Mr. Quinn to his feet and then pushed and shoved him forward in the direction of his office at the corner of the lounge. A third gunman manned the front entrance. The staff and patrons were alarmed but as ordered, stayed in position, whispering to each other. Shane was anxious, but for everyone's safety Bernie and he remained in place and kept calm as they had been trained.

"Remember just stay calm and don't intervene," Bernie said, "This is best for all concerned."

"Got it, Bernie. Mustn't escalate the issue."

The hooded men continued to push Mr. Quinn toward his

office where the safe was located. They passed the bar behind which Shane and Bernie were standing. Shane could hear Mr. Quinn explain that protection money was regularly paid and that the collectors were due in about an hour. One of the gunmen replied, "We are fully aware of that. Now do what you're told, and no one will get hurt."

They kept forcing Mr. Quinn unceremoniously forward and entered the office. The door was left ajar, and Shane could just see through the gap that Mr. Quinn was on his knees. Then he saw a gun placed on his temple and heard a command,

"Open the safe!"

Shane felt that there was no bluffing here. Bernie came over to Shane and both looked over through the gap in the door.

"I recognize the one holding the gun to Mr. Quinn's head," Bernie said.

"What?"

"Despite the mask, I can see a strange scar around his left eyelid. He was in my class in St. Joe's."

"Did he get the scar then?"

"Yes, he was in a fight in the school yard and the other lad grabbed a piece of glass that was sitting on the ground just outside the school railings and pushed it into his head."

"Jeez."

"He was a hooligan then and a rebel without a cause. He now has a cause. I've seen him around since, and the scar has grown as he has grown."

"So, do ya think he would pull the trigger?"

"Sure of it. However, Mr. Quinn is smart, and he'll handle the situation OK."

Shane could just see through the crack in the door that Mr. Quinn was opening the safe. "Bernie looks like the gunmen have their spoils. I can just about see them putting the money into a bag."

The gunmen exited the office, told Mr. Quinn to stay put until they had left, and off they went. This episode lasted all of twenty minutes. Bernie and Shane rushed over to the office to help Mr. Quinn. He was bleeding from a couple of cuts to the head where a gunman had wacked him with the sidearm.

"Are you OK?" Shane asked.

"A bit dazed but otherwise alright."

"I'll ring for an ambulance," Bernie said.

Within fifteen minutes Mr. Quinn was taken to the Royal. On the radio news the following day Shane found out that as surmised by many, the group that had orchestrated this event was from the Provisional IRA. They had deliberately and provocatively taken funds reserved for the Official IRA. I'm sure this will not be the end of things, he thought. Don't want to be around when the Official IRA catches up with the Provisionals.

Mr. Quinn was given leave for a few days because of his ordeal. When he returned, he was a shadow of himself. Shane noticed that he was nervous and shaking a lot. One evening the following week Bernie was talking about the incident to Shane.

"You know I was speaking to Mr. Quinn. He's gutted that this could have been done by freedom fighters for a united Ireland."

"I'm sure he is. He doesn't make a secret that he's a supporter of the cause."

"I've seen him leave the last few evenings with a bottle in a brown paper bag. He's hitting the booze badly."

"Awful. What a terrible experience."

Several weeks later Mr. Quinn was placed on extended leave. During this time, Bernie was given the role of running the pub, a job he had neither sought nor wanted.

Lily's younger sister Deirdre was cleaning her front windows in her terraced house situated on the Crumlin Road. Opposite the three-story block of large, terraced properties high above the Crumlin Road on a hill stood the Ardoyne Roman Catholic Church, the Holy Cross. Mr. Baxter, a neighbor who lived higher up on the Crumlin Road, was coming back from work as usual at about one-thirty. He worked the early shift in the cotton mill in

Flax Street, about a mile closer to the city center. He often passed by her house just after lunchtime. Deirdre greeted him, "Hello Mr. Baxter. Beautiful day."

"Isn't it lovely?"

Deirdre was standing outside on a wooden box she was using as a step and was polishing her sitting room windows. She noticed the reflection of a beam of light in the window coming from high up in the church grounds. This was unusual. As Mr. Baxter moved past her, she turned to look up to the church to see what was causing the blinding reflection. Then a loud shot rang out followed by a second. Deirdre was stunned, frozen to the spot. Just five yards away she watched the gentleman fall to the ground.

There was a delayed scream from Deirdre. She ran to the dying victim and cradled his head in her arms. "Hold on there Mr. Baxter. I'll get help."

There was a semblance of a mumble or groan from the victim. Her husband Declan, who was just about to head off back to work following his lunchbreak, ran out. She bellowed, "Ring for an ambulance, Dec! And bring a pillow and some blankets!"

"On it." A few minutes later Declan returned with the pillow and blankets and handed them to Deirdre. "Ambulance on the way," Declan said.

Deirdre laid the pillow under the gentleman's head. Blood was streaming down from a head wound onto his shirt and tie. He was just barely conscious. She spoke the rosary into his ear. He grabbed her sleeve and then the life drained out of him. In a couple of minutes an ambulance arrived from the nearby Mater Hospital. The medics checked the gentleman, nodded their heads, and covered his face with a blanket. They lifted him into the ambulance. Deirdre stood, blood spilling down her bright yellow frock. She was in shock. Declan helped her inside the house. This was a shattering experience and one that would last with her forever.

After a couple of cups of tea with more sugar than usual to ease the shock, Deirdre went to the bathroom, had a shower, and put on fresh clothing. Declan called in to his work to explain that he had an emergency and could not come back that afternoon. They both sat and discussed what had happened.

"My God. That could have been one of us, or worse still one of our children, Dec."

"Yeah, Luv. Thanks be to God that it wasn't."

"I don't feel safe, Dec."

"Understand, Luv. The shock."

Deirdre went to ring her elder sister, Lily. She was trembling as she lifted the receiver.

"Here, Luv. I'll do that. You sit down."

Declan rang and explained what had happened.

"I'll be over early evening, Dec. I'll call Liam to give us a lift."

"Thanks, Lily."

"Now, please make sure that Deirdre gets some rest. Better to put her up to bed. I'll do dinner when I come along."

"Thanks Lily. Will do. See you soon."

Lily rang their younger brother Liam, who came over at about five-thirty to drive the McMahon family to Ardoyne. Brendan got into the front seat, while Scarlet and Tyrone squeezed in between Lily and Shane in the back seat. When they arrived, Lily went over and hugged her younger sister.

"How're you doing, girl?"

"Getting over it now, Lily. The sleep helped."

"Don't worry about a thing. I'll do dinner. Here's Shane with all the groceries."

"I'd love to help," Dierdre said.

"Come on then."

Both disappeared into the kitchen with the bags of groceries.

One of Deirdre's teenage daughters, Brenda, turned to Scarlet. "Come on up with JoAnn and me to our room, Scarlet. We can get up to some mischief."

"Sounds good. Coming."

Deirdre's youngest, Paul, about the same age as Tyrone, beckoned him over. "Want to play with me, Tyrone? We can build with my Meccano set in my bedroom. I've started on a bridge."

"Wow. Coming Paul."

Brendan and Declan went into the sitting room for a chat and cracked open a couple of Guinness's. This left Shane and Dan in the parlor.

"And then there were two," said Dan. "Fancy a quick half before dinner? The Harp should be opening soon."

"Let's go for it."

As they were about to leave, they heard a shout from Lily. "Be back in an hour."

"Will be," Shane said.

Shane and Dan walked half a mile down the Crumlin Road and then turned left into the estate where the pub was located. As they entered the street, Shane looked down the hill.

"Holy God!" he said. "See that?"

"Massive riot. News must have gotten round quickly about the shooting."

"Gosh. There must be about fifty youths rioting."

"And about the same number of soldiers. Let's get a bit closer to see better."

They stepped onto the road to cross. Then suddenly there was a loud shriek of sirens. They jumped back to the curb as two ambulances and a fire engine turned the corner and whizzed by. They were about to cross again when two more ambulances and another fire engine passed, followed by what looked like a news crew. Shane and Dan progressed about fifty yards closer, and from their vantage point had a good view of the proceedings.

"Gosh. What is that ball of flames shooting across the street?" Dan asked.

"It's a soldier. Look, petrol bombs are being hurled in their direction. Other soldiers are coming to his aid with blankets."

"Pains me to see these British fuckers all over our streets as if they owned the place."

"If they weren't here, Dan, there'd be a civil war. They're here to keep the peace."

"Some peace. Want all these English people out of our country."

"You weren't saying that a few months ago when you and I were down at the front of the Ulster Hall at the Led Zep concert, and you were shouting to that English guy Robert Plant that he should be King of Ulster."

"That's different."

"Is it?"

"Yes."

"Got it."

Shane and Dan stood and watched.

"God, people are getting shot," Dan said.

"It's the plastic bullets. They take a chunk out of people."

"Wow. I can see blood flying through the air."

"Peckinpah would be impressed."

Shane could see the army lashing out at the demonstrators, taking no prisoners. Many civilians dropped to the floor. Rubber bullets hailed across the street. Many people were injured. The rioters replied with bricks and petrol bombs. Cars were burning. More ambulances came and parked on the periphery. The global press had arrived and stayed near the ambulances.

"Look. See those poor medics carrying stretchers into the heart of the confrontation? Soldiers and civilians are being carried side by side to the ambulances," Dan said.

Some medics, braving their lives to aid the wounded, themselves became victims. The crisp, dry, and bright night had a tinge of red in the air once again as cars were set ablaze. Saracens arrived to help drive the crowd back. Two armored vehicles had water cannons and began pushing back the rabble.

"Think we should be getting back now," Shane said.

"Yeah, let's go."

Shane and Dan returned and told the others what had been

going on. "Don't go down the Crumlin Road when you leave, Uncle Liam," Dan said. "Better to go up the Crumlin and then cross over by the West Circular."

"Thanks, Dan. Will do."

"Let's turn on the TV and see what's brewing," Declan said.

An extended news was bringing live footage from the riot in the Ardoyne. Declan called out. "Deirdre, Lily, better come for a few minutes and see the news."

The kids heard the call and came down from their bedrooms. Everyone crowded into the parlor. The news started off with a recap of the shooting that led up to the riot.

A forty-seven-year-old man was shot and killed on the Crumlin Road at lunchtime. The shooting took place just outside the Holy Cross Church in the Ardoyne area of Belfast. Security forces believe that a sniper was positioned in the raised area of the church. No one has taken responsibility for the shooting, but the forces believe that it was carried out by an extreme wing of the protestant Ulster Volunteers Force. A spokesman for the security forces confirmed that there will be an army presence from now on in the vicinity to prevent such atrocities happening again.

The dying man, whose name has not yet been released, was aided in his dying minutes by a resident of the area, as shown by this photograph taken by a passerby.

"My God, Deirdre," Lily said. "That's a photo of you with the victim. You have blood all over that new yellow frock you bought last week."

"Don't know how they got the photo, Lily. People came out and gathered round, but I didn't see anyone with a camera."

"You were focused on the poor man," Declan said. "Can't expect to know all that is going on around you."

The newscaster continued.

And now we will pass to Peter McGonigle who is on site in Ardoyne, close to the riot.

Pete McGonigle stood with his back to the riot, looked into the camera, and described the scene.

Local people, angry at the death of a neighbor early this afternoon, came out to the streets to protest. Youths joined in and started burning cars and hurling bricks. The security forces were quickly deployed and then became the focus of attention. The youths hurled bricks and petrol bombs in their direction. Up to the present time fifteen civilians and five soldiers have been taken to hospital. The rioting is continuing vigorously as can be seen from the scenes behind me. Army Saracens and water cannon arrived about fifteen minutes ago and can be seen behind me quelling the disturbance. More later. Back to you in the studio, Jim.

"Wow. That's going on now less than a mile away?" Lily said.

"Yes, Auntie Lily," Dan said.

"Is it likely to spread up to us?"

"Not likely, Mom," Shane said. "The forces seem to have a good handle on it. However, as Dan said, we should avoid going down the Crumlin on our way back."

"OK everyone. Dinner is ready. Come gather in the kitchen," Lily said.

Tensions continued to grow in Belfast, and violence was escalating. One evening the television news provided footage on disturbances in the center of Belfast.

The paramilitary groups have moved their focus to planting bombs within the city center once again. The bombs have been positioned to cause maximum disruption. An unnamed member of Sinn Fein, the political wing of the IRA, informed the BBC that the aim is to significantly disrupt businesses and bring attention to their demands. Shocked and distraught businesspeople in the city are seeing their livelihoods once again crumble in front of them. A boutique owner in the city center told the BBC that businesses were going to sell off their stock at rock bottom prices to the public and then board up their premises.

On hearing this Shane decided to visit the city center the following Saturday morning to see if there were any bargains in the clothes boutiques. As he traveled through the side streets and lanes where the boutiques were grouped, he noticed in a boutique front window the Kid Curry jacket, now reduced to fifteen pounds. That's ten percent of the original price, he thought. Yes, this is the shop window that Mom and I looked at when we bought the new stereo system. Can't believe that the price is only fifteen pounds. I'll check. He went in.

"Is this really fifteen pounds?" Shane asked the boutique manager who was busy brushing the floor.

"Unfortunately, yes. Considered damaged goods and I'm obliged to sell it at a knock-down price. No problem, insurance will make up the balance."

"May I try it on?"

"Be my guest."

Shane put on the jacket.

"Looks to be a perfect fit," the manager said.

"Wow. I'll take it."

It was almost pristine apart from two farthing-sized spots where foam, deployed to put out the fire, had spluttered. They were hardly noticeable. He bought a couple of shirts and a pair of Levi's, also at reduced prices. He proudly wore the jacket back home.

Shane was still comfortable training in West Belfast but was now modifying his routes to stay clear of hot spots where violence had erupted or was likely to erupt. That afternoon he went out for a brisk ten-mile training run around the Hannahstown area. He then decided to walk down to the Royal Victoria Hospital to visit Paul. He proudly wore his new jacket.

"Nice jacket. Where did ya get that?" Paul asked.

"Just been down to the boutique area after the recent bombings. Good bargains there."

"Well, I'll have to wait a bit to pucker up my wardrobe."

"How're you feeling?"

"Coming along well. The doc says that I should be discharged in a couple of weeks' time. Can't wait."

"Way to go. Here's some fruit to help your recovery."

"Thanks, friend."

They chatted and laughed at the irony of the situation that

brought this good fortune to Shane. They were having their usual discussion on running schedules when a loud crack cut through the air. Shane looked over Paul's head to the other parallel wing and saw a flash of blue light. Then another crack rang out. "Wow! I believe there's a gun battle in the next wing!"

"What should we do?"

"I don't know. There's no way I can wheel you to safety. Let's hope the gun battle doesn't pile into this ward."

 "Keep yer head down. If they come this way, don't look at them."

"No eye contact. Got it."

The hospital had long wards on several wings. Each ward housed about twelve patients in evenly spaced beds, balanced each side. The gun battle appeared to be in the adjacent ward in the next wing. The ward ran parallel to the one Paul was in, with a corridor of about eighty feet separating them at right angles at the front ends. Each ward had entrances at the front and back. The rear entrance exited to a stairwell, normally used for evacuation.

In all Shane heard four shots. Then there was calm.

"Do ya think they've gone?" Paul asked.

"Pretty quiet now. Just let's give it a bit longer."

"I can hear something."

"Me too. I hear the pounding of running coming towards us.."

"Jeez. Yes, they're coming closer."

Other patients in the ward were expressing concern. Then the entrance doors broke open and two hooded gunmen plowed through. The first one in shouted as he ran, "Keep your heads down and you'll be fine!"

Shane and Paul kept still with heads bowed. The gunmen hurried past them. One looked over at Shane. "Like the jacket." he said.

"Thanks."

Luckily, the gunmen kept moving ahead. Shane peeped to the side and saw that the two gunmen exited through the rear doors. He then heard the clanking sound of them descending the metal steps outside to the car park. Danger was averted. Shane and Paul spoke for a while. Then hospital officials came in and asked all visitors to leave.

The evening BBC news carried the story.

It transpired that a prominent member of the newly formed Provisional IRA was in the Royal Victoria Hospital in Belfast for an appendix operation. Sources close to the Official IRA informed us that two of their gunmen carried out a hit on this prominent member. Their mission was accomplished, and they successfully escaped. This appeared to be a tit-for-tat assassination. We've just received news that the victim was Belfast's Provisional IRA leader, Maria Dern.

Shane woke up early as normal on Tuesday, August 10. He went downstairs at about seven o'clock and into the parlor where he knew his mother would be.

"What was that ruckus last night, Mom?"

"Ssh!"

The morning news had just started on the wireless and Lily was listening attentively.

Operation Demetrius was launched by the security forces yesterday. Houses in different Nationalist areas of Belfast were raided, and over three hundred people thought to be connected with the Provisional IRA were arrested and interned. They were brought to a newly built detention center at a former Royal Air Force base in Long Kesh, some ten miles outside Belfast.

Later yesterday evening there were disturbances in Nationalist areas, the worst of which was in Ballymurphy. Several people were shot and killed by the army in what is being referred to as the Battle of Ballymurphy. This followed protests and disturbances in the area. Security forces released a statement that those killed had guns and were shooting at them. This has been vehemently denied by the families of the deceased. One of the men killed was a Catholic priest. His name has not yet been released.

"Jeez. Can't believe that a priest was shooting at the security forces," Shane said.

"Bet the army wasn't aware when they made their

statement that a priest was shot by them. I doubt we've heard the end of this."

The news continued.

The Northern Ireland Government has issued a statement advising all residents in the Belfast area to stay indoors for the next few evenings.

"Aren't you due to train with John this week?" Lily said.
"Yes, in fact this afternoon."
"Isn't his house in the thick of it?"
"Sure is. I'll ask him what went down from his perspective."
"Let me know what he says, Son."

Shane was working on the quality aspect of his training. He had arranged to do two high-intensity sessions a week with John McGee who was much faster than him over shorter distances. This would help develop the speed in his legs and aid him with sprint finishes. They would separately each jog up to the front of St. Theresa's Church on the Glen Road in the early afternoons of Tuesday and Thursday, where they would meet up and then progress further up the Glen Road for their session. One was a hill session on the steep incline at Hannahstown, and the other, interval work around the grass Gaelic football pitches in St. Mary's Grammar School. The two met up as planned.

"Heard about the riots and shootings near you last night John. Hope you weren't too close."

"You'll never believe what went down. Following the raids by the army earlier in the day, word went around that there'd be a silent protest outside the army barracks in the evening."

"Were you there?"

"Yes. The protest started off silent as planned. Father Mullan was among those at the front. I went over and had a brief chat with him. He was confident that the press which was gathering would see Ballymurphy at its best with a silent protest against internment without trial. However, the Provos turned up and started hurling petrol bombs at the barracks. Others joined in throwing bricks. I went to the back of the protesters against the wall. Soon all hell broke loose."

"Did you get out of there?"

"I was pinned to the spot with what I saw. A man beside me went down. I went to his aid. He was shot. More shots rang out. A couple of us grabbed the injured man and carried him away to the grass area about thirty yards away. We laid him down and checked him. He was dead!"

"Jeez!"

"A few of the guys said we should see if any more people were hurt. We went to go back, but there was a stampede toward us. Then I saw my twin sisters further down the safe part of the street shouting at me to come home."

"What did ya do?"

"I thought it better to be out of it and I was concerned about them, so I went over to them, and we went home."

"Sounds like you did the right thing."

"Yeah, but I found out this morning that one of the men shot and killed was Father Mullan."

"Jeez. It was Father Mullan!"

The two kept a comfortable running pace as they progressed up the Glen Road but discussed no more on the riots. Soon they reached St. Mary's School and ran up the driveway to the grass pitches. As they did, Shane saw one of the Christian Brothers in the distance. He waved over to him.

"I take it we're good to train here, what with you now having graduated and left the school," John said.

"No problem. I had a chat with the Brother who heads up Sports and he said any time. That was him over there, the one I waved to."

"Grand."

"Anyway. It's a bit of a quid pro quo. He asked me if I would give a talk to the students at assembly one morning when the school starts back next month."

"Better you than me. What do ya have to talk about?"

"It's about extracurricular activities and the balance with studying. In the last academic year two of the students were killed and several more injured in street riots. They're trying to get the students off the streets and into other activities such as sport, chess, theater. You know what I mean like?"

"Yeah. Sounds good. Are ya prepared?"

"Well, I've got to talk about running. So, I'll think of something."

They reached the grass pitches, took off their tracksuits, and started to pound around the three-quarter of a mile perimeter. They completed a tough session of twelve sixty-second stints, each approximately four hundred meters long, with a thirty-second jog between. When they finished, they made their way back down the school driveway and then down the Glen Road.

Just before they split up to go their separate ways, Shane said, "I heard on the news that there may be more riots up your way this evening. Probably better to stay off the streets."

"Certainly will. See ya Thursday."

Shane met with Siobhan on Sunday, September 19. This was the day when Siobhan would travel to Liverpool in preparation for her courses at the university. Shane agreed to meet her at her home and take her at lunchtime to the Milk Bar on the Glen Road. They arrived at the Milk Bar, were shown to a table, and placed their orders.

"Can't believe this day has come so quickly," Shane said.

"Yes, the summer has flashed by. I'll miss you," Siobhan said.

"Hopefully the time will fly by until you return in three months."

"Hope so."

"So will you join any societies?"

"Plan to. I believe there's a car sports club, so that will be my prime aim. In fact, that may be enough as the sponsorship means that I'll have to do assignments with local companies."

"Makes sense. Will you go to the Liverpool Freshers' Ball?"

"Probably will, but don't be concerned. I'll pick the most

unattractive guy to go with. What about you?"

Shane smiled and then continued,

"Me too. I'll go to the Queen's University Ball with the most unattractive fella also!"

Both laughed.

"Didn't you say that Dan was lining something up?"

"Yeah. Well, ya know Dan. Got a call from him during the week to clarify. Apparently, he had asked two young ladies to go with him, and he just realized that both accepted. So, he was begging me to go with them to accompany one in, as of course he is only permitted to accompany one."

"Yes. That doesn't surprise me. Typical Dan. What degree was he accepted for?"

"Can you believe, Political Studies?"

"Hard to believe. Would he make a good politician?"

"Wow. That would be something. Doubt the country is ready for so much excitement!"

"Well, good luck to him."

They both had an enjoyable meal, albeit with emotions rising. Both were shedding tears as they walked back to Siobhan's home. At the end of Siobhan's street where it met the Glen Road they stood for a while.

"I don't know how I'll manage when you're gone," Shane said.

"Same here," Siobhan said.

They kissed and held each other close.

"We'll get through this together, Siobhan."

"I'll ring you once a week on Sundays as we discussed."

"Yeah. I'll look forward to it. In any case, I'll only be away for a few months at a time so we will be together before long."

"Suppose so."

They kissed again, exchanging tears. Then they walked up to Siobhan's house. After another embrace at the front gate Shane walked back down the street to the Glen Road and took a taxi back to the Falls Road. The O'Connell's had agreed to swing by Shane's house and pick him up on the way to bring Siobhan to the ferry so that he could also say goodbye. It was a tough evening for all. Nevertheless, Siobhan had a good send off.

One bit of respite for Shane following Siobhan's departure and the escalating problems of Belfast was the pending arrival of a group of athletic coaches, certified by the British Amateur Athletic Board. They would be coming to Belfast during the following week. A couple of them specialized in long-distance events. With the Olympics just several months away, athletics coaches were in a great position to gain lucrative sponsorships to support the local athletic communities across the British Isles. Northern Ireland was one of those lucrative stops. Shane signed up for the four-day session. My hard-earned Eagle Inn funds were being put to a great use, he considered. The event was planned to take place in the Mourne Mountains in County Down and the surrounding beaches. Tom Clyne was a big supporter of these visits. He did his best to get as many of his proteges as possible to attend, often raising sponsorship money to assist.

The athletics coaches arrived as planned on the Friday. Tom Clyne and his team arranged for four cars to take his group down to Newcastle, County Down, for the rendezvous. From there they were taken to log cabins in the Mourne Mountain. Each cabin was set up for two people. Shane was paired with Pete McGuirk from St. Malachy's. Both had had good battles for their schools against each other that year and there was mutual respect.

On the following day there was an early morning five-mile run, followed by coaching tutorials in a large conference-style cabin. That afternoon a session was arranged on a Newcastle beach. It was cold and so heaters were blazing in the cabins while they were away. In that respect it was very cozy for the athletes when they would return to their digs. However, later that afternoon as the cars carrying them approached the cabin park, Shane heard sirens and saw fires blazing into the sky. As they came up the entrance, he could get a good line of sight from a distance. The cars stopped and the athletes got out. Shane looked over to see two of the log cabins ablaze! The athletes showed great concern and were discussing the issue.

"Has there been a paramilitary attack?" one asked.

"The visit of athletics coaches would not cause such an interest outside of the athletic community. This has got to be something else," Tom Clyne said.

Shane and some of the athletes walked up the lane toward the cabins. There was a cordon around the area that the fire brigade was working, and they had to halt there. To Shane's surprise Brendan was on-site with the fire crew. Shane waved over to his father who in turn came to the barrier to speak with him.

"Let's walk over here where it's a bit more private. Better to be out of ear's shot," Brendan said.

"What's the problem?"

"Nothing too serious. Looks like someone did a makeshift wiring repair behind a radiator. The wiring of the radiator was faulty. A wet towel was left on it, and we think a spark lit it as it dried."

"Oh. So, that's why's the second cabin's on fire."

"The cabins are very close together, and it seems like the wind got up and blew the flames across. Anyway, we have a couple of electricians on-site now, and they're checking all the wiring on all the cabins and the assembly hall cabin just to be sure. In fact, I just heard that we've finished with the assembly cabin, and it's fine if people want to move over there."

"My God! Hard to believe."

"Stranger than fiction! Good job we arrived soon, or they all would've gone up in flames."

"Glad it wasn't a paramilitary attack."

"No. No concern there."

"How come the Belfast center crew turned up? This isn't your patch."

"We heard about the fire and offered to help as the local crew was attending another incident. Anyway, it was a good opportunity to see how you were getting on."

"Thanks, Da."

"Well, a decent portion of your hard-earned cash is funding the long weekend. Don't want that investment to go to waste. And your mother would never forgive me if I didn't check it out."

"Know what ya mean."

"Yes, that would be more dangerous for me."

They both laughed.

"I'll tell Tom Clyne that he can get everyone together now into the assembly hall," Brendan said.

Brendan had a chat with Tom and the British coaches. Then he came back to Shane, and they discussed how the training had gone so far. The fire was controlled within a further thirty minutes, all the wiring was checked in the park and given a clean bill of health, and the fire crew left. The runners got on with their course. First, they were allowed to shower and change into their clothes. Dinner was served as planned in the assembly cabin and was followed by further training strategy discussions. Luckily not all the cabins had been fully occupied, so the people affected by the fire were able to relocate.

The following day the course moved to a beach backed by sand hills. The sessions focused on sand hill training for resistance work. This evolved into team races over the dunes. The hill work on the dunes was excruciating. The coaches were pushing all the athletes to run harder. Shane was to learn that this was a very effective form of endurance training. He decided that where practical he would incorporate this type of training in his off-season training.

Unknown to the participants, a camera crew from the BBC had been arranged. As the runners plowed up the sand hills and then sprinted along the beach, the crew gathered footage. That night Tom asked Shane to help him, and they got together and placed a large television set that Tom had delivered in the assembly cabin. During the team debrief the TV was switched on. There was a ten-minute special on the distance-running course in Mourne Mountains on the BBC Northern Ireland community program that followed the national news. The runners watched and joked as they one by one came into shot. The program was played to Cliff Richard music, starting with *On the Beach* and for some reason progressing to *Summer Holiday*.

"This's no summer holiday!" Pete whispered to Shane.

Shane nodded in agreement. He was thinking, as he rubbed his aching leg muscles, that this was the furthest thing from a holiday. The rest of the training weekend was also helpful. Training tactics from a range of different top coaches, including some who had trained Olympic champions such as Arthur Lydiard and Percy Cerutty, were discussed and critiqued by the visiting experts. Shane found a couple of ideas that he would apply going forward. I'll fit in resistance work on the sandhills, he considered, and will also include some trail running. Really enjoyed running through the woods, he thought. He was encouraged that it was possible to do runs of over twenty miles in the woods without covering the same path twice and especially without seeing any cars or Saracens. He considered that during the racing season, he could incorporate shorter hill sprinting sessions. Based on some of the training he had just experienced, he would choose hills that had a flattish runoff on top. This would help to train him in pivoting off the gruesome hills into a steady cadence with smooth breathing. This is where he could make race progress, at the stage where most runners slowed down just before the top of the hill in anticipation of a rest period. This would help to enhance the effectiveness of his training and racing.

The Queen's University term had a start date of Friday, October 1. Registration was open from September 29. In preparation for the first term, Shane was getting everything he needed together the weekend before. Following Mass on Sunday morning, Shane saw Liam and Clodagh arrive outside his house. He welcomed them in, and Lily made a pot of tea. As they were finishing their tea, they invited Shane, Lily, and Brendan out to the back alleyway. This seems strange, Shane thought. Liam opened the back gate and, in the alleyway, stood a white Volkswagen Beetle. Liam threw the keys to Shane. "It's yours," Liam said. "Ready now to get you to Queen's and back each day."

"What?" Shane asked. "Thank you very much Uncle Liam and Auntie Clodagh."

"Don't thank us. Thank your parents," Clodagh said, "They bought it."

"Wow. Thank you, Mom and Da. Best present ever."

"What, better than the stereo?" Lily said.

"Certainly, on a par."

"Now, the thanks to Clodagh and Liam are most appropriate as they got us a very good deal," Brendan said.

"It's four years old, Shane," Liam said." Good single owner, an elderly lady. Has been well looked after."

"Yeah. I can see that. It looks almost new."

"Not many miles on it. In fact, less than ten thousand. Just nicely broken in."

"Jeez. Looks great!"

"I replaced the battery. This one should last several years. The rest I checked over. Rock solid. Here's a container of distilled water. You may need to top up the battery a couple of times a year. Don't use tap water. Must use distilled. Now, you know how to get to the battery?"

"Sure do."

Shane opened the door, pulled forward the driver's seat, and lifted the back seat. "There you are."

"You got it."

"Strange place for a battery, Liam," Lily said.

"Yes, a VW Beetle thing. There's a reason why it's there. Who knows?"

Scarlet and Tyrone had just come out to see the car.

"It's because the engine is at the rear, just like a racing car," Scarlet said.

"Way to go!" Liam said.

"My word. So where do you put the cases and groceries?" Lily asked.

"In the front, Mom," Scarlet said.

Brendan walked over and opened the front hood.

"See. There, Lily."

"Well, who would've thought that?"

"Shane, we think it's better if you park it in the backyard," Brendan said, "Better not to leave it on the front street or it'll get battered in those football games. Liam, you, and I are going to spend the afternoon widening the back entrance and laying a foundation between the lawns just inside the wall. I have two gates specially made."

"Can I have a spin first?"

"We thought you'd say that. Course you can," Liam said.

Liam sat in the front passenger seat, with Brendan in the back with Scarlet and Tyrone. Lily and Clodagh went into the kitchen to catch up and prepare lunch. Shane demonstrated his excellent driving skills with a drive up to Hannahstown and back. Then Brendan, Shane, and Liam got to work in the backyard.

Shane had concerns about running through the Andersonstown and Glen Roads because of the recent skirmishes with the forces. Although he now had the means to drive over to other locations to do his runs, he knew he still needed to continue some runs from home for convenience. Because of his concerns, he changed his main routes. For his longer runs he decided that he would aim to cross over via Stockman's Lane past Musgrave Park Hospital, cross Balmoral Avenue, and make his way to Malone Road. From there he could run down to the Embankment, progress to Belvoir or Lady Dixon Park, or take advantage of the university playing fields. He reasoned it was a much safer world in these parts. He had done this successfully on many occasions. However, on an unseasonably warm and sunny autumn day in late October as he ran down the hill of Stockman's Lane, his experience would greatly make him question if it was safe to run in Belfast at all. As usual army Saracens would come past from time to time. On this occasion, as three of the thick metal vehicles passed, a shower of bottles was thrown by a group of youths higher up from the other side of a large hedge in one of the properties on the other side of the road. The bottles smashed as they hit the armored vehicles. The vehicles came alongside Shane, and a succession of smashed bottles broke apart on top of the armored roofs and poured down on Shane who was poorly protected while running in just a jersey and shorts. He was cut to bits, mostly with superficial injuries. However, several larger bits of glass penetrated deep into his skin. He carried on for several yards covered in blood and then fell. As the Saracens sped ahead, people in nearby houses could see Shane's predicament and came to help. Shane could see that some ladies had arrived with towels.

"Quickly Mabel, run back and ring the ambulance. I'll tend to his injuries as best as I can. What's your name, young man?"

"Shane. Shane McMahon."

"Do you live close?"

"Falls Road, close to the bottom of Whiterock."

"Have you a number I can call to alert your family?"

"Yes. Thanks."

Shane gave the number and repeated it when asked. Mabel came back.

"Ambulance called. Should be here in about ten minutes. How's the patient, Carol?"

"He's badly cut, but I think he'll be OK. Can you stay with him while I head home and ring his parents?"

"Will do."

Other concerned people gathered around and waited with Shane until the ambulance came. The paramedics arrived soon after and applied some temporary dressings. They then helped Shane into the ambulance through the back doors. Shane was soon taken to the Royal Victoria Hospital, where he was tended to straight away. Ambulance deliveries always had priority. He required several stitches in each of five larger cuts to his legs and arms and a cut on the right side of his jaw. The rest of the cuts were minor not requiring stitches. Brendan and Lily arrived in a taxi and brought some of Shane's clothes and a duffle bag for Shane's bloodied running kit.

"How did this happen?" Brendan asked.

"Three Saracens passed me, and all I felt was a hail of broken glass pieces pierce into my body. Apparently, some youths were throwing bottles at them from higher up on the other side of Stockman's Lane."

"So that's what you get for taking a so-called safer route for your run. What's this place coming to?" Lily said in disgust.

Shane felt shattered and was slurring a bit as he spoke with an angst nervousness. He was shaking. One thing was clear in his mind; this incident had hit so badly that he was seriously contemplating leaving Northern Ireland.

The family took a taxi home and entered through the back door into the kitchen so as not to disturb Shane's siblings. Scarlet was in the sitting room with some friends from school listening to some of Shane's records, which of course he had given Scarlet permission to do earlier. Tyrone was in the parlor watching *Thunderbirds.* Brendan, Lily, and Shane sat down at the table in the kitchen and had a serious discussion.

"I'm really finding it difficult to run on the streets of Belfast. As much as I try to find a safe training route, danger seems to follow."

"We understand, Son," Lily said.

"I'm seriously considering leaving Belfast. I'm thinking of enquiring if I can get transferred to a university on mainland Britain to continue my degree."

"Fully understand, Son," Lily said sympathetically.

"Let's give it some thought before making a rash decision in the heat of the moment," Brendan said.

"Will do, Da."

Shane's mind drifted a bit as they sat together. Deep down he considered that he didn't particularly want to leave Belfast as he was excelling at his courses during his first term at Queen's, with the help of an excellent tutor. Then he jolted up when he heard Lily's voice again.

"Is the offer for a place at Villanova in the U.S. still open?"

"Don't know. However, I've heard the universities in the U.S. take their pound of flesh when students go over on a scholarship. I don't like that mechanism," Shane said as he picked minute fragments of glass from his thick locks that had been missed in the hospital. "Although I give everything to running in training and racing, I prefer to be my own master when it comes to how I apply my time."

"Understand, Son. You don't want to be restricted in that way," Lily said.

"My preference would be to go to an English university if I was to make a change. As I mentioned earlier, I'll think this over."

"We understand. Why don't you head upstairs and get some rest now?" Brendan said.

"Good idea. Will do."

Shane agreed to speak to his parents in advance of taking any action if he wanted to pursue this option. As they were finishing their chat, he could hear through the walls of the sitting room the recording from the local group *Them* beating out "Please Don't Go". Was this a sign?

SHOCK OF THE NEW

It was a beautiful autumn evening with the sun glinting down on a quiet Belfast. To ensure the youth in West Belfast had a semblance of a social life, the Gaelic Athletic Association (GAA) would allow their facilities to be used for evening events when games were not being played. One such facility, which the kids called "the Brier", was in the upper Glen Road. Youths would take a taxi to the bottom of a two-hundred-yard rough stony lane and then walk up to the building. Some who had the use of cars would park on the Glen Road at the base of the lane, while others would walk up from home. On this Friday evening with the week's school behind them, many took advantage of a disco in the GAA building. Students from schools from around West Belfast would make their way there. It was one of the big attractions for young people in the area.

Fiona Callaghan from St. Dominic's Grammar School met outside the Eagle Inn with two of her friends, Jane from St. Genevieve's High School, and Colleen from St. Louise's Secondary Girls College.

"Is Scarlet coming?" Jane asked.

"No. She has her granda's seventieth birthday party tonight down the Falls. She'll not be able to make it," Fiona said.

"Shame," said Colleen. "This'll be the first time we go without her."

"Yes. We were hoping all the girls from the neighboring schools would meet up this evening," Fiona said.

They started off on the half-mile walk up the Glen Road to the Brier.

"Glad we can get a good break from doing A-level revision," Colleen said.

They were in fine form, joking as they progressed up the road. They had arranged to meet other friends from around the area at the foot of the lane as normal. As they ascended the slope on the Glen Road that led to the lane, Fiona could see their four female friends some eighty yards away waiting for them. In the far distance beyond them, Fiona noticed an army Saracen coming down the Glen Road in their direction.

"Can you hear that rustling in the hedge just up there to our right?" Jane asked.

"Yes. Is it a dog?" Colleen asked.

"No, it's a couple of lads in there on the field side of the footpath," Fiona said.

"What are they doing," Colleen asked.

"Probably playing with themselves," Jane said.

The three girls burst out in laughter. As they passed by, Fiona looked closer. "Seems weird. Something seems off."

"They seem to be looking up at that army Saracen in the distance coming this way," Jane said.

Fiona looked over at the Saracen and then back to the youths in the hedge. "Something's brewing." She looked over at their four friends standing at the base of the lane beside a couple of parked cars. Then Fiona yelled to them, "Run, Run, Run!!!"

The puzzled girls at the base of the lane looked her way, and one of them, Julia, put her hands palms up, shrugged her shoulders, and shouted back, "What?"

Then Julia saw the Saracen approaching and the panic in her friends faces some fifty yards away down the Glen Road. She started jumping up and down and shouting frantically.

"Run! Run!" she said to her other three friends, as they stood beside a row of parked cars. "Jill, Meg, Lindsay come on. Run!" The four began to sprint down the road toward Fiona, Jane, and Colleen. They were too late! A loud explosion rang out. One car just behind them shot into the air in a blaze of fire as the Saracen came alongside. The Saracen was blown onto its side, the four girls were blown forward into the air, and their friends fifty yards away felt a strong blast of wind shove them into the adjacent hedge. As they collided with the hedge, Fiona could see the two male youths they had noticed suspiciously lurking behind the hedge sprint off up a grass hill. The girls fell to the ground with their ears tinging. Fiona was dazed. Jane came over to her. "Get up! Get up!" Jane's voice seemed distant and progressed from near silence to a powerful pounding. Fiona pulled herself up to her feet.

"Is Colleen, OK?" She asked.

Colleen was also rising to her feet, brushing off dust from her clothes. "I'm fine. What about Jill, Lindsey, Meg, and Julia?" Colleen said.

They looked up the hill and ran in the direction of their friends. The three girls approached their friends and then cringed in horror. Two of them were motionless and missing limbs, and the other two lay reeling on the ground in agony with serious injuries. They had become the most recent child victims of the Troubles. Fiona looked toward the Saracen and could see two soldiers extracting themselves from the armored truck.

"Oh, my God. Those soldiers have flames on their backs," she said.

"Look, they're rolling on the grass border," Jane said.

All three stared over at the soldiers who had run to an adjacent grass border as they worked frantically to put out the flames. Jane with tears streaming down her face hugged her two friends. Then she watched in disbelief as the soldiers who had just been in flames limped back to the Saracen to help remove two more colleagues from the armored vehicle. She watched them lay the two injured soldiers on the road, both still alive but groaning in pain. The three girls, despite being distraught and in shock, comforted their two injured friends as best they could until help arrived.

"Any sign of the ambulances yet?" Fiona asked.

"I can hear sirens in the distance," Colleen said. "Should be here soon."

Three Ambulances and police jeeps arrived within a few minutes of the explosion. Paramedics jumped out with medical bags in hand and ran to the victims. One group went to the young ladies lying on the ground, another to the stricken soldiers, and a couple of the paramedics came over to tend to

Fiona, Jane, and Colleen.

A female paramedic came over to Fiona and gently sat her on the curb. She checked her over.

"No broken bones, a few cuts but they'll heal. How do your ears feel?"

"They're tinging. Can't hear clearly."

"That's normal in these cases. Let me check them."

The paramedic took out an instrument, placed it one at a time in Fiona's ears, and looked through a sight."

"Should settle down in a couple of hours' time. We'll get you checked out better at the Royal. You're also in shock. This is normal too. Stay patient and we'll get you sorted out."

She then went to check on Jane. A colleague was already examining Colleen. The policemen who had arrived interviewed witnesses and took statements. Fiona, Jane, and Colleen were escorted to an ambulance and taken to the Royal Victoria Hospital a couple of miles away.

High up on a hill some six hundred meters away, Seamus Rooney looked down on the carnage. He had a smirk of achievement on his face as he surmised his work. He watched as his two men came up the winding path through the bushes.

"Mission accomplished, Sir," one of his men named Bobby Sullivan said.

"Couldn't wait until the kids were out of the way, Sir," Mickey Gorman the other team member said.

"No worries. There'll always be casualties in a freedom fight," Seamus said.

"Will the boss be OK with that?" Mickey asked.

"Leave that to me," Seamus said. "Jimmy told me the adjutant made it clear we had to send a strong message today no matter what the cost."

"So, something's in play?" Bobby asked.

"Bet so, but don't know what," Seamus said. "Well done, soldiers, on your first field mission."

"Thank you, Sir."

The McMahon's arrived back home at nine o'clock from Joseph McKeown's house. They entered the hallway.

"Great party this evening. Can't believe that Granda is now seventy years old," Shane said.

"Me too," Lily said. "I remember him still playing top-class football for Armagh when I was a little girl. Where's the time flown?"

"Great to see all of Deirdre's family there," Brendan said.

"Yes, wasn't it? Also, really pleased to see Clodagh have a night out. Taking on too much work."

"Well, seamstresses are in great demand these days. She really seemed to enjoy herself," Brendan said.

"Think the sherry helped," Scarlet said. "She seemed to have a fondness for it."

"Didn't she just. A little bit of sherry now and then fuels the spirit," Lily said.

"Granda liked that bottle of whiskey you brought down, Mom," Tyrone said.

"Yes, he's quite fond of whiskey. And that was no ordinary whiskey. That was a single malt."

"What's a single malt?"

"It's a special version not blended with any others. It's very expensive. Great for the taste buds."

"Wow."

"Now, who'd like a cup of tea?"

"Me."

"Me."

Lily walked toward the kitchen. The phone rang.

"I'll get it," said Shane, "Hello, the McMahon household. Oh, hello Sister Matilda."

Then Shane waved over toward Lily. "Mom. It's for you. It's Sister Matilda at St. Dominic's."

"Coming. Wonder what she wants at this time of night?" Lily took the receiver from Shane. "Hello Sister Matilda." Lily listened attentively but said nothing. Brendan, Scarlet, Tyrone, and Shane watched her. Her face turned pale. Lily gently replaced the receiver. "Tyrone, off to bed please."

"But Mom."

"Now, Tyrone!"

Tyrone made a beeline up the stairs.

"The rest of you, in the parlor please. Something terrible has happened." Lily spent the next five minutes explaining what had transpired by the Brier.

The next morning just before seven o'clock Shane came down to the parlor. Lily was there twiddling the tuning dial on the wireless. Shane sat down but said nothing. Then the radio blurted out,

> Good morning. This is the seven o'clock Northern Ireland news. Two female teenagers left this world last night following an attack on security forces in the Glen Road. The girls were waiting with friends at the base of a lane leading to the Brier dancehall when a bomb in a nearby car was detonated. Two other teenage girls were severely injured and are being treated in hospital. They are still in intensive care. The children's names have not yet been released to the press. Late last night the Provisional IRA claimed responsibility.

"They're killing our children on our streets! So much for a freedom fight," Lily said.

"Tragic Mom. No stopping this escalation of terror it seems," Shane said.

"Yes, they're a law unto themselves."

"Any word on the funerals?"

"No further details yet. Sister Matilda said she'd ring later today."

"Most likely the schools will get together for a joint funeral procession."

One week later a joint funeral ceremony was arranged for the two teenagers who had died. The funeral procession featured on the evening television news. The McMahon's sat down to watch.

> All schools in West Belfast were shut today and students from girls'

schools in West Belfast formed a procession for the funeral of Jill McAteer and Lindsay Curran from St. Dominic's Grammar School. The funeral procession left from Clonard Monastery following a service at noon and stopped for tributes at St. Dominic's on the way to Milltown Cemetery. Thousands of people lined the Falls Road as hearses slowly progressed. Students followed in an orderly fashion. It was another sad day in this great land.

"Look Scarlet. There's you at the front just behind the families," Tyrone said.

"Yes, all the girls at St. Dominic's were in the procession, together with close friends of Jill and Lindsay. Fiona, Jane, and Colleen were alongside me at the front." Scarlet said.

"Any word on the other two girls?" Brendan asked.

"Both are out of intensive care. Meg is making a good recovery and should be home in the next day or two. Julia still needs a couple of operations on her legs, but she is otherwise recovering well," Scarlet said.

"When they have fully recovered, please invite them round Scarlet, together with Fiona, Colleen, and Jane," Lily said.

"Will do, Mom."

Siobhan returned to Belfast in mid-December for her Christmas break. Shane had been looking forward to being with Siobhan again, and it brought much needed positivity back into his life. They spent as much time together as they could. When Shane called up to Gransha one pleasant morning, Siobhan's mother met him at the door.

"Shane, please feel free to use the sitting room any time when you meet with Siobhan," she said.

"Thank you, Mrs. O'Connell. Will do."

Because of the escalating atrocities in Belfast, Siobhan's parents showed more concern than ever about the safety of their children. They encouraged Siobhan not to spend too much time in an environment where danger lurked. Shane's parents showed the same caution. When Shane and Siobhan were alone Shane said, "D'ya think if we spent time in your sitting room your parents will have glasses to the walls trying to eavesdrop on our discussion?"

"Don't be daft!" Siobhan said.

On this occasion they decided to not go far. They took a stroll down to the Falls Park and enjoyed a very sunny but chilly afternoon. When they returned and Shane was departing, he said to Siobhan, "Your mother has a good point there. Maybe we should take advantage of the sitting rooms in our places."

"Yes. Will ease their minds a bit. So long as we get outside sometimes."

"Agree. Better if we go outside in the daylight."

During daylight hours Shane and Siobhan would often go to the parks up by the university, or up the Cave Hill, or take in some of the attractions such as the city hall and the zoo. One Saturday morning before Christmas they met to go to the city center to do some Christmas shopping.

"Let's visit the city market first," Siobhan said. "There're often bargains there, just right for Christmas."

"Yes, of course. I remember spending many Saturday mornings in the marketplace with my mother when I was much younger. She would take me there to shop for clothes. I was always in shirts, tee-shirts, pullovers, and jeans that never had labels."

"Why was that?"

"Apparently the vendor, as a condition of selling these top-brand goods at knockdown prices, had to either remove the labels or cut through them."

"I know the market also sells top brand products fully intact with labels at reduced prices."

"Yes, that's true as well. However, to get the best deals the labels had to be removed or cut through. I was always embarrassed to go to school with a cut-through label, so I would always remove them completely."

"Understand."

"In addition, if I ever came across an intact label, I would sew it onto the appropriate garment."

"No way!"

"Yes, it's true."

"Well, we'll go for the ones slightly reduced that have all their labels intact."

"Deal."

At the city markėt they first checked out lunch. Siobhan was aware of a stall that served good Irish stew, so they headed there. They sat up at the bar on high stools and ordered their lunch.

"So how do your parents feel about you going downtown?" Shane asked.

"They're always anxious when I go out but try hard not to restrict my freedom. How do your parents feel?"

Shane thought for several seconds and then replied. "Pretty much the same. However, I tend to keep it quiet if I come close to danger. I don't want them to worry any more than they normally do. So better that they don't hear about near misses."

"I remember you telling me that before. So, they never know where you're going then?""

"Well, generally they do. They know for example that I'm meeting with you today and going into town. But I don't give them more details."

"Oh, see what you mean."

The Irish stews arrived after a few minutes.

"There you are now. The best Irish stews in Belfast," the server said wiping off the countertop.

"Actually, not the best. Maybe the second best," Shane said.

"Go on then, why's that?"

"My mother makes the best Irish stew from a recipe handed down from generation to generation."

"Yeah, I bet she does. If she ever needs a part-time job, Please ask her to contact me."

"Will do."

As Shane was about to tuck into the stew, he heard a commotion in an adjacent lingerie stall. A middle-aged lady was arguing with the stall owner, Mr. Sullivan. Mr. Sullivan sold good-quality goods (with the labels included) at better prices than the High Street stores. Siobhan often bought garments from his stall. She whispered to Shane, "Mr. Sullivan's a very decent man. Wonder what this lady's problem is?"

Shane couldn't hear the full details of the debate, but it appeared to be that the lady had found the same garments she had bought there a few weeks earlier at a store in the High Street at a lower price. Mr. Sullivan was asking clarifying questions. The lady shouted out in annoyance to Mr. Sullivan, "I was done in those knickers!"

"If she was done in those knickers then why is she complaining?!" Shane said to Siobhan.

Siobhan nudged him in the chest as she whispered, "Oh Shane! You are awful."

They followed their meals with coffees and then headed off around the stalls in the market. Having bought a few presents, Siobhan and Shane moved on to the High Street stores, where they picked up some good bargains. They now had large bags in each of their hands.

"Better head back now. Can't carry anything else," Siobhan said.

"Yeah. Let's call it a day."

As they exited Robinson and Cleaver's, an upmarket department store just across from city hall, a very loud explosion rang out close by, and dust spread in the air! Due to the surrounding noise Shane shouted to Siobhan, "Jeez. What was that?"

"Seems to be further up the road but close by. Must be around the post office area in Royal Avenue."

Pandemonium broke out, and a busy city center public started to run in all directions.

"Better get out of here," Shane said.

"Can't agree more."

"Let's make our way to Divis Street, and we can grab a taxi there."

"OK. Let's make haste."

As they began to make a move, a second bomb went off also in Royal Avenue, much closer at just a hundred yards away. Shane and Siobhan watched as a car parked by a hotel was just suddenly lifted into the air ablaze. Siobhan screamed out, "Oh my God!"

"Must be a major attack on the center. There may be more bombs. We'll need another route back."

Soon after, a third bomb could be heard detonating about half a mile at the other side of city hall.

"My God. They're going off all around us. Where's safe?" Siobhan asked.

"Let me think a minute. I'll find us a route out."

As Shane had often run through the city center, he knew many of the roads, alleys, and short cuts. He thought carefully. "Let's take a detour away from the Royal Avenue area and work our way up to the old St. Mary's school where we were dropped off. Taxis should be waiting there."

"Good idea. Let's get away before anything goes off closer to us."

Off they set. As they looked up Royal Avenue from a distance, through a light cloud of dust, they could see buildings and cars burning and smoke rising into the air. As the dust started to settle, the bright late afternoon sky had a reddish haze, fueled by the flames below.

"Rome is burning," Shane said.

Although it was not completely safe to take side streets, Shane knew they had to vacate the city center as soon as possible. He led them up some alleyways, out past Moore's Sports Shop, down another narrow street past Bertolli's Electrical Store, and eventually approached St. Mary's old school. As they came closer, there was a stampede for the taxis. Shane stopped and beckoned Siobhan to halt.

"This's not going to work. Are you up for the three-mile walk back to my house?"

Siobhan pointed down to her new Adidas Gazelles and said, "These boots were made for walking. Let's go."

Dusty bags in each hand, they set off. To avoid the main crowd, they had to take some more side streets to the other side of the old St. Mary's school. To the din of fire engine sirens, they made progress and eventually came back onto the Falls Road by Andrews Flour Mill.

They progressed up the Falls Road covered in dust. Their presents were also covered in dust.

"Good job the presents are nicely wrapped up," Siobhan said.

"The packages look OK. No damage."

"Yes. And I'm pleased they placed them all in plastic bags. Should make it easy to dust them off."

"Yeah."

As they walked up the Falls Road, Shane turned to look back on the city center from the elevated vantage point. He nudged Siobhan. "Turn round and have a look. Have you ever seen such a sight?"

"Not from such close range. The flames seem to be reaching into the clouds."

"Yes. I saw the city blazing once before."

"When was that?"

"At the start of the Troubles at the end of the summer in sixty-nine. Our family was returning from holiday in Carnlough. When we arrived back at the city train station, Belfast was ablaze."

"I remember that time but didn't see it firsthand."

"A pretty sight for van Gogh maybe but frightening for us!"

"A frightening time for all of us."

As they continued up the Falls Road, youths came out and started scuffles. As normal, the army was patrolling as well. The youths then vented their frustration on the security forces. Once again, the situation descended into a street battle. On one side the youths were throwing stones, and on the other the security forces were resisting and advancing behind plastic see-through shields. This was becoming a regular Belfast event.

"Better stay clear of any scuffles with the forces. Let's detour through the side streets," Shane said.

They diverted off the main road and took the back streets and alleyways toward Shane's house. Mr. O'Connell was there when they arrived. He was relieved to see that both were unscathed. "Oh my God. I'm so please to see you both."

"Where were you when the trouble hit?" Lily asked.

"Outside Robinson and Cleaver's. We weren't sure where the next bomb was likely to explode," Shane said.

"We came up with a plan to get the hell away from there as quickly as we could. Luckily Shane knew all the back roads and shortcuts," Siobhan said.

"Where's Da?" Shane asked.

"Where do ya think at a time like this? He was called out straight away. I guess he's in the city center now tackling the damage."

"We better be getting you home. Your mother will be worried," Mr. O'Connell said to Siobhan.

"Will you not have time for a wee cup of tea. You can ring Geraldine from here and let her know Siobhan is safe," Lily said.

"Ach. Go on then."

After a quick cup of tea, Mr. O'Connell left with Siobhan. A great day out for Shane and Siobhan had a sting in the tail. Thereafter, both carefully took full advantage of Siobhan's stay in Belfast largely indoors until she had to return to Liverpool. Occasionally they would venture outside and had a couple of trips down to the Milk Bar just before Christmas. However, they were wary not to go too far afield from their homes as the situation in Belfast was getting worse. Because of the recent experience in the city center they reconciled themselves to this restriction. Shane was also dreading the day that Siobhan would leave for Liverpool. Must cherish whatever time we can spend together. Luckily, we'll be together before too long when I go over to England for the British Students Cross-Country Championships in February.

Shane was continuing well with his training and feeling much stronger. He had upped his schedule to over seventy miles per week to be ready for key cross-country races coming up. The British Student Championships would be followed closely by the Northern Ireland Championships and then hopefully the World Championships in March if he qualified. Adding an extra five miles to my longer runs on Wednesday and Sunday should boost my stamina, he thought. Got to get more pace into my hill and fartlek sessions. One Sunday morning in late December he started out on a fifteen-mile run. Things were going well until he approached the Gransha estate via the adjacent fields. Children were playing with a German Shepherd dog. As Shane passed by, the dog lunged out and bit him on his right calf muscle.

"Aah." Shane cried out, his leg stinging. He looked down and saw blood seeping from several wounds where the teeth pierced the skin. He was hurting badly and fuming. He approached the kids and demanded authoritatively, "Which of you owns this dog?"

"It's not ours, mister," said one of the lads.

"Well then, who owns the dog?"

"It belongs to the man in that house over there in Gransha Way," he said pointing along the road.

Shane was annoyed. That ruins my run for today, he thought. Just two miles to show for it. Now I need to head back to the A&E for a tetanus injection and some stitches. He marched off in the direction of the house to confront the owner of the dog. As he approached, he remembered seeing this house on a recent BBC *Panorama* program. It focused on a profile of the leader of the IRA in Belfast. This was the house the leader had exited from in the program on his way to Sunday Mass. Shane stopped, thought better of it, and decided to walk away. Better start the run down to the Royal Victoria. Should be there in about twenty minutes, he considered. He started off and soon realized he could not progress at his normal pace. He continued with shorts bursts of running followed by walking spells. When he arrived, he checked in at the reception. "I was bitten by a dog while out for a run. Will need a tetanus jab and maybe some stiches."

"Here. Take these swabs and tissues and mop it up. This should stop the bleeding for a while." The receptionist then proceeded to check him in. "There are seven people before you. Should take about two hours maximum for you to move up the line and be seen by a doctor."

"No problem. Many thanks."

Shane sat down and waited. A few of the patients were seen within the next half hour and he progressed to fifth in line. Then pandemonium; ambulances arrived with bomb victims. It appeared that car bombs had exploded outside some churches that morning as worshippers were exiting. The stretchers were wheeled in right in front of him. Looks like a major blast, he thought. The carnage was significant. One ambulance after another came. All medical staff were redirected to the emergency. Guess I'm going to have to be here for a bit longer now, he considered. I'd better make a call home to Mum to let her know. He rang.

"Collect call, please."

"Number please," the operator said.

Shane called out the home phone number and then listened as he heard the operator connect and ask Lily if she would take the collect call. He heard her affirm. "Hello, Shane. What's happened?"

"Hey Mom. I was bitten by a dog up by Gransha not long into my run. Had to detour down to the Royal Victoria. I'm here now. I need a tetanus jab. Unfortunately, there have been some bomb blasts in the city this morning, so ambulances are arriving with victims. Don't know how long I'll be."

"How bad is the bite son?"

"A few teeth marks with blood trickling down. May need a stitch or two and a tetanus jab. Should be fine."

"OK. Hope so. I heard on the wireless that something went down toward the city center an hour or so back. Let me know when you're finished, and I'll ask Liam if he could pick me up and we'll collect you."

"No need for that, Mom," Shane said. "I'll be able to run back within ten minutes."

"OK, Son. Let me know if anything changes."

After four more hours, things seemed to calm down a bit and the queue was active again. Two people were seen, and Shane was now third in line. He had been in the queue at this stage for almost five hours. Then another alert! More ambulances descended! It was all hands on deck for the medical staff again. This took another four to five hours. Shane again rang back and updated Lily.

"Hey, Mom. Things aren't looking good here. More bomb victims coming in. I need to hang on here for my injection. Please don't bother Uncle Liam. I should be able to run back OK once I've been seen."

"OK, Son. However, do give me a call when you're leaving the hospital so I know you're on your way."

"Will do, Mom."

Eventually his "number" was called, eleven hours after he signed in at reception. He was shown to a cubicle. A young doctor, most likely a registrar, met him. "You'll need a tetanus injection," she said.

"Not surprised at that."

"The teeth marks should heal up without any stitches, but we'll put an antiseptic bandage on and give you a few more to change the dressing each day. A nurse will be in soon to treat you."

"Much appreciated. Many thanks."

The doctor left. Fifteen minutes later a female nurse entered the cubicle. She asked to Shane, "Would you prefer the tetanus injection in your arm or your backside?"

"My arm please." I don't want to drop my pants in front of a female, he thought. The nurse departed to get the tetanus vial and syringe and returned a few minutes later. Shane started to roll up the sleeve on his left arm.

"OK. Drop your pants," she said.

"I thought that you said I could have the injection in my arm?"

"I just asked you if you had a preference. I didn't say you had an option. This is our little joke!"

"OK. I get it."

Shane reluctantly obliged, and down his pants came. He said silently to himself as if speaking to her, just hurry up. Within a few minutes he received the injection and had a firm antiseptic adhesive dressing applied. The nurse gave him a small bag with a handful of packages of antiseptic dressings.

"You can shower each day. Take the dressing off before showering and apply a new one after the shower. Please do this for the next five days."

She then accompanied him back to the reception and arranged for him to be discharged. Shane once again called Lily to let her know he was on his way and slowly ran the one and a half miles back home. Eleven and a half hours of my day spent here for less than thirty minutes of treatment, he thought as he passed through the swing doors of the main entrance. Never mind, I'm the lucky one. Those poor victims. Just grateful I'm not one of them.

Sectarian and political issues increased in Belfast. One evening, just before the new year when Shane was working in the Eagle Inn, Nolan and Mike came in and sat at the bar as normal. Both were forty-something and dressed casually. Mike took out a local tabloid newspaper from his parka and began reading aloud an article on a mob raid on a politician's house the night before.

"Hey, Nolan. This is about that politician, Jeremy Finn. Seems there's been an attack on him."

"Oh, sure. Isn't that the fella who lives up the Falls Road?"

"Yeah. He's one of us. In fact, he lives just down the road from me in a terraced house."

"Oh, I know where you mean. I've seen that chap around the area. Nice guy."

Mike read out details from the article. "Appears to be that at about midnight a mob broke through the front door. My God, the mob was comprised of masked females."

"Jesus. Now the fairer sex is getting involved. What's the world coming to?"

"Looks like they went up the stairs while Mr. Finn and his wife were in bed."

"What? Were normal surgery times not good for them?" Nolan said with a grin on his face.

"It doesn't say, but most likely they intended to ransack his house to send a message, or worse."

"Yeah. Those Social Democratic Labor Party politicians are under pressure to include a future united Ireland as a central platform for any political discussions."

"Do they not do that already?"

"No, they're focused on civil rights and bringing further employment to the province."

"Well, that can't be all that bad, surely?"

"So, what happened?"

"It says the middle-aged politician was in bed upstairs with his wife. When he heard the commotion, he got out of bed and ran to the stairs with a hurling stick in his hand."

"Good for him."

"This is how the story goes, as explained by an anonymous female from the mob to the newspaper, 'Mr. Finn came to the landing and met us part way down the stairs. He had risen from bed with just a short vest on. His manhood was clearly in display as we ascended the staircase and was almost straight in our line of sight. It was shocking! So, we decided to turn around and depart. It's hard to believe that a grown man would go to bed in just a short vest and no pants!'"

"He has my vote," Nolan declared.

"Mine too. Here's the conclusion on the topic, 'Never has such a defense of territory with this type of weaponry been successfully staged since *Carry On Up the Khyber*!'"

"Love that movie. Love Sidney James and Kenneth

Williams. Love all those British slapstick comedy films."

"Yes, me too. They're all airing now on the BBC."

The gentlemen settled back down to their drinks and Shane continued washing glasses under the counter ledge.

One evening just after the new year celebrations Brendan came home distraught. He called Lily into the sitting room. Shane wondered what the big issue was about. He and Scarlet lingered close to the sitting room door out of sight. They had never seen their father in such a state, and this greatly concerned them. Brendan had tears streaming down his face. Shane was astonished by what he heard.

"What's wrong?" Lily asked as she furrowed her brow.

"Barry was found shot dead earlier today on wasteland in the Shankill Road area of the city."

"Mother of God! You were just drinking with him in the Eagle Inn a couple of days ago. I'm so sorry to hear that, Bren. Why was he in that Orange area?"

"With his job selling beers and spirits he works across mixed communities in the city."

"Has there ever been a threat on him before?"

"No, not that I'm aware of. Sure, we've been friends since primary school. He would have told me. He was well liked and respected by the people he did business with from what I remember."

"Yes, that's what makes it so shocking."

"It seems like only a few years ago we were both playing hurling together for the Mitchells."

"Yes, I remember. I was often taking both of you down to the A&E. If one of you didn't get injured in a match, the other did."

"I've spoken with Laura. As he left home yesterday he told her he was going to see the manager of a bar on the Shankill Road just after lunch. From details I've heard later, a Protestant paramilitary group pulled him out of the pub and dragged him to the wasteland. There in broad daylight he was executed. His crime was that he was a Catholic."

Shane whispered to Scarlet, "Promise me that you won't repeat to anyone what you just heard."

"I promise."

Both then scurried up the staircase before they could be seen.

THREE STRIKES

It was the morning Saturday January 8, 1972, and the new year celebrations were in the rear view window. Shane was awake early as normal lying and thinking in his bed. Was dreading this day, he thought. Siobhan will be going back to Liverpool. I'll go with her parents to see her off from the ferry port before I head for work at the Eagle Inn. Don't know how I'll manage another three months without her. Didn't realize how much I'd miss her last term. It's been great being with her again. Aah, yes, it won't be three months. I'll see her when I come across for the British Student Cross-Country Championships in February. Just a one hour train ride from Liverpool. OK, better get ready for a good performance in this race. Need to peak at the Northern Ireland Championships but can use this as a good practice race. Finishing strongly over the last half-mile would be useful so I'll take it steady at the start and then blitz that final stint.

Shane arrived early at Gransha for Siobhan's departure.
"Can I give a hand with the case to the car," he asked.
"Just finishing up, Shane," Siobhan said. "I'll have it ready in a minute."
Siobhan soon came downstairs with the case and Shane brought it out to the car where Mr. O'Connell was waiting to take it and place it in the trunk.
"Has she got any more bags, Shane?" Mr. O'Connell asked.
"Just her backpack I think."
"Grand."
Shane walked back up the path to the hallway.
"All ready now?" Mrs. O'Connell said to Siobhan.
"Almost there," Siobhan said.
She then came downstairs carrying her backpack and pocketbook. "Shane, can you stick that in the car?"
"Got it."
Shane brought the backpack down to Mr. O'Connell who

was standing by the open trunk.

The backpack was placed in the trunk, and all got into the car with Shane and Siobhan in the back seat. Siobhan took hold of Shane's hand out of sight of her parents and gently rubbed it, then held it firmly. Shane could feel her trembling.

"OK?" he whispered.

"Don't want to go," she said softly.

"Won't be long until we're together. I'll be over on February the eleventh on the ferry."

"Can't wait, Shane. You'd better be ready for a good race."

"I'll be ready, but my main focus may be elsewhere," he said as he looked into her eyes.

Siobhan dropped her head onto Shane's shoulder.

The ferry was on time. Siobhan stood on the upper deck waving back to Shane and her parents. Then the ferry departed.

"We'll drop you off at the Eagle Inn then Shane," Mr. O'Connell said.

"Dead on, Mr. O'Connell."

"Won't be long till you see her again then, Shane" Mrs. O'Connell said.

"Yeah. Early February for the Student Cross-Country Champs," Shane said.

Shane visited his Uncle Liam at his car service center on Stockman's Lane the following Friday. Liam closed the shop, and then both practiced racing each other in go-karts on the wasteland behind Liam's business.

"Clodagh asked me to invite you back for dinner, Shane, "Liam said. "Do you have time to come along? She has a shepherd's pie cooking."

"Sure do, Uncle Liam. It'll be great to see my godmother again."

Liam lived in the residential part of Stockman's Lane about a half mile from the industrial sector. They walked back and continued the conversation.

"Clodagh always looks forward to you coming over. She

doesn't get out much, so this brightens up her day."

"Why doesn't she get out much?"

"Well, she's taken on a lot of orders for wedding dresses recently. People seem to be getting married these days as if it's going out of fashion. Also, I feel she has a bit of agoraphobia. She sometimes feels uncomfortable outside."

"Uh. Sorry to hear that. However, she seemed to be fine when she was over recently and at the cross-country races earlier this year."

"Yes, she has good days and bad days. I think it's a mild version."

"Well, it'll be great to see her again."

They crossed the roundabout beneath the M1 motorway and made their way up to Liam's house. As they came toward the house, an ambulance pulled up. Out of the back of the ambulance, two paramedics helped the next-door neighbor's eldest son, Geordie Doyle, down from the ambulance in a wheelchair. Geordie was a year younger than Shane and in the same school but a year behind. He had a broken leg and a broken arm, each strapped up in plaster of Paris, plus a bandage on his face covering one eye. Shane was close enough as they passed by to notice bruises on the rest of his face. He was taken aback. Once Geordie was brought inside, Shane said to Liam, "What on earth happened to Geordie?"

"I was speaking to his father the day he was taken to the hospital. He said Geordie was brutally beaten by the security forces."

"What? How come?"

"Apparently, a patrol stopped him by a row of shops, took him round the back away from the public, questioned him, and then beat him to a pulp!"

"Jeez. Is he in the IRA?"

"His father is adamant that he's not, and I believe him."

"Why would the security forces do such a thing? Surely, they would be called out."

"I believe it was in retaliation for an attack on an army base where a couple of soldiers got killed."

"So why pick on Geordie?"

"Wrong place at the wrong time. He was coming home one evening and was stopped."

"Weren't there other people around?"

"Not many and in any case they took him around the back of the shops where they couldn't be seen. His father told me he said that the guy in charge looked ferocious. He looked beaten up, a bit like a boxer. Geordie is a quiet lad who focuses on his studies. He's never been in trouble. However, he has a quick tongue on him, and it's likely he reacted badly to the questioning."

"Jeez. Did his family complain to the security forces?"

"Most people around here don't complain. They believe it's a waste of time."

Shane thought this whole episode was odd but knew that Liam believed it, so he believed what Liam had said. Things were getting more dangerous on the streets from both the IRA and the security forces.

The following day was a race-free Saturday. Shane trained on his own. He had decided to do a steady long run of about thirteen miles up towards Dundrod where motor cycle races took place in the spring and summer. It was a crisp and clear day. Shane's thoughts drifted to Siobhan. He then felt a tune come into his head, so he toyed that around. Lyrics flowed freely so he put them to the tune. Fittingly the lyrics were about a distant love affair. As he pushed on he developed them further. Without realizing it he was running to the beat of the tune. He had covered ten miles in a breeze and had the basis of a new song. Must get this laid down when I get home, he thought. OK. Let's focus on running now. Three miles to go. Let's pick up the pace to sub-six. Shane was feeling good and striding effortlessly. He pushed along the upper Springfield Road and then eased down the Hannahstown hill to the Glen Road. OK, press now. Let's up to five-and-a-half pace. He covered the next couple of miles to home with the new song playing in his head. When he arrived home and before his shower he put pen to paper.

Brendan was out at work on a cold and crisp January night. It was a busy night in the city with several buildings on fire following bomb attacks. Lily sat with Shane and Scarlet watching her favorite program, *Alias Smith and Jones*. Suddenly there was a frantic knock on the door, and then another frantic knock.

"Coming, coming," Lily said.

Betty Dornan from down the street was standing there. "Quickly, quickly, Lily. Ring for an ambulance and bring some blankets. Two teenage girls have been tarred and feathered by the lamppost at the base of our street by the Falls Road!"

The McMahon's household was one of the few in the street with a phone. Lily quickly moved into action.

"Ambulance on its way, Betty. Should be here in less than five minutes."

Then Lily joined Betty, blankets and pillows in hand, and ran off down the street. Lily had the foresight to bring scissors. They got to the lamppost. She said in a soft voice to the distraught teenagers, "Hold still. I'm going to cut your binds."

The girls were crying but held still and Lily removed the ropes. Both were tied to the lampposts and had feathers stuck to hot tar on their heads, some of which was trickling down their faces. Their assailants were long gone. Lily and Betty eased the victims down onto the blankets and pillows. They were still crying and petrified.

"Help is on the way. You're safe now. Just lie still," Lily said.

One of the girls said with a hint of relief in her voice, "Thank you."

Soon the ambulance came, and the paramedics took over. Lily and Betty stepped back into the crowd that had gathered. Neighbors in the street who lived near the lamppost were discussing what had happened. Lily overheard them saying that four masked men jumped out of the back of a minivan and grabbed the girls as they walked down the Falls Road. They then shaved their heads, tied them together to the lamppost, and applied the tar and feathers which they took out of the minivan. They then placed a placard around each of their necks with the words, "Touts Out!"

Ethel from farther up the street came over to Lily and Betty. "The word is that the two girls were seen dancing with soldiers in a bar in the city center," she said.

"I've heard there are a lot of tar-and-feathering punishments in West Belfast as revenge for females who are suspected of colluding or mixing with the security forces," Hilda said in broken English, with a German accent. Hilda and her family lived next door to the McMahons.

"Yes, I've heard that as well, Hilda," Betty said. "There are also a lot of kneecappings going around for fellas for the same reason."

"In fact, the news was saying the Royal Victoria Hospital is becoming the world's foremost center for the treatment of gun shots to the leg," Lily said.

"Jesus, Mary, and Joseph," Betty said. "What is this place coming to?"

During January Shane took a leaf from Mary Peter's book and was developing a strategy to peak in the race he considered most critical. However, he had a dilemma. He knew he had to give his best in the Northern Ireland Cross-Country Championships to qualify for the World Championships. I need to plan my training to peak at the Northern Ireland Champs, he considered. No point in peaking for the World Champs if I don't get there. I'll then adjust my training regimen to remove the longer runs and have a greater focus on speed to excel again at the World Championships, Shane thought as he lay on his bunk strategizing. He then developed a training schedule that worked back from his main races and established which other races he would run in. All was carefully logged in his running diary. I must make sure that everything is aligned to peak first in the

Northern Ireland Championships. However, if I enter a race, I must take it seriously and give my best. I'll plan these races to make sure I'm physically and mentally right for the big ones. I'll therefore need to be rested and eager for the competition. I can still take in the critical university events but will reduce the number of club races to one per month. Seems like a plan, Shane concluded.

One of the races that Shane was eager to perform well in was his first British Student Cross-Country Championships. The event was on mainland Britain, and Queen's University had arranged for the athletes and trainers to travel by ferry from Belfast to Liverpool. The coaches would bring their cars and then drive to the event on exiting the ferry. However, Shane had arranged to meet Siobhan in Liverpool and take the train with her down to the race. The Queen's University officials were supportive of this. Shane had prepared his training well and was in good shape. It would be a good stepping stone to his main race of the season, the Northern Ireland Championships. Nevertheless, this would be a race in which he would give his all.

Queen's University had arranged for Tom Clyne to accompany the team. Tom had planned to pick Shane up on the Thursday evening before the race to take him to the ferry with some of the other runners. Shane had never competed outside of mainland Ireland before and was eagerly looking forward to it. This in fact would be only his second trip outside of the island. Late Thursday afternoon he was busy getting his running kit together. Lily was in the parlor with her ironing board doing the final touches to his running clothes. Scarlet and Tyrone were home from school watching *Blue Peter* on the television.

"Mom can't find my red socks," Shane said.

"I washed them yesterday. They should be in a basket in the kitchen."

Shane went to get them. As he did, he heard Scarlet ask, "Mom, why does Shane need red socks?"

"Some running hero of his only races in red socks. He

always takes a couple of pairs to races."

"Which runner is that Mom?" asked Tyrone.

"Oh, don't know his name," Lily said. "But he's one of the runners Shane has a poster of in your bedroom."

"I think I know the one."

"Sounds daft having to run in red socks," Scarlet said. "There's stacks of white ones over there."

"I heard that," Shane said as he came back with socks in hand.

"Eejit!" Scarlet said.

"If you weren't a girl, I'd make you suffer for that," Shane said, busy packing his bag.

"If I weren't a girl, you'd be the one suffering, eejit," Scarlet said.

"Now, kids. Enough," Lily said.

Shane could just hear Scarlet whisper "eejit" under her breath, so he looked sternly at her.

"Mom, can I have red socks?" Tyrone asked.

"No."

"Why not."

"They'd end up in Shane's kit bag and you'll never see them again."

"Oh."

"Tell you what. I'll get you some blue socks. Then you can be in Everton colors."

"Great."

Five-thirty was approaching, the time Tom Clyne said he'd call for Shane. Lily was busy ironing his Queen's University running vest.

"Mom, Tom will be here in five minutes," Shane said. "Are you ready yet?"

"Don't worry son. If Tom said five-thirty, then we'll have an extra ten minutes as he's bound to be late."

Shane continued packing his duffle bag with clothes and his running kit bag with his running shoes and spikes. In the background he could hear a whisper, "eejit", and was getting further flustered.

"Ready now. Here you go," Lily said, as she threw Shane's vest to him.

"Thanks Mom," Shane said. "That's me ready now."

It was now twenty-to-six and as Lily predicted Tom Clyne had arrived right on time, ten minutes late. Tom pumped the car horn but stayed in his car. Shane grabbed both bags and went over and gave Lily a kiss. Then he patted Keeper who had been lying quietly on his rug all the time.

Shane walked past Tyrone and Scarlet and quickly dropped his bags. He then went over and grabbed Scarlet by her sides and started tickling her in the ribs.

"Mom! Mom! Help!" Scarlet cried out.

Lily laughed. Shane stopped and picked up his bags again. As he departed, he heard Scarlet say, "Good luck, Big Bro."

"Over here Shane" came a voice on the dock as people disembarked from the ferry to Liverpool.

Shane looked around and saw Siobhan waving. "Hi Siobhan."

He eased his way past people and met up with Siobhan. They held each other closely and kissed for over a minute.

"Are you up for a thirty minute walk to the university halls?"

"Hope I can manage that far. If not I'll have a big problem tomorrow."

They set off talking on the way.

"Got you a room in the halls. One of my friends is heading back to see her parent this weekend and offered her room."

"Grand."

"I know you'll need an early night so we can grab a bite to eat this evening at the union bar."

"That'll work well."

"There'll be a local acoustic group playing there this evening, so I thought you'd like that."

"Way to go."

Shane and Siobhan caught the train on the one-hour journey to the race. They then took a fifteen minute bus ride to the venue. They held each other closely. The bus stop approached where they needed to get off.

"Better leave you to warm up now. I can mind your running kit bag. I'll come across to the finish line when you have completed your warm down."

"Thanks. Sounds like a plan."

Shane performed admirably in the race coming home a most credible eighteenth. Many of the runners ahead of me are seasoned international runners so not a bad performance, he thought as he warmed down with some of his teammates. Shame we just missed out on the medals.

Shane said his goodbyes to the Queen's University officials and his running friends and headed back with Siobhan. They had a most enjoyable Sunday together before he caught the evening ferry back to Belfast.

The Northern Ireland Cross-Country trials were quickly approaching. Paul Nairn had managed to get back into training over the Christmas period, and Shane helped him with his rehabilitation back to running. Unfortunately, Tim Callaghan decided not to come across from America. Although Villanova would have released Tim, he had just broken into the first team and was reluctant to leave at this time. Tim would comfortably make the team, Shane thought. He has his reasons for not coming. Doubt that the selectors will pick him at junior level without him running the trials. They'd be more flexibility at senior level, as the runners are better known, but it's unlikely they'll make an exception at junior level. It's up to Paul and me to hold the fort for us three amigos, he thought. Paul is making great progress now. He'll qualify, alright. I'll have to be on my best form to beat him, he thought.

The Northern Ireland Championships took place on the first Saturday in March. The Junior race took place as normal over a course of four-and-a-half miles before the senior event. This was good for Shane and Paul because after their race finished, they could warm-down and run around the course for the senior race in reverse to see how it was unfolding. When their race started, Shane held back to ensure that Paul was in a good position. Shane was feeling refreshed and strong. Halfway around the five-mile course when he and Paul were running comfortably in fourth and fifth position with a large gap behind, Shane could see that Paul would easily qualify. "You're in good position now, Paul. Do ya feel you can hang on and qualify?"

"No worries, Shane. You press ahead and see if you can medal. In fact, first place is not that far in front. Go for it."

"OK. I'll move on and see if I can medal."

He pressed ahead and passed a couple of competitors. Feeling good today, thought Shane. Feels like a runners' high. I've only experienced that a couple of times before. Feels like I'm running on air! Closing in now. As he entered the final straight, there was just one runner some ten yards ahead between him and victory. I've got him, Shane thought. Must dig deep. He upped the pace. Beat yourself, beat yourself, he kept saying to himself. He smoothly accelerated past to move into the lead before the opponent knew what had hit him. Shane crossed the line and became the Northern Ireland Junior Champion. Once finished, he ran back outside the ropes and shouted to Paul. "Almost up to the medals, Paul. Push. Push."

As Paul passed, Shane saw him push forward to fourth place. Shane greeted him soon after he finished.

"Excellent sprint, Paul. Fourth place. Not bad for your first competitive race back."

"Yes, very pleased, Shane. Thanks for pulling me along."

"Cheers."

They then put on their track suits and warmed down watching the senior race unfold.

Shane was excited he had made his first Northern Ireland team, and would be competing in his first international race, and a world championship at that. Doing so as champion and with his lifelong friend, Paul, was a bonus. Shane had followed his grandfather's advice and planned carefully to self-improve to achieve his dream. At this moment he felt on top of the world. He decided to ask the driver to leave him off at his granda's so he could see him first.

Shane made his way down to his granda's house. He knocked on the door but didn't enter. Joseph came to the door. He looked straight at Shane's face. He hadn't heard any results; however, Shane's face told the story. He smiled. "Well done, Shane. Made your first international team?"

"With your help, of course, Granda. In fact, you're looking at the Northern Ireland Junior Champion!"

Joseph's eyes lit up. He embraced Shane. "Well done. I had every faith in you."

"I followed your advice, Granda, and kept pushing myself on by saying just beat yourself, just beat yourself. I believe I beat my best self several several times in that race."

"That's my boy!"

"I really appreciate you coming over to visit and tell me first, Shane."

"My priority, Granda."

Shane stayed for tea and then walked home. He felt invigorated and positive about his running.

On his way home, Shane thought about his journey to this success and considered that this was not the end of his journey, rather the end of the first stage. He must now concentrate on giving his best at the World Cross-Country Championships. Nevertheless, it was important to celebrate successes. He reached home. Lily and Brendan had seen him approach the front door and went into the hallway to meet him. Lily opened the door just as he approached. "Well?"

"I did it, Mum, and Dad!"

"Wow, you qualified for the World Champs?" Brendan said.

"Not just that. I'm the Northern Ireland Junior Champion."

"Wow! That's my boy. Bren where's that other bottle of champagne?" Lily asked.

"Coming along. Well done, Shane."

Scarlet and Tyrone joined in the celebrations and made sure that their glasses were full, with sarsaparilla soda in their cases. As the celebrations commenced, Liam and Clodagh popped in for ten minutes on their way to a dinner dance.

"Heard the news, Shane. Well done," Clodagh said.

"Thanks, Auntie Clodagh."

"Well, all the hard work has paid off Shane," Liam said.

"Sure has, Uncle Liam. Now I must get ready for the World Champs."

"Don't worry about that tonight, Shane. Tonight is for celebration."

The Belfast Telegraph sports supplement, *The Ireland's Saturday Night,* was published later each Saturday evening and could be picked up from the newsagents after seven-thirty. This supplement was printed in the early evening when most of the sports results were in. It would carry the results as well as pre-prepared articles on forthcoming events. Following dinner, Shane grabbed his coat and shouted into the parlor, "Heading down to the shops to pick up this evening's *Saturday Night.*"

"OK. Son. Give our regards to Mr. Miller," Lily said.

"Will do."

He walked down to the Falls Road and onto the row of shops where the newsagent was located. On the Falls, Glen, and Andersonstown Roads, the shops were often located in front of wasteland. This was the case for the row of shops that Shane was approaching. Darkness had crept in as Shane arrived at the newsagents after a ten-minute walk. Good to see a full moon is out tonight, he thought. He entered the newsagents and went up to the counter where the proprietor was arranging the newspapers.

"Hello Mr. Miller."

"Well done on winning the race and making the team!" said

Mr. Miller with a beam on his face.

"What? How'd you know?"

"It is on the front page of the *Saturday Night*."

"Really?"

Mr. Miller pulled out a copy of the paper. In the bottom right-hand section was the title, "Northern Ireland Cross-Country Championships." Following the main discussion on the senior race was a paragraph dedicated to the junior event. Then, Mr. Miller read aloud. "Up and coming Belfast talent Shane McMahon triumphs in the
Northern Ireland Junior Championships. He makes the team for the International Cross-Country Championships and is accompanied by his Belfast United Harriers teammate Paul Nairn who came in fourth."

"I'll take a copy, Mr. Miller."

"Here you go, Shane."

"How much, Mr. Miller?"

"Tonight, it's complimentary, Shane. Well done! Give your parents my regards."

"Of course, Mr. Miller. They also sent their regards to you. Many
thanks."

With that, Shane left the shop with his eyes fixed on the article.

As he started to make his way back home, attempting to read snippets in the moonlight, Shane noticed an army foot patrol coming toward him. This was becoming more regular these days as trouble mounted in the city. OK. I'm sure to be stopped and quizzed, he thought. He was reminding himself that the protocol was that they would stop you, ask for your identification, check it via walkie-talkie with the barracks, then give the document back, and send you on your way. As Shane approached, they predictably stopped him. There was a sergeant and six privates. The sergeant looked to be in his late thirties, but the privates were about the same age as Shane. The sergeant walked over to Shane.

"Identification please."

"Here you go."

Shane took out his gleaming new driver's license and handed it to the sergeant. "Over here," he said, and beckoned Shane to come with him to the wasteland behind the shops. The privates followed. Shane was puzzled by this but as tutored by his parents, followed the sergeant's instructions. "Stand by the wall." There was a grass bank several yards away, and the privates sat themselves down there, removed their rifles, and placed them on the ground. It was dark and nothing could be seen clearly despite glimmers of moonlight shining through the adjacent trees. The sergeant then took out his flashlight and shone it onto the license to read it. He studied it, perusing the details.

"Shane McMahon, eighteen years old, Falls Road," the sergeant said. "So, Shane how many brothers and sisters do you have?"

"One brother and one sister, Sir." Shane was groomed by his parents to be polite, answer all questions in full, and not get flustered when being interrogated.

"Where does your father work?"

"He's a fireman in the central city center facility."

"Where does your mother work?"

"She's a housewife and stays at home."

The sergeant used his walkie-talkie to communicate with the barracks. Shane could hear faintly the response and knew that his details were confirmed.

"Well, that's alright then," said the sergeant as he handed Shane his license back. He then turned and approached his men resting on the bank several yards away, with his back to Shane. It was about a ten-yard walk to the end of the back wall and then about a further fifteen yards along the side of the shops back to the front road. Shane headed off. As he was about to turn the corner, he heard the click of rifles behind. He turned round and to his horror saw in the moonlight the six privates standing and pointing their rifles directly at him, fully cocked. He was petrified. One loose finger and I'm dead, he thought. What's all this about? He remembered there had been a couple of similar incidents in the press where so-called terrorist youths had been found dead in wastelands. It had been concluded that they had been stopped for a routine questioning, and the general thought by many was that things then had gotten out of hand. The sergeant called him back. As Shane approached, the angry looking official walked over to him, stood inches from his face, and looked straight into his eyes. The sergeant was a few inches shorter than Shane and was staring slightly up and into him. In the moonlight Shane could see that he looked ferocious. He had an almost flat nose (most likely from boxing) and a side tooth missing. He was one angry man. Shane was quaking but kept his focus, ready to answer any further questions.

"Who said you could leave?" the sergeant barked.

"You did, Sir."

"I did not. Now you told me you have three brothers and two sisters, that your father works in the shipyard, and that your mother runs a boutique in the city center."

At this instant, a cold feeling hit Shane as thoughts of stories he had heard ran through his head. I'm not going to get out of this, he thought, starting to tremble. They may shoot me. There's no one else around. At best they'll give me a severe beating. I may miss the World Championships.

The night before, a barracks had been blown up by the paramilitaries, and twelve members of the forces had been killed with several badly injured. Belfast was a tense place when such incidents happened. Shane had heard about the previous night's incidents on the news. He realized that invariably there would be blood for blood. He remained surprising calm, despite shaking within. "I have one brother and one sister, my father works in the fire brigade, and my mother is a stay-at-home housewife," Shane said.

The sergeant moved closer, right into his face. "Well why didn't you say that in the first place?" He took his walkie-talkie and spoke into it. This time there was no crackling of interference. Shane realized that he was pretending. Then for a second time the sergeant said, "Well, that's OK then." Once again he turned his back to Shane and walked over to his troops. Shane walked off to the corner of the shops as before, and as he was about to turn the corner, he heard the click of rifles from behind. He turned around to see the privates aiming at him and the sergeant summoning him back. "Who said you could leave?"

"You did, sir."

"I did nothing of the sort." He got in Shane's face once again, looking meaner than ever, like a confrontation at a prize fighters' weigh-in. "You told me you have four sisters and one brother, that your father works in a pub, and that your mother works in a launderette. That does not tie up, mate."

Shane calmly replied that he had one sister and one brother, his father was a fireman, and his mother was a stay-at-home housewife. Once again, the sergeant asked Shane why he hadn't said that before. For a second time the sergeant pretended to call through to the barracks for confirmation.

"That's alright then," he said once again to Shane.

The sergeant again turned to his men and ignored him. Shane stood in position. Five minutes passed. Then the sergeant turned back to Shane, went behind him, kicked him in the back of his knees, and shoved him to the ground. "Get on your knees!"

BREAK THE CHAIN

"We don't want these terrorists attacking our people, the sergeant said." That's all Shane could hear. The sergeant was at this stage back over with his men as Shane stayed kneeling on the dirt. He listened carefully, but the sergeant was speaking quietly to his men several yards away by the grass bank, and Shane could only make out bits of the discussion. Words such as beating, hospital, and teach him a lesson sent Shane into despair. He remembered what his Uncle Liam had told him about his neighbor Geordie Doyle and shaking nervously was preparing for the worst. Geordie had been badly beaten by a patrol led by a ferocious character who looked like a boxer. He wondered if this could be the same person. This panicked him even more. Then he heard the sergeant say to his men, "Let's get on with it. Let's teach this . . ."

Shane wondered why the sergeant had stopped speaking. He heard approaching footsteps, but his head was bowed, and he feared looking up to see who had approached.

"Good evening sergeant," said a rather jovial voice. "Just passing by in a Saracen when we saw light behind this row of shops. What do we have here?"

"A potential terrorist, Sir."

"Well, we don't like terrorists. Isn't that right sergeant?"

"Certainly not, Sir."

The higher-ranking official shone his flashlight in Shane's direction to take a better look. He could see his bright blue Adidas shoes and could make out an inscription in neat black ink, "Go Pre".

"So, Mr. eh! Sergeant, please be a gentleman and tell me our guest's name."

" Shane McMahon, Sir."

"Well Mr. McMahon. Are you a terrorist?"

"No, Sir!"

"Sergeant, Mr. McMahon says he's not a terrorist! How am I to establish the truth?" The official moved closer to Shane. "I see you have fancy Adidas shoes. Do you run?" he said to Shane in his posh voice.

"I do, Sir."

In a theatrical-type style the senior official continued. "Well then let's see if Mr. McMahon is telling the truth. Shall we, Sergeant?"

The sergeant nodded in submissive agreement.

"So, if you are a runner, Mr. McMahon, you will know about the winners on the track in the big Games," the official said.

"Agree, Sir."

"So, who is the reigning 5,000-meter champion in the Commonwealth Games, Mr. McMahon?"

Shane was puzzled at the question. Something seemed familiar, but he couldn't quite grasp it in his fear. "That's Ian Stewart, Sir."

Then the official turned to the sergeant. "Is Mr. Mahon correct, Sergeant?"

"Don't know, Sir."

"Well, that doesn't help us."

He turned to the privates who were standing to attention in a line by the grass bank. "Gentlemen, do any of you know the answer?"

"No, Sir," they all replied in turn as the official walked down their line.

The official came back, stood beside the sergeant, and looked down at Shane who still had his head bowed ensuring no eye contact. "Luckily, I know the answer. You see Ian Stewart comes from Birmingham, and I come from Burming-gum also. Mr. McMahon is correct; Ian Stewart is the reigning Commonwealth Games 5,000-meter champion! You are certainly a runner, Mr. McMahon, and I do not believe you are a terrorist. We are all God's people, gentlemen! Don't you agree?"

The troops meekly nodded in agreement.

"You may leave, Mr. McMahon," the official said.

There was something familiar to Shane with the official's delivery and words, but he was so confused and frightened that he couldn't quite work it out. However, it did sound comforting to Shane in this experience of incredible terror. With tears trickling down his cheeks he picked himself up, head still bowed, and walked to the end of the row of shops. As he was about to turn the corner, the official called after him. "Hold on Mr. McMahon."

Shane shrieked and stopped. Thankfully the official did not ask him to come back, rather the official came over to him. He was dusting something off in his hand. As he approached Shane, he could see him emerge in a beam of moonlight. It was Captain Green.

"You forgot your newspaper, Mr. McMahon," he said.

He handed Shane the newspaper, and Shane safely departed. As he hurried home, badly shaken, he wondered why Captain Green was still in Northern Ireland following his prior ordeal.

Shane returned home. Lily could see he was deeply distressed.

"Something terrible happened when I went for the newspaper, Mom."

"Let's go into the sitting room, Son, and tell me all about it."

Shane explained what had transpired. He told Lily he needed to get out of Northern Ireland. For Shane this was the third and final strike following the shooting of Paul and the injuries sustained when broken glass scuttled off the Saracen and cut him sorely.

"I can't take any more, Mom," Shane said in a stuttered voice as the tears poured down his face.

Lily put her arm around him and hugged him closely.

"I know you're in shock now, Shane, and deeply concerned. Let's discuss this further when you father gets in."

Brendan was on a late shift. The younger children were in bed when Brendan returned later. Lily, Shane, and Brendan sat in the parlor and had a frank discussion. Brendan and Lily advised Shane to go to bed, get some rest, and sleep on it.

In the cool light of day, Shane still knew he had to leave the province. The next morning was a quiet and lazy Sunday. Shane considered carefully what had transpired the previous evening and what his views were as he lay in his bunk. His siblings were having a lie-in as normal at the weekend, so he went downstairs. Both Lily and Brendan were in the parlor fixing a fire in the grate.

"May I speak with you both a minute?" he asked.

"Of course, Son," Lily said.

Lily and Brendan sat down on the settee, and Shane pulled a chair close. "As much as it pains me, Mom and Da, I know I have to move away."

"Yes, we understand," said Brendan.

"How will you go about it?" asked Lily.

"I'll discuss with my tutor next week. I'll see what is possible for me after I complete my first year at Queen's."

"You have our support," Lily and Brendan said.

Shane was rather trepid when he met with his tutor at Queen's University to discuss a move to a mainland university. The tutor was sympathetic with Shane's situation and asked for a couple of days to pursue this further. To date there had not been an official mechanism to aid students who had already started on a degree and felt they needed to move away from the province, but the tutor mentioned there had been discussions to establish one. He said he would get back by the end of the week. To his word, a message came from the tutor to Shane for a meeting on Friday morning. The tutor then advised him that this had been discussed at the highest level in the university and that the pro vice-chancellor wanted to meet with him. An appointment had been arranged for that afternoon.

The pro vice-chancellor expressed sympathy to Shane and stated that many students wanted to move away.

"I've been working with universities in the British mainland to establish a pilot. This had been agreed in principle.

However, it has been difficult to get it off the ground as many English universities have concerns about taking students from Northern Ireland, largely because of what has been seen in the news."

"I understand, Sir."

"Nevertheless, several universities are supportive. We are discussing with them the option for crediting the first year at Queen's so that the students may move straight into the next level. What we need is a suitable individual for the pilot. I've looked at your grades and discussed your case with your tutor. He in turn has had discussions with your lecturers. They all agree you are a top-class performer. Would you be willing to participate in this pilot?"

"Absolutely, Sir."

"I cannot give any guarantees. However, leave this with me for a few days or so and I will pursue it. Please expect to receive a call from my office in about a week's time."

"Many thanks, Sir."

"Please see Gillian on your way out so that she knows how to contact your directly."

"Will do, Sir."

Shane met with Gillian, the executive assistant to the pro vice-chancellor and provided her with his address and telephone number.

"Now if you don't hear from me by next Friday, please ring or pop in and I can give you an update," she said.

"Dead on. Will do. Many thanks."

The following week the pro vice-chancellor's office contacted Shane for a follow-up meeting. The pro vice-chancellor once again met with Shane. He mentioned that he was discussing his case with three universities in Great Britain, two in England and one in Scotland. He was not yet in a position to divulge the specific universities and couldn't guarantee when a conclusion would be drawn but promised to keep him updated. Another week passed without word, so Shane stopped by the office. He spoke again with Gillian.

"The office isn't yet in a position to reply to you, Shane."

"Are options still open with all three universities?"

"I shouldn't really be saying this, but two of the universities have pulled out. Nevertheless, things are progressing well with the other one."

"Is that one of the English universities?"

"For confidentiality reasons I can't mention which university. However, the one still looking good is in England."

This felt good to Shane as he was hoping he could get a university somewhere close to Liverpool where he could see Siobhan more often. Gillian once again recommended to Shane to stop by each Friday lunchtime for an update. He duly did this, but for the next couple of weeks there was no progress. He was becoming disheartened and was concerned that this opportunity would pass him by. Having resigned himself to leaving the province, he was now on tenterhooks as to whether he would get the chance. This occupied his mind daily. Brendan and Lily regularly discussed this with Shane and advised him to remain patient.

The following Thursday Shane was once again preparing himself for disappointment when he would visit the office the next day. However, there was a call to his house that afternoon, and Lily took it while Shane was out on a run. The pro vice-chancellor's executive assistant simply stated that progress had been made with one university in England and requested that Shane attend the office at nine o'clock the next morning. Shane turned up in eager anticipation. The pro vice-chancellor was there to meet with him.

"An English university recognized for having a high standard music degree has offered you a place. Based on your performance, results, and references, this university is prepared to accept your first-year credits from Queen's University and move you straight to their second year."

"Wow, that's great news! Many thanks. I'm so relieved. May I ask which university?"

"Yes, of course. I was just coming to that. It's Liverpool

University. With the history of the Beatles and the *Mersey Beat*, Liverpool University is excelling in its music degrees."

"Yes, I'm well aware of that, Sir."

"Would this be acceptable to you?"

Shane was almost speechless but quickly replied, "Absolutely, Sir."

"Please take some time to discuss this with your parents and ring back with final confirmation to my office by, say, close of business on Monday. Upon your confirmation, I will advise this to the pro vice-chancellor of Liverpool University and set up the arrangements. Congratulations, Shane."

The pro vice-chancellor then stood up and shook Shane's hand. Shane was almost in a trance. He thanked him and exited the office to the executive assistant's area. He then thanked Gillian and headed back home to inform his parents. Liverpool, of course, was perfect for Shane mainly because Siobhan was there. Then he realized that he would also be able to see his team, Everton, play live. Finally, it dawned on him that Liverpool was the heart of progressive music in the western world! There couldn't be a better solution, he thought. He went home in a most positive mood and discussed this with Brendan and Lily. They were so pleased for him. He rang into the university and discussed this with the music professor at Queen's University, who was a great inspiration to him. Later that Friday evening he rang through to Siobhan and he could tell that she was jumping for joy at the end of the phone. Shane rang into the pro vice-chancellor's office on Monday morning and confirmed his acceptance.

Shane was working in the Eagle Inn on the Saturday evening of February 26. The black-and-white television sets around the lounge and public bars were on. There was a keener interest than normal in the main program on the televisions. It was the final of the World Snooker Championships from Birmingham, England. A couple of guys agreed to meet that evening in the lounge of the Eagle Inn. They were regulars of Shane's, and he was aware they ran a glazing business together in the city center.

"Would somebody please smell that man's breath," Norman, a well-dressed and distinguished middle-aged gentleman, said as he entered the lounge, pointed across, and walked over in the direction of Damien.

Damien, who was also neatly attired in a suit with shirt and tie, was all smiles. "Great to see you, Norm. Ready for some education in snooker?"

Norman came over to the bar, and they both looked up to the screen, as many in the lounge were doing. "My God. We have a Belfast kid in the World Snooker Final," Norman said as he scratched his greying goatee beard.

"We do Norm, one of our own."

"They say he plays faster than the eye can follow, Damien."

"He sure does. Just watch." Damien ran his fingers through his greased jet-black locks and turned around to Shane who was washing glasses behind the bar while peaking at the screen. "Do you know much about this guy, Shane?"

"Only during the last couple of days. Saw something about him on the TV as he was moving through the rounds."

"I thought these snooker players are supposed to take a lot of time between shots to size up their next moves. How does he play so quickly?"

"They normally take their time. But this Belfast guy sizes up his next moves much, much faster."

"What's he called?" Norman asked.

"The Hurricane," Damien said.

"What's his real name, Shane?" Norman asked.

"Alex Higgins."

"Boy, look at him clear the table! Must have only taken a couple of minutes," Damien said.

The final took place over a few days and was a marathon event. Only brief highlights were presented in the television news together with interviews, and there was a keen interest. Despite the balls in snooker being colored, people were glued to the black-and-white images. In fact many became experts in determining the correct color from the shades of grey on the screen.

"Look, he's going for the green ball now," a customer said.

"No, that's the blue ball. Worth an extra point," another customer said.

"How do ya know it's the blue ball?"

"It's a bit lighter and is sitting on its spot separate from the others."

"Oh. I see."

The game certainly created a lot of debate, but one thing they all were united on was that the province would have its first World Snooker champion within the next day or two. For the final two days of the event the music system in the Eagle Inn was diverted to the sports news on BBC to pick up the commentary. Customers packed the pub to listen and watch the news bulletins on TV. Higgins, despite a keen contest with an experienced opponent, romped away to victory. There were celebrations in the pub and across the city for the victorious Belfast Child. His charisma and swashbuckling approach made him an instant success; something to put a silver lining on the cloud that had descended over the city. Belfast had a world champion, who became better known as the People's Champion.

The World Cross-Country Championships were fast approaching. Shane and Paul would be competing in the junior event. The competition would be held in Cambridge in England. The two friends trained together on the run-up to the event. While they were out on a ten-mile steady run on the Monday before the event, they struck up a conversation as normal.

"I heard we'll be flying over to London on Thursday to get ready for Saturday's race," Paul said.

"Looking forward to it, Paul. I've never been on a plane before."

"Me neither. It'll be great. A short flight from Aldergrove, about forty-five minutes."

"So how are you feeling, Paul? Ready to beat me now?"

"As ready as ever, Shane."

"Game on."

They moved ahead.

"So, we'll be famous, Shane?"

"What d'ya mean, Paul?"

"This'll be the last ever International Cross-Country Championships. Next year the IAAF is officially taking it over."

"Oh yeah. From next year it'll officially be called the World Cross-Country Championships."

"That's right. Must qualify for that as well, and then we'll have something more to be famous for."

"I've been calling it the World Champs all along."

"Me too."

Paul had been training well with Shane and was progressing back toward his best. Although Shane had beaten him in the trials, Paul's natural talent and return to fitness would push Shane all the way. They prepared well for the race in Cambridge. On the Friday they had a gentle run around the course.

"Proper cross-country course," Paul said.

"Yes, should be a good test," Shane said.

Race day came along, and both had an excellent start. In fact, they were comfortably running together for most of the race.

"Not pushing forward this time, Shane?" Paul said.

"Not at this pace. I'll leave my push for the final straight."

"Me too."

Both were coming toward the end of the four-and-a-half-mile race and entered the homestretch together. Each accelerated and piled it on, taking several places. At the line Paul just edged Shane to finish thirteenth with Shane a place behind despite a mass finishing pack around them.

"Gosh. Where did ya get that sprint from, Paul?"

"Been working on it."

"I thought I was going to get you before the line."

"Dug deep. Anyway, in that last fifty yards we both passed

three competitors. So can't be bad."

"Agree."

Shane felt he had left most of it out on the course and was most happy. He too had dug deep in that final straight, but on this occasion, Paul just had that bit more. Shane was pleased for him and pleased that he also had given a good performance.

They returned home as local heroes within the running community, and an article was written on both in that evening's *Ireland Saturday Night*. Despite this most credible performance, Shane still felt he could have given a bit more. He didn't experience the runners' high that carried him to victory in the Northern Ireland Championships. He believed he could do better. He reasoned to himself that a fresh environment might open his running potential further. This helped to reinforce his decision to leave. Having said that, running alone was not his main goal, although he wanted to do his best at it. He was coming to the realization that running was just a balance in his life and that more important things awaited him. He felt his real goal was to be with Siobhan and enjoy a life together in a more liberal environment. Siobhan had been able to see this clearly and the haze was just starting to lift around Shane.

Easter time arrived with great spring cheer. Siobhan returned for a few weeks. The Eagle Inn had an annual excursion day and held it as the good weather came in around the Easter period. Each employee or temporary employee was allowed to invite a partner, and Shane was delighted that Siobhan could join him. He met up with Siobhan earlier in the week and explained. "The excursion normally is held within Northern Ireland. We usually visit key places such as the Giant's Causeway, Bushmills Distillery, Cushendun, and Cushendall. However, I just heard that because of the Troubles the main part of the day out will be held in the Republic."

"Sounds good to me, Shane. I always enjoy it in the South."

"Not sure which places we'll visit, but I've heard that Dublin is on the list and that we'll stop off at a beach in the vicinity on the way back."

"Looking forward to it."

"You'll need government-issued identification with a photograph to cross the border. A passport or a driver's license will do."

"Got it. I'll bring both."

"I'll come over to your place at say a quarter to seven in the morning. I can park at your house, and we can walk down."

"Sounds like a plan."

Shane met up with Siobhan as planned and then convened with the others at the Eagle Inn at seven o'clock on the Sunday morning. The inn was closed on Sundays because of licensing laws, so the event was always held on a Sunday. Bernie oversaw the trip as Mr. Quinn was still off with his "nerves." They all got on a hired coach and then embarked on their journey. The first stop on the agenda was Drogheda in the Republic for breakfast at a seaside hotel. Then it would be on to Dublin where a large part of the day would be spent. Before they departed Bernie provided a bit more details on the places they would visit.

"The main part of the trip will be in Dublin. You'll all get a chance to walk along the river Liffey, visit the Guinness brewery, and see the historic post office on O'Connell Street."

"Just checking," Shane said to Siobhan, "that you're aware that the post office we'll visit was the scene of the main battle in the 1916 Irish Uprising."

"Of course, Shane. Know it well. I was brought up in a Catholic school as well," she said.

"Oh, of course. Should've known," Shane said.

Bernie continued, "Following lunch in Dublin, the next stop will be at a beach in Bray, just north of the city. Then off to Dundalk where dinner has been arranged in a plush restaurant. This will be our final stop before crossing back over the border again. We'll then head back to the Eagle Inn."

A big cheer rang out from all. "Hip, hip, hooray for Bernie!"

"Hey team. You need to thank Mr. Quinn when he returns. He set this all up."

One of the team stood up and started a chant. Everyone joined in. "There's only one John Quinn! There's only one John Quinn!"

The day was moving along well, and everyone was in great spirits. Everything was going great until the evening meal was finishing up in Dundalk on the party's way back home.

"Unfortunately, it's now time to leave for our coach and go back over the border," said Bernie. "I hope you've all had a good day out here down South."

"We have Bernie," one day tripper said. "Thanks for everything, Bernie."

Cheers rang out, and the party got up to leave.

Outside the restaurant a man and a woman, both in their late-thirties or early-forties, approached the group as they returned to the coach and asked for the organizer. Bernie stepped forward. The woman came over to him. "We need a trip over the border to Belfast. You know what I mean like?" she said in a strong Belfast accent.

"Well, we're just out on a day trip and were stopped at the border on the way here. They have details on all of us and know exactly how many will be on the coach."

The guy stepped forward and looked Bernie in the eyes. "We stated this politely. However, it's not a request. Figure it out."

He then opened his jacket to quietly reveal a pistol. Bernie quickly realized the predicament. Although they didn't need to spell it out, the duo was from the IRA and needed the camouflage to travel back to Belfast. Bernie stepped away and spoke with his party. Several of them were staunch IRA supporters.

"Yeah, of course. Go for it," they said.

Several others were petrified.

"This will not be good for us if we get caught with terrorists at the border, Siobhan," said Shane. "It could affect your sponsorship at Liverpool and my offer to go there."

"Yes, most worrying, Shane," said Siobhan. "However, we could always explain and hopefully that will be understood."

"Well, I know that a few universities had cold feet about taking me on. Don't want Liverpool to be scared off too."

"That was probably because the universities would have had to change their protocols to take someone mid-course. They take in students from the province straight from A-levels. I don't think there'd be a problem with Liverpool now that they have the procedures in place."

"Hope not."

"Still, I agree. Better not to be associated with terrorists."

"I'll have a quiet chat with Bernie and see what he can do."

The group was debating the issue among themselves. Shane tugged Bernie on the sleeve and beckoned him across out of earshot. "Siobhan and I are worried about our Liverpool University places if we are caught harboring terrorists."

"Know what ya mean, Shane. However, these people are quite serious. The guy showed me that he's carrying a gun."

"They'll hardly start shooting in broad daylight and on this side of the border."

"Likely not, but it has happened before. My first concern is for our welfare."

"Understand, Bernie."

"Let's get back and see what the consensus is."

Shane and Bernie moved back to the group. Shane waved to Siobhan to come over.

"We don't want to be caught smuggling terrorists over the border. We've got our families to think about. What if they are identified by the security forces at the border?" a distraught lady asked.

"Good point, Gemma," another lady said.

"Do we have a choice?" Bernie asked.

"Doesn't look like it. They can see we're from the Eagle Inn from the sign at the front of the bus. They'll know where to find us," Barney said.

A significant debate erupted. Bernie was a nice man but not strong enough to enforce an opinion. Nevertheless, he concluded on the matter. "On that basis we'll have to oblige. We need to have the same numbers of men and women on the bus when we cross back over the border. We need a man and woman to travel back by train. Any takers?"

There were plenty of volunteers from those who were dead set against harboring the terrorists. Although all the names were taken at the border, not all identification was examined; rather a sample was reviewed. It was imperative that the identification matched the names given. Of course, this had to be a man and a woman. One couple, the most distraught at the predicament, was chosen as their passport photos bore the closest resemblance to the intruders.

"You can have our passports, but please make sure to get them back. We'll return by train," they said. "We'll use our driver's licenses to get across the border if identification is asked for."

"I'll make sure to get them back for you, Paddy and Susan Bernie said, "Thank you for volunteering and understanding."

"No worries. We're so glad to do so. Don't want to be around any terrorists. We have our children to think about."

Bernie went back to the terrorist duo and confirmed to them that they would be taken on the coach.

"The security forces will check the bus. They'll search around it for explosives, open the hold and examine bags, conduct a head count, and then sample identification from the passengers," the female terrorist said.

"Yes, I'm aware of that," Bernie said. "Based on the way the identification was sampled on the way down, it will be best if you are toward the center of the coach. Also, better not to sit together."

"No problem."

"May I ask you, madam, to sit beside another female, and you, fella, to sit by another man? That will look reasonably normal to the border guards."

"Got it. You're the man," the IRA man said.

The IRA duo sat about midway back in separate rows, the female at a window seat beside another woman and the man a row back in the aisle beside another guy. Shane and Siobhan sat together three rows behind the male imposter. Shane sat by the aisle and had a good view of the rows in front of him. The coach arrived at the border check. Two security guards boarded, pleasantly said "Hello," and did a head count from the front.

"I take it you're in charge," one of the security guards said to Bernie, who was sitting at the front just behind the driver.

"Yes, that's right," Bernie said.

"Did you have a good trip down south?"

"Sure did."

"So now back to the old grind."

"Tell me about it."

"OK. We need to check a few people for identification. Don't want any terrorists traveling back with you," he said with a cheerful demeanor.

"Of course. Be our guests."

The two guards moved down the aisle of the coach and stopped every few rows and examined identification. They had a short, pleasant chat with each person they examined. Shane was nibbling at his fingernails and breaking out in a cold sweat as they approached the terrorists. The female guest was the closer of the two to the front of the coach, so they approached her row first. Luckily, the guards walked past that row without stopping.

"Phew," Shane said.

Siobhan nudged him and whispered, "Calm down or the guards will know something's awry."

The male terrorist was two rows back. One of the guards stopped by him in the aisle. "Identification please," he said.

The male terrorist was about to go for the borrowed passport when the guard bent over and then specifically looked at the person by the window. The man sitting there gladly produced his passport.

"So is the Guinness better in the south?"

"Unfortunately, I have to say yes. I'm told it's the water."

"Shame, but I bet they can't beat our Bushmills."

"Absolutely no way. Nothing beats Bushmills."

The guard smiled and then moved further down the coach. Shane and Siobhan were sitting together and had their credentials examined. The guards sampled a few more people to the rear and then made their way back. Shane could see the male terrorist let out a sigh of relief as the guards passed down to the front.

"Sorry to disturb you. Enjoy the rest of your trip," one guard said as they disembarked satisfied.

All on the coach were much relieved and chatter broke out. The coach went on its way. In a small town in Northern Ireland just a few miles from the outskirts of Belfast, the female terrorist stood up. "Stop here," she said.

The coach pulled to a stop. Both in turn went over to Bernie at the front and handed back the passports. As they disembarked the female turned back around. "Sorry to have disrupted your day's excursion. You've made a big contribution to the freedom of our country."

"Goodbye," Bernie simply said.

The atmosphere in the coach improved for the rest of the journey back. Many were relieved just to get home. It transpired later that the guests were both near the top of the security's most-wanted list. They were known as experts in bomb making. What a near miss for the day trippers from the Eagle Inn. The coach returned to the inn, and all went on their way. Shane walked Siobhan back to her house.

"So glad to be back," Siobhan said as they stopped at her front gate.

"What an ordeal! Great shame."

"Well, you said it'd be exciting, Shane. You're a man of your word."

"It's late, so I'd better head straight off."

"See you Tuesday at ten in the morning."

"Yes, I'll come over then as planned."

They embraced and parted. As Siobhan entered through her front door Shane drove off for home in his VW. It had been a most tense and frightening experience. This was the last annual day out that the Eagle Inn ever had because of this bad experience.

SLÁN LEAT

Easter disappeared into the rearview window and cross-country running was put to bed for another season. Shane turned his attention to track and road races. He lay in his bunk on a sunny spring Sunday morning planning his schedule. Got to participate in some track events, of course, but I prefer the road races. Don't like running around in circles, better to be going somewhere. I really like the relays. Enjoyed the Portadown-to-Belfast Road Relay last year, so that's definitely one for the calendar. I ran a three-mile stage last year. Wonder if I can get a longer stage this time? I'll discuss with Tom. The relay was one of the most popular in Northern Ireland. Juniors competed with the seniors to ensure a complete team. There were twelve stages, half approximately three-to-four miles long and the remainder from six to nine miles. Each stage had a prize for the fastest runner. I'm unlikely to be among the fastest this year, but the longer distance will be a good experience. I'll likely be shown a clean pair of heels by the seasoned runners.

Shane spoke with Tom Clyne later that day. "Shane, before you ask, I'm thinking about giving you a longer leg this year. You did well last year at three miles, but I think you could really help our strategy on the longer fourth leg this year."

"Great minds think alike, Tom. I was going to ask you for a longer leg this year."

"Grand. Then we'll plan for this."

"So, what's the race strategy, Tom?"

"Gerry will start the first leg of four miles to get us up in the top half dozen, so that we're in the hunt. Then we'll have some of the least-experienced runners on the second and third stages. I think you'll be handed over around tenth to twelfth place. You should then be able to have some easy pickings in front of you."

"Where do you need me to be at the end of the stage, Tom?"

"If you can get into the top six, that'll work. The aim is to hit the front by the eighth or ninth stage."

"Got it, Tom. I'll be ready." Extra pressure, Shane thought, but bring it on.

The race took place three weeks later. Shane was in great form taking over in ninth place and moving through to fourth, just twenty-five seconds off the lead. He performed much better than expected, and when the times came in later, he was actually the fastest runner on that stage. He had felt exhilarated on this run and pulled out all the stops to help his team. Belfast United Harriers expected to medal in the team event and were well on track. The remaining colleagues of Shane's, bar a couple, had good chances of setting fastest legs on their stages.

Following his stage, Shane got a lift by one of the coaches to a couple stages ahead. He warmed down running back along the sixth leg to see the leaders come through. When they eventually arrived, he could see that his friend Pete McGuirk had moved into third place. All is going according to plan, he thought. The leaders approached.

"Go for it, Pete. Closing in now. The leader is only fifteen seconds ahead."

Pete pushed forward. Shane then turned back and ran to the end of the leg. One of the coaches was just about to drive to the end of the next stage, so he hitched a lift. Paul Nairn was on that stage, a three-mile leg. Once again Shane ran back to where the leaders were coming. From a distance he could see Paul advancing on the lead. As the runners approached, Paul was just a few seconds behind.

"You've got this Paul."

Paul nodded over in acknowledgment. Then he pushed into the lead, handing over a six-second advantage at the end of his stage, also taking the fastest time on his leg.

Belfast United Harriers extended their lead on the next stage. They now had a commanding thirty-second advantage. This was both good and bad. Their runner on the tenth leg, comfortably in the lead, took a wrong turn and didn't realize it for nearly half a minute until he noticed a couple of the team's coaches running to the side and frantically waving at him. He doubled back and was ushered by officials back onto the correct course now in second place. He returned to the course close to where Shane was waiting. "Go Jim. You can make the gap back up."

Jim was some ten seconds behind a runner from North Belfast Harriers. He pushed hard and brought the team back into the lead by the end of his seven-mile stage. With just two stages to go, the team was in good shape to win. Despite some good competition on these last two legs, they held on for the win. In fact, Shane and Paul ran the fastest legs on their stages. They got together at the finish in the center of Belfast.

"Well done, fella," Shane said to Paul.

"You set it up for us, friend," Paul said.

They then moved on to meet up with the rest of the team. They joined in the celebration. However, following the race, there was an appeal. Shane could see there was a serious discussion close by with Tom Clyne in the midst in the officials' area. Tom came back to the Belfast United group looking dejected.

"What's the problem, Tom?" Shane asked.

"Turns out the officials who had ushered Jim back onto the correct course brought him some ten yards before the point where he went off," Tom said.

"Is that a problem? Jim must have run more than an extra couple of hundred yards anyway," Paul said.

"These AAA officials are not applying pragmatic rules. They say he didn't cover the full stage. They're keeping to the letter of the law. There's nothing more we can do."

"What a shame after all that effort," Shane said.

"There's one silver lining on that cloud."

"What's that?"

"The fastest runners on each stage, apart from Jim, will still receive their prizes, as these legs were run correctly. So, you will get a prize for stage four, Shane, and you for stage seven, Paul."

"Good to hear, Tom, but little consolation," Shane said.

At the awards ceremony in a school assembly hall near the center of Belfast, Shane had the pleasure of moving to the stage amid applause and receiving an electric coffee pot. He was proud to take this back and give to his mother.

The inter-university track events were fast approaching. Queen's University had picked Shane for the 5,000 meters in the head-to-head with Trinity College Dublin at the latter's grass track in the Dublin campus. Shane had never visited the university before and was very impressed. The campus grounds were well groomed, and the track in excellent condition. It was the first time this year that Shane had some serious competition on the track. There were three runners for each team, and two of the Trinity runners had represented Ireland. Shane needed to make up fifteen seconds on his best time to have a chance of winning. As the race progressed, he was elbowed in the ribs, tripped, and spiked, and deliberately in most cases. Halfway through the race a top-rated Trinity runner moved to the front. "Sod this," the Trinity runner said.

He shot off. Must go with him, Shane thought. First, I must get out of this boxing match. He moved to the outside and accelerated past the others. He pushed hard and caught the breakaway runner. Got to get into an easy breathing pattern now. He moved behind the leader's shoulder and eased off the pace a bit. Soon he was running at a comfortable cadence.

"Hope you don't mind some company?" Shane said.

"Be my guest. I was expecting you to come with me. I'll, of course, expect you to share the lead."

"Of course." Shane was surprised that this top international athlete would even know him and felt quite privileged. "Well, I didn't want to remain amid the Battle of Bannockburn!" he said.

"Yes, these university races tend to get a bit frisky."

Shane held on gallantly and tried to overtake on the final lap, but his adversary was just that bit too strong for him. He came in a credible second and broke his personal best by twenty seconds. A very successful outing, he considered.

Following a warm-down running around the campus, Shane headed back to watch the remainder of the events. He was a connoisseur of field events. Got to see the actual competitions, not just hear the results, he thought, as he moved to a vantage point.

That evening all competitors were invited to a banquet in the main refectory hall at Trinity. Thereafter, everyone was let loose to enjoy themselves. As Shane and a couple of guys from his team walked around the campus on the beautiful warm summer's evening, they noticed a group of students playing instruments under an oak tree.

"Mind if we join you?" Shane asked.

"Be our guest. Here borrow this one," said one of the Trinity guys who was sitting under the tree. "I'm Brian. You must be Shane."

"That's right. Thanks Brian."

He handed Shane an acoustic guitar. Shane and his colleagues from Queen's joined the group. They all introduced themselves.

"How do ya know I play guitar?" Shane asked.

"We get the *Athletic Weekly* as well. Saw the article on you after the Northern Ireland Cross-Country Championships."

Shane was slightly embarrassed. He was surprised that his reputation ran ahead of him. He sat down under an extended broad limb of the tree, tuned up the guitar, and joined in the fun playing Irish music.

"OK. Now we've to each play a song," said Brian.

Each musician was asked to do a solo. A couple of guys from Galway and Coleraine went first.

"Now your turn, Shane," Brian said.

Shane had been thinking about what he should play. Must be something they recognize, he thought. Better to be a traditional Irish song. Now the Dubliners have some great songs to choose from. Yes, got one. Shane did some final tuning on the guitar and then began a rendition of the traditional Irish song "Whiskey in the Jar." This went down very well with the crowd who sang along. When he finished, everyone applauded enthusiastically. Friendships were made that night, some of which would last forever.

The final event in the Irish Universities Track and Field calendar was the Irish University Athletic Championships in mid-June. These were held two weeks later in another well-groomed grass track in Cork, and Shane was in attendance. He knew that Cork University had one of the country's top steeplechase runners, Donnie Craig, who had represented the country the previous year in the Helsinki European Championships. Shane was also aware that even though he was highlighted to go to the Olympics he had not achieved the qualifying standard, and he would make his push here. Shane had an opportunity to discuss this with Donnie the evening before over a drink. "So not concerned, Donnie, about trying to get the qualifying time on a grass track?"

"I know it won't be as fast as a synthetic surface, but I should get the time OK, Shane. If not, I have a few more good opportunities in races over the next few weeks, all on synthetic surfaces."

"Understand. Go for it, Donnie."

"I may need some help. I could do with someone taking me out for the first four laps. Would you be up to that, Shane?"

"I'll give it a go. You'll have to nudge me a bit if I'm not on pace."

"You'll be fine."

"Glad to help."

"I just need to have a word with the officials in the morning. I must make sure that all is in position for an official time."

"Any concerns there?"

"Just need to make sure that the barriers are at the correct locations and that the water level in the water jump is correct."

"Amazing what one has to think about to get an official

time."

"Normally it's just left to the officials, but I can't take a chance. Must be sure to be sure."

Track and field was an amateur sport and relied heavily on volunteers to organize the events and take the timings and measurements. About thirty minutes before the race, Donnie went around the track for a final check. Shane heard him shout over to the officials as he warmed up, "The water level is two inches short."

"What. We checked that," one official said.

"Well, it's not at the correct level now. Must have the minimum level. Better fill it up about an inch above what's needed."

"Will do, Donnie."

Donnie was a veteran of the university, having competed for the last six years and now in the final year of a PhD. He was well respected by all involved. The whole university was very supportive of this qualifying time attempt. The local press was in attendance to report on the race, and on the championships in general.

The steeplechase started. As promised, Shane went to the front. Now, if I can just deliver Donnie through the first four laps, I should be clear of the field and able to hang on for the silver, he thought. Shane knew he had no chance of staying with Donnie for the full race. He had assessed the rest of the field and knew he needed a gap because there were a couple of runners known for fast finishes. The race was going well. Shane hit his marks through the first four laps, and then Donnie moved ahead.

"Thank you, friend," Donnie said to Shane on his way past.

"Go for it, Donnie."

Shane checked his Casio wristwatch timer and could see that with three laps to go he was on for a personal best by some ten seconds. In addition, he remained comfortably in second place with two runners some thirty yards behind. He knew one of them from Trinity University, and he was one with a superfast finish. He was not familiar with the other runner from Galway University. Need to keep the gap, he thought, as he continued with a smooth cadence. He was feeling strong as he came halfway down the home straight with just over a lap to go. He could see Donnie on his own up front moving into the last lap, but he couldn't hear the bell. As Shane passed the finish line with one lap to go, there was no bell. He looked over at the timekeepers, two elderly gentlemen in Irish athletic blazers who were helping themselves each to a wee Jameson. He didn't know what to do. He was ready to push forward but was unsure if he was on the final lap. He looked at his watch and deduced that he had to be on the last lap and moved briskly forward. He pushed on the final lap, entered the final straight, and powered forward. He could see Donnie cross the line some sixty meters in front of him. Then he heard a bell and noticed the officials beckoning Donnie to keep going. Donnie Craig pressed his watch as he crossed the line and ignored the bell. He checked his time. Shane knew from a glance at his watch that he had comfortably beaten the Olympic qualifying standard. Donnie stopped, and the officials came over to him.

"Go on. You need to do another lap."

"I certainly do not. You have your count wrong."

The officials snuffed at that rebuff. Shane soon crossed the line in second place and stopped also and checked his watch. He had beaten his steeplechase personal best by fifteen seconds. He was very pleased; however, the officials shouted to him, "One more lap."

He looked in Donnie's direction. Donnie was shaking his head in utter disgust at the officiating. The reality hit Shane that he would not medal without another lap, but he couldn't go any further. He realized that the first four laps of pacing had burnt his legs out. The other runners who had kept a constant gap behind Shane kept going at the bell. He went over to Donnie and stood beside him breathing heavily to catch his breath.

"What went on here?" Shane said.

"A complete cluster..."

Donnie stopped in mid-sentence and went over to the officials. Shane from close by could hear an abusive onslaught of cursing from Donnie at the timekeepers. The officials were so upset they nearly spilled their whiskies.

"That's all the thanks we get!" one said.

Donnie didn't let up. In his soft Cork accent, his verbal lambasting was like poetry in motion. When he was done, he came across and apologized to Shane for the poor officiating and for his outburst. He mentioned to Shane that he would make it up to him. Donnie was one of the prime organizers of the two-day event, and he had something special planned for everyone that evening. "I hear you like music," he said.

"Yes, absolutely!"

"Then keep yourself free for a concert this evening."

"Great. Who's in the concert?"

"That's a secret for the time being."

That night all the athletes and officials were invited to an open-air concert in a Gaelic football stadium in the Cork athletic grounds by the marina. Following an early dinner at the university, buses took the delegation to the concert. When Shane got there, he realized the concert was that of a new band formed by one of Cork's own, Rory Gallagher! Wow, Rory Gallagher live, he thought. That's right, he split up with Taste just over a year ago following the Isle of Wight festival. This must be his first solo gig. Gallagher had just released the eponymous first solo LP, *Rory Gallagher*, and blasted off the concert with the first track from the album, Laundromat. The concert lasted for over three hours. Strangely, not many Taste tracks were played, Shane thought. He certainly has enough top-quality material for several new albums. Shane then remembered back to the time when the late, great Jimi Hendrix had been interviewed a couple of years earlier and was asked what it was like being the world's best guitarist. His response was, "Ask Rory Gallagher!"

Shane rationalized that the evening certainly made up for

the disappointment of losing a medal to a poor lap count earlier in the day.

As the university track season finished and the exams were close to completion, Shane would often get together with the A-team of Paul and Tim, the latter now back in Belfast after having had a most successful first year at Villanova University. Tim had been a regular in the scoring six for the cross-country team at Villanova and had markedly improved his 1,500-, 5,000- and 10,000-meter times on the track. Ironically all three mates were performing at about the same level. The summertime was effectively their off-season.

One Sunday, when they met to go over to Dub Lane, Paul spoke with them. "Let's take advantage of the off-season to get some good conditioning for the cross-country season. Queen's University's Embankment sports center is well equipped with gyms and a weight room."

"That's right. We'll be allowed access with Shane's pass," Tim said.

"I'm in," Shane said. "I'll get us signed in. We have a big year coming up in the senior ranks."

"Are you both up to meeting there say twice a week?" Paul asked.

"You got it," they both said.

They started doing the conditioning sessions the following week. Following an approximate one-hour period in the gym, they would then warm down with a thirty- to forty-five-minute run up and around Belvoir Park. Paul and Shane were most interested to hear about Tim's first year in the United States. Paul was set to attend Villanova University on a scholarship reserved for him and would leave for the States in early September. Shane would often take appropriate stories back to Lily, who was eager to hear what the Philadelphia area was like.

The three amigos took full advantage of training together, prior to all preparing to leave for different pastures in September.

One day toward the end of June the three amigos were out on their warm down after a session at the Embankment sports center.

"Did you hear about that atrocity at the weekend when three teenage army soldiers were lured to their deaths by young Catholic women in the Antrim Road?" Tim asked.

"Yeah, heard it on the television news," Shane said.

"Heard a bit on it," Paul said. "Any further details, Tim? You live close by."

"The soldiers were off duty and attended a disco. The three females invited them back to the apartment they shared for a few drinks. When they were there, the ladies exited the sitting room and a gang of eight or nine paramilitaries entered. They tied up the soldiers and then took them to a nearby waste ground and tortured and shot them," Tim said.

"Jeez!" Shane said.

"Can't shed any more light on what happened that evening, but something happened the next day."

"Go on," Paul said.

"That was on Sunday, I was running along by the Water Works on Cliftonville Road," Tim said. "I was coming toward the end of my training session and cutting back through Hopefield Avenue toward Antrim Road. As I approached an alleyway, a youth sprang out at top speed. Ten to fifteen yards behind, two men in their early thirties in jeans, jackets, and running shoes were belting after him. I was knocked to the ground in the furor."

"Wow. Were you hurt?" Paul asked.

"No, just shaken a bit, wondering what this was all about."

"Who were these guys in pursuit?" Shane asked.

"Didn't recognize them. However, I did recognize the guy who appeared to be running for his life. It was John Robertson. You know, the top-class hurling player for the Antrim minor team, who also attends St. Malachy's Grammar School."

"Ah, yes. Wasn't he in his final year? I believe he's due to go to Queen's in the autumn to study mechanical engineering,"

Paul said.

"Yes, that's right. Well, he would normally nod over or say Hello to me, but he looked terrified and just kept going," Tim said. "Anyway, he carried on up the road toward his own house. I could see his mother was on the path by the front garden. I heard him shout, 'Open the door!' as he approached. She did this, and John shot into the house petrified. The two men followed, pushed his mother out of the way, and entered the house."

"My God!"

"The guys followed him into his own house?!"

"Not only that, but as they brushed John's mother aside, she fell from the path into her rose garden. I could see that John and the two men had exited through the back of the Robertsons' garden and were heading up the alleyway."

"I was really concerned. I shouted over to Mrs. Robertson to ask if she was OK. She picked herself up with some minor scratches from the roses and said she was fine. Then she asked me if I could check on what was going on as she was concerned about her son and worried about whom these pursuers could be."

"I told her I'd head up the street parallel to where they were now hurrying in the back alleyway. I must admit, I wasn't sure how safe it would be. Nevertheless, off I sprinted."

"Were you able to see behind the houses?" Paul asked.

"Well, the houses are three-story semis, so I could see in the gap between the houses. I kept my distance but tracked them," Tim said. "John made a beeline for the back path of a neighbor's house several gardens along. The pursuers kept pace. I was coming around the side of the next semi as John reached the back door, a full glass panel door. I saw him jump into it to kick it open but instead he went through it, badly cutting himself!"

"You've got to be kidding!" Shane said.

"No, not at all. I then hurried over to the house to help John. I arrived there just as the two men arrived."

"Who were they?" Paul asked.

"One of the pursuers took out a walkie-talkie and called for an ambulance. It transpired that they were undercover army policemen who had been assigned to the area following the execution of their colleagues. Their mission was to check out any youths who fitted the profile of the abductors."

"How did they know the descriptions of the paramilitaries?" Paul asked.

"Apparently, they'd spoken with witnesses at the disco and had identified and arrested the females who had been involved, and they in turn gave general descriptions of the paramilitaries. John matched one of the descriptions with his bright curly orange hair, so when he got off the bus on his way home from town, they started to follow him."

"So why did John run?" Shane asked.

"Ironically, they asked John that while they were tending to his cuts and waiting for the ambulance. I was still there at the time. John said he noticed them following him and thought that they were paramilitaries, got scared, and so he started to run."

"So, a completely innocent person is now another victim of the Troubles?" Paul said.

"Sadly, yes."

Following this episode John Robertson had to spend two weeks in the hospital recovering from deep cut injuries. This event spooked Shane. It would only be a matter of a couple of months before he would leave the province. However, he felt that violent occurrences were becoming more widespread. He was seeing horrors all around and felt that they were suffocating him. He was counting the days until he departed.

Summer was in full flight, the exams were successfully behind, the three mates continued their training, and most importantly Siobhan was coming back home. Shane agreed to pick Siobhan up at the ferry terminal. They met up when she disembarked, embraced, and kissed.

"Great to see you, Shane. Hope you've kept out of trouble."

"Can't seem to shake trouble, but the last couple of months

have been fine. Looking forward to joining you at Liverpool University."

"Can't wait," Siobhan said. "However, I just heard before I left that I must return early for some industrial foundry experience. So, I'll only be back here for one month."

"Shame. However, let's just take full advantage of the time we have together."

They walked down the road to Shane's VW and then drove to Gransha. Shane and Siobhan would meet up as often as possible, in fact almost every day during Siobhan's truncated summer break.

With his move to Liverpool University confirmed, Shane now turned his attention to making some more money in advance. Going forward he would need to fund his own accommodation, food, and travel. Although he would have a government grant, he was aware that they tended to spread thinly, so he needed additional funds. That will be my primary focus until I depart, he considered.

Lily encouraged Shane not to take any more bar jobs as there were more and more reports of dangerous events in pubs in the region. "Is there something you could do outside, away from parked cars and the city center? Your Uncle Liam may have some good contacts. I can ask him."

"Understand, Mom. Yes, please do ask Uncle Liam." Shane knew that Liam serviced cars for local businesses and was hoping that he might come up with something appropriate. One of those businesses was the local golf course, Balmoral Golf Club, and some of the officials and members had their cars serviced by Liam. At Lily's request he made some enquiries and found out that he could get Shane an interview as a caddie. "Caddies spend about four to four-and-a-half hours on a round of golf and usually make two to three pounds in tips," Liam said when he met up with Shane.

"Wow. Much better than what I earn at the Eagle Inn for about the same number of hours work. Yes, I'm most interested,

Uncle Liam."

"Great. I'll get in touch with them and see if I can arrange for you to meet with them soon."

A couple of days later Shane was duly interviewed and was offered the opportunity. "You will have to do some training, learn the golfing rules, and take two sessions of caddying for me on a couple of evenings," the head caddy said.

"Understand, Mr. Murphy. Sounds good. When can I get started with the training?"

"Come back tomorrow morning at eight, and I'll get you started. I'll take you through the rules, and then you can go out and track one of the other caddies."

"Many thanks, Mr. Murphy."

All went well. Shane became well versed with the rules of golf. For background knowledge he decided to read up on some of the top golfers of the time. He was impressed with some of the most notables such as "the King," Arnold Palmer; the athlete known as "the Black Knight," Gary Player; the new sensation known as "the Golden Bear," Jack Nicklaus; and the one he really admired for his wit the "Texan," Lee Trevino. Shane thought all four should do a spaghetti western movie with those nicknames. Within a week Mr. Murphy confirmed that he was ready and to expect a call any day to get started.

A few days later Shane received a call from Mr. Murphy. He asked him to come over to the golf club the following Saturday morning as he had an assignment. "You'll be caddying for a local businessman who owns a string of bakeries in Belfast. He's Des McKern."

"Thanks Mr. Murphy. I believe I've heard of him. He does a lot for the area."

"That's right, Shane. A pillar of society, so we must impress him," Mr. Murphy said. "He'll have a solicitor as a partner, and they'll be paired against an optician and an estate agent."

"Looking forward to it, Mr. Murphy."

Shane arrived about an hour before the tee time. He took a bit of private time to refresh on the rules and work through a bag of clubs to be fully familiar. Shane went to the drop zone as the golfers arrived. "I'll take your clubs Mr. McKern," he said as the car pulled to a stop and the driver got out.

"Thank you, son. What do I call you?"

"Shane."

"Call me, Des," Mr. McKern said.

"Will do, Des."

"My teammate here is Frank."

"Hello, Frank. Jimmy will be caddying for you. He'll be along shortly."

"Thank you, Shane."

"Danny and Domal, our opponents, will be along shortly."

"Yes, the other two caddies will come out when they arrive."

Shane brought the golf bag around to the practice area. He quickly went through the bag to get acquainted with the clubs that Des has brought along.

The four golfers starting out on their round had placed a wager on the game. This seemed to be the norm for competitions. Each of them had a similar good standard, between two and four handicaps. The game started. After a few holes, Shane's impression of the game was that each player played two or three strokes to the greens, took a putt, missed, and then started to curse profusely. He also had to experience the debates as to whether a ball was technically inside or outside a hazard line, where to drop the ball if it was inside, and how many club lengths to use for the drop, and in what line. As the game wore on, the gamesmanship continued. "What a stupid sport," he muttered out of earshot. "Can one really call this a sport? The only ones who seem to be getting any decent exercise are the other three caddies and me?"

On the seventeenth hole there was a long debate as to whether someone putted the ball when it was microscopically moving. What a bunch of morons, Shane thought. By the eighteenth green where a five-minute debate had taken place on who was furthest from the hole, Shane thought to himself, I've had enough of this. I'll wait the game out, but never again. The game ended with a narrow victory for Des and Frank. Shane cleaned Des's golf clubs and returned them to his car as requested. Des then went over to Shane and thanked him and presented a tip of three pounds.

"You helped me out there, Shane, with your knowledge of the rules. Much appreciated. Here you go."

"Thank you, Des."

Despite the nice tip, twice as much as he would make later in the week at the Eagle Inn for a night's work, he was resigned to this being his last caddy assignment. Shane had a quick shower, changed his clothes, grabbed his duffle bag, and then went to the back of the club house to track down Mr. Murphy. He found him in a small shed, fitting grips. "Sod this for a bunch of soldiers! I am one and done! I'm off and
not coming back!" Shane said.

"Sorry to hear that, Shane," Mr. Murphy said. "Mr. McKern was just in here and was singing your praises."

"Thanks for the feedback, Mr. Murphy, but my mind was blown away with all the gamesmanship. Just can't take it."

"Know what you mean. Hey Shane if you change your mind just give me a call."

"Thanks, Mr. Murphy."

Shane left thinking it was strange that Mr. Murphy seemed to understand. He then decided to visit his uncle Liam to explain to him before he heard from anyone else. Following that he informed his parents. Both understood.

The following week Shane heard from a friend that a pub in the city center was looking for a guitar player for a couple of evenings a week. As Shane was a talented performer, he decided he would check this out. He secured a meeting with the manager of the Anchor Bar on Glengall Street. "Now, I just want you to know that there is no payment for the evening from the Anchor. Basically, you would play for tips," the manager explained.

"Oh. OK. So how much does one normally make on tips?" Shane asked.

"On a good evening one could make up to five pounds. Should make at least three pounds."

"Sounds good. I'm in. What evenings are available?"

"The prime evenings are Friday and Saturday, but unfortunately I have people in place for them. I also have a guy who can only do Thursdays. How does Tuesdays and Wednesdays sound to you?"

"Sounds great. When do I start?"

"Can you start next Tuesday?"

"Yeah. Dead on."

Shane was most pleased with the arrangement and eager to get started. In addition, he would continue to work at the Eagle Inn on Fridays and Saturdays. Although the money each night was less, he was loyal to Mr. Quinn and enjoyed the atmosphere. When he arrived home, he informed his parents.

"Just a bit worried, Shane, about you going into town in the evenings," Lily said.

"The center is pretty safe now, Lily," Brendan said. "Security's most effective these days."

"Can't quite trust it, Bren. Anyway, Shane has made up his mind, and it's only for a couple of months."

"Thanks, Mom and Da."

"I've got a nice Irish stew for dinner tonight. It's in the oven and should be ready any minute. Let's set the table," Lily said.

Over the next few days Shane practiced up on various songs, some popular and several from his own pen. Really excited about this, he thought.

On the first evening Shane played, which was the following Tuesday, there was a fair-sized crowd. The pub was close to the newly built hotel, the Europa, the largest in the city where most of the international journalists stayed. They needed to be entertained and would frequent the city center pubs where music was on the menu. Shane went through his prepared repertoire. Dylan featured heavily. There was also Joni Mitchell, Neil Young, Cat Stevens, plus some traditional Irish ballads. Toward the end of his session, four gentlemen came in and sat near the front at an empty table. They were American journalists. One blurted out in a brash American accent, "Play a song from America." They had been drinking in other pubs and were a bit merry.

"What would you like? Dylan, Kristofferson, Morrison?" Shane asked.

One of the other journalists, a quite jovial character, piped up. "No, someone we haven't heard of."

Shane thought for several seconds. "Have you heard of Tim Buckley?"

"Tim who? No haven't heard of him! Go for it."

Shane hadn't practiced his preferred song from Tim Buckley for a while, so he took a minute to clarify it in his head. His audience was starting to believe he didn't know any of Buckley's songs. Shane could hear some murmuring in the crowd. Just before he was about to be hurried, he began singing the *Song to the Siren*. The pub fell quiet. Everyone was spellbound. When he finished, he received a standing ovation from the thirty-odd people in the bar. The American journalists came over, and each put a five-pound note in his hat, which sat at the front of the small stage just in front of him. Others came up and contributed. That evening Shane made over twenty-five pounds, more than Brendan made in a week while risking his life putting out fires. I'm all in, Shane thought. He continued playing at the Anchor for the rest of the summer.

Lily switched on the wireless one morning in early July as her children were eating their breakfast.

> The Women's Peace Drive has been gathering momentum in Northern Ireland, with marches successfully carried out without any violence in Belfast and Derry. Leaders of the Drive told our correspondent that they had had meetings with the leaders of the provisional IRA who

acknowledged their concerns about children being hurt in the Troubles. They said that the IRA leaders have agreed to revise their operational strategy as a consequence.

"Wow. We may be getting somewhere after all this time," Lily said.

"Sounds most positive, Mom," Shane said. "Also, that lady they interviewed; didn't you say you know her?"

"Sure do, Son. Tess and I were at school together. Really proud of her."

Thirty minutes later there was another news bulletin on Northern Ireland on the wireless.

News has just come in that the annual Orangemen Twelfth of July March has been cancelled as part of a ban on sectarian. Concern was raised in Parliament that the Orangemen insisted on taking the parade through the traditional route into certain Nationalist areas.

"Wow," Lily said. "That'll be a first. Never thought they'd cancel the Orange parade."

"Sure, didn't you often take us down to see it as it passed by before the Troubles?" Scarlet said.

"Yes, sure did. You kids loved it."

"Yeah, I remember, Mom. We often looked forward to it," Shane said. "Of course, we didn't understand the purpose of it when we were younger."

The news continued,

Following consultation between the Northern Ireland Government and the British Army, it was felt that uncontrollable major violence may occur and consequently it was announced yesterday in parliament that the twelfth of July parade has been cancelled.

"The Orange community will not like that," Brendan said, as he entered the parlor, "Wonder what Mr. Paisley thinks of that."

The news continued on the radio,

The Orange leader, the Reverend Ian Paisley, was most annoyed that the Orange-led Northern Ireland Parliament had delivered the order to cancel the event. His anger was cast in their direction. He approached the bench in parliament and read out a statement. "The government has capitulated to the policy of terror. Today the IRA has won!"

"Well, the BBC must have been listening to you, Bren. There's your answer," Lily said.

"Need to prepare now for unrest among the Protestant community following Dr. Paisley's words. Will probably be called out over the next few nights."

"Wow. What a provocative statement from Ian Paisley. He was certainly directing his venom at his own parliamentary leaders," Shane said.

"I suppose the government was between a rock and a hard place," Lily said. "They didn't have a better option, if there was real concern of trouble during the marches."

"I suppose so, Mom," Shane said. "As they say, 'Damned if you do, damned if you don't.'"

"What happens next is the question," Lily said.

Shane was concerned about the escalation of violence in the city and was counting the days until he left for Liverpool on September 16. Predictably riots broke out in several Protestant-focused areas in Belfast and Derry. His father was called out for a couple of nights to put out fires in the areas affected in Belfast. The beat goes on, Shane thought. After all, this is Belfast. Shane's concern was well justified as the summer of 1972 became a story of unrest and devastation in Northern Ireland.

There was a respite from the terror in Belfast with a cease-fire announced by the Provisional IRA on July 3, following the impact of the Women's Peace Drive marches and secret discussions with the British Government. However, the cease-fire was short lived. The McMahons were regular listeners of the news. One morning carried horrific news of the return to violence.

Good morning. Here is the Northern Ireland news on Saturday, July 22. Yesterday, destruction took place in Belfast which will go down in history as 'the Bloody Friday Massacre.' Within an eighty-minute period the Provisional IRA triggered over twenty bombs around the city, with its plan to rock the financial structure of the province. The IRA, in a statement sent to the press, said this was a response to the breakdown in secret peace talks between the British Government and Sinn Fein, their political wing. They went on to say that the massacre yesterday demonstrates to the government that they have the power to make a commercial desert of Belfast.

"God's truth," Lily said. "Where will this end?"
"Listen. There's more," Scarlet said.
The news continued,

Nine people died, and over one hundred and thirty people were maimed and injured. On the back of Bloody Sunday, which occurred earlier in the year in Derry City, leading to fourteen deaths and over fifteen injuries, the province has been deteriorating rapidly.

"You tell me," Shane said. "I was hoping the destruction would ease out following the impact of the Peace Drive, but it seems to be getting worse."

"You made the right decision, Son, to go to Liverpool," Lily said. "Only a couple of months now until you're on that boat."

"Yes Mom. Thank you for your support."

Following Bloody Friday, the British Army forced a significant presence in Nationalist strongholds. Belfast was becoming a difficult place to live and move about in. Shane was wondering how much longer he could hold out. The stale air was driving him crazy.

Shane and Siobhan spent as much time together as they could, largely going outside when it was daylight. They often walked together in the beautiful Belfast parks, discussing what they would do together when Shane came across for his courses. Siobhan only saw Shane perform at the Anchor once with a special dispensation from her parents on the basis that they accompanied her. Shane and Siobhan enjoyed the summer made easier by the knowledge that they'd soon be together in Liverpool. Shane was comforted about that and kept his positivity. The stay of Siobhan in Belfast seemed to fly by and in what seemed like the blink of an eyelid Shane was back down at the ferry port with the O'Connell family seeing her off at the end of July.

As summer came to an end, the Munich Olympics commenced on August 26. This provided some respite to the athletics community in the province. The track-and-field events did not start until the second week as normal. One of the early athletic events was the Women's Pentathlon, which kicked off on September 2. At the end of the first day, the athlete from Belfast, Mary Peters, had a good lead. On Sunday September 3, most of Northern Ireland, never mind the rest of the world, were glued to their television sets. Mary had a slender advantage going into the final day. Shane invited Paul, Tim, Pete, Phil, and John around to watch. Scarlet and Tyrone also squeezed into the parlor to watch, and Lily from time to time popped in for an update.

"So, Heide Rosendahl has cut into Mary's margin following the long jump," Phil said.

"Not surprising," Paul said. "She's the best at the long jump and just won the Olympic Gold at it."

"Yes, and she has home advantage," John said.

"So, what does Mary have to do going into the last event?" Tim asked.

"Basically, she has to run the race of her life," Pete said. "Her advantage is down to fifty points. That's not much."

"So, what's the final event?" Scarlet asked.

"The 200 meters," Shane said.

"Basically, she has less that one second to play with," Paul said.

"Wow," Tyrone said.

Over a million people in Northern Ireland ran those 200 meters with Mary and felt her pain as she drove down the finishing straight. Rosendahl won the race as expected. It seemed like an eternity before Mary crossed the line. The will of the Northern Ireland people was blowing her to the finish line. The occupants of the McMahon parlor were on their feet shouting into the TV.

"Did she get it?" Shane asked.

"Don't know," Paul said. "They're all standing there on the track wondering."

Lily had come in to watch. "She certainly ran the race of her life," she said. "Made us all proud whatever the result."

"I'm confident, Mom," Scarlet said. "She's the best."

"You got it, Scarlet," Shane said. "When a few of us were down at the university gym last year, we saw her training. It was phenomenal what she was doing."

"They're all looking up at the score board," Paul said. "The results are going up one by one."

All held their breath. Then Mary's time went up on the screen. The commentator called out that she just edged the German for the multi-event. The whole house erupted. Everybody was jumping and cheering. In fact, the whole street could be heard doing the same, as was the whole of the country. Mary had prevailed by the smallest of margins. The activity in the streets of Belfast that night was now of celebration. The province had an Olympic champion! For a moment all Northern Ireland was as one.

The great start to the Munich Olympics was indelibly scarred by the massacre that occurred on September 5 and 6. A terrorist organization, Black September, attacked the athletes' village and killed competitors and held others hostage. The Olympics were halted. The world watched as sporting events resorted to terror. The McMahons were listening to the wireless on the day the news broke.

"Gosh. What's going to happen now?" Lily said.

"I think they'll postpone until the siege is brought under control," Brendan said.

"Can't believe we were jumping around and celebrating just a couple of days ago and now disaster," Shane said.

"Shame," Lily said.

A couple of days later the news was once again blasting out in the McMahon household.

After two days of bartering and expert action, the German security forces seized back control at the Olympics.

"That's great," Shane said.
"Will the games resume?" Lily asked.
"Hope so."
A later bulletin was broadcast.

It has been decided by the Olympic Committee after discussion with the German authorities that the Olympics will continue tomorrow.

"Excellent!" Shane said, as the family listened. "Let's get back to something good."

Later that evening the BBC TV news reported on the terror in Munich.

The heart has been cut out of the celebration of the world's youth. Despite the announced resumption of the games tomorrow, many athletes do not want to compete. Some will not and some will reluctantly. It is likely that results of some events will be different because of the attack. Nevertheless, for the sporting world, there are still a lot of events to get pumped up about.

"One of these events is the one I've been waiting for," Shane said to his family. "It's the Men's 5,000 meters and will be on the final day."

"Better invite your running friends around again, Shane," Lily said.

The day arrived, and the McMahon household was once again filled to the brim. Cousin Dan came over to watch.

"All the big favorites are in the race," Tim said.
"Who do ya all fancy?" Dan asked.
"The hot favorite has to be the flying Finn, Lasse Viren," Paul said.

"Can't see anyone beating him. He picked himself up off the floor and had to catch up about sixty meters to win gold medal in the 10,000 meters earlier in the week," Phil said.

"Yes, and he set a world record to boot," Shane said.

"Look out for the current 5,000-meter champion from the Mexico Olympics, Mohammed Gammoudi of Tunisia," Pete said. "He's bound to have a say."

"I agree," Paul said.

"Bedford may well take it out and make them all suffer," Tim said. "He'll want to make up for a poor performance in the ten."

"Don't ignore Ian Stewart," John said. "He's a winner, with a blistering finish."

"Agree John. But also look out also for the American, Steve Prefontaine. He's got the heart of an ox," Shane said. "He'll have something to say about the race."

As the race unfolded, Prefontaine grasped the nettle and was making sure that anyone who would finish ahead of him would suffer and earn it.

"Bedford's dropped off," Tim said with disappointment.

"Go Pre! Go Pre!" Shane shouted.

"Go Ian!" was a shout from John favoring the Scottish runner.

"The Finn's coming," Phil said.

"No, the Tunisian is pushing hard," Paul said.

"The Finn's in position to pounce," Pete said.

All in the room had stood up, shouting at the television as a pulsating final lap unfolded. They listened to the BBC commentary from David Coleman.

Prefontaine is pushing hard down the back straight. Has he got much left? The Finn is moving past him. The Tunisian is going with him. Prefontaine is fighting hard to hold on. It's between these three for victory. They're entering the home straight. The Finn is surging ahead. The Tunisian is with him. Prefontaine's legs have gone and he's running backwards! Coming to the line now. Viren is moving away. He's the champion. Gammoudi is second. Now here comes a fast-finishing Ian Steward looking for the bronze.

Shane was jumping up and down. "Go Pre! Go Pre!"

Prefontaine gave everything and held on gamely pushing to the line in the hope of medaling but was pipped to the post by the fast-finishing Ian Stewart. Shane looked over to John and shook his head. "You were right about that fast finish."

John grinned and replied, "Wish I was wrong. However, Pre's much younger than the others and less experienced."

"He showed his cards too early," Tim said.

Shane was most disappointed that "Pre" hadn't medaled.

"Disappointing. Pre almost got there. He left everything out there. That's all that can be asked," Shane said. "Nevertheless, I feel we may have seen the event's next gold medalist in the Montreal Olympics in four years' time."

"Here, here. Here, here," a couple of the guys said.

On the morning of Saturday, September 16, a football game was arranged in the street as a sendoff for Shane. It was a glorious sunny day. Many from the Belfast United Harriers turned up, as did Cousin Dan, and the O'Connell family. This was the largest participation ever assembled for a Gaels versus Champions match, with close to thirty people on each side. The street was cleared of all cars. For this special game a referee was arranged, none other than Ciarán O'Loughlin. Ciarán had been recovering well from his injuries; however, he still needed to rest regularly. On that basis an armchair was brought out to the footpath on the street and placed just outside his front door.

"Dan, why don't you and I go in and help Ciarán out?" Shane said.

"Coming, Shane," Dan said.

"Come on Ciarán give me your arm and Dan the other."

"Thanks guys."

Ciarán was sat down with a woolen blanket to keep him warm. He was prepared with a whistle to adjudicate on the game. Scarlet came out in her properly attired Everton kit. However, on this occasion she was carrying a small white flag on a cane stick.

"I'll be your linesperson, Ciarán," Scarlet said.

"Much appreciated, Scarlet."

She was ready to run up and down the footpath and draw Ciarán's attention to issues that required his attention.

"OK," Paul said. "We'll have to extend the length of the pitch."

Coats were duly moved. The pitch then covered nearly three-quarters of the street.

Ciarán addressed the crowd. "Rather than each half being decided by goals, on this occasion there will be two thirty-minute periods."

"Got it."

"Ready," Ciarán said. "Let's do the toss." Ciarán threw a coin in the air. "It's Shane's day so he can call."

"Heads."

"The Gaels have won the toss," said Ciarán. "Please kick off on my whistle."

Ciarán blew and it was game on. Scarlet was most active as there was a lot of gamesmanship, no doubt a takeoff from the topical Leeds versus Derby encounters recently seen on TV. At half-time it was five to three to the Champions. Refreshments were brought out by the residents at the conclusion of the first half for this special occasion.

"Please line up in an orderly fashion," said Hilda, as she brought out a small table and poured the lemon barley water.

Betty, Ethel, and Lily lined up with Hilda behind the table and handed out the drinks. Five minutes elapsed.

"Two-minute warning," Ciarán said.

Ciarán sounded the whistle, and the second half commenced with the same intensity. Partway through, an army patrol group came up the street. The game had to have a temporary halt as the soldiers walked past. One soldier leaned over to Scarlet as he passed by and whispered something. Many saw this and were puzzled and inquisitive. As the patrol departed up the street and exited through the alley at the top of the cul-de-sac, a few people came over to Scarlet and asked what had been said.

"Go Toffees!" Scarlet said.

The game progressed and ended in a very credible and satisfactory nine-all draw. Then makeshift tables and chairs were brought out from the houses and a street party continued for the next hour. To Shane's great surprise Liam and Clodagh had arrived with his Granda McKeown. Shane thanked all for the great send-off.

In the early sunny evening Shane was about to leave for the ferry. Liam and Clodagh had taken Joseph McKeown home and then returned to drive him down with Lily and Brendan.

"So, it's adios, Big Bro," Scarlet said.

"No, it's au revoir," Shane said. He then threw over the VW keys to Scarlet. "The white chariot is now yours, Scarlet," Shane said. "When is your driving test?"

"Thanks, Big Bro! It's next week. Just need a couple more lessons with Uncle Liam."

"Yes, she's doing very well," Liam said. "We'll have her ready."

A tearful Tyrone came across. "I'll miss you, Shane."

"I'll miss you, too, wee man. But don't worry. I'll be back every few months."

"Can't wait."

Then the adults climbed into Liam's Ford Escort and headed to the city center for the Liverpool ferry. The McMahon's and McKeown's arrived at the ferry terminal as the sun glinted down on the vessel.

"Belfast has a habit of delivering its best weather when people are leaving," Clodagh said.

"Doesn't it just," Lily said with tears starting to swell.

"Now Shane, remember that you can contact our cousin Gerry McKeown at any time when you're over there," Liam said.

"Got it, Uncle Liam. I've his phone number and his address in the Childwall area."

"Just give us a call, Shane, if you need anything," Brendan said.

"Will do, Da."

Lily came over and gave her son a hug. She held on tight. The tears were trickling down her cheek. She eventually let go.

"Please ring, Shane, when you reach Liver . . ." Lily burst out crying and couldn't continue. Shane put his arms around her and gave a big hug again. Then Brendan gently peeled her away from their son.

A loud horn rang from the ferry indicating that it was time to leave. The ferry master was calling out, "Final boarding!"

Shane walked up the ramp as his family looked on. He turned round to wave to them. Brendan was holding Lily, who looked on in distress. Shane felt for her; however, he knew he'd made the right decision. Nevertheless, he was heartbroken to be leaving them.

Ferries were considered neutral ground. Belfast travelers and the army alike would travel back and forth by ferry. There was no conflict during travel, and in fact the rival factions would often have a drink together and play cards or darts. As it was relatively expensive to book a berth, most people stayed up through the night for the eight-hour crossing. Some would grab a bit of sleep on a bench.

The ferry pulled away from the dock. Shane checked his bags at storage, took a ticket, and stepped out onto the upper deck. He looked back at Belfast. He knew the city had a magnet that would always draw him back. He loved the place, but he had no regrets on leaving. It had never been clearer in his mind that he was right to leave. The vessel progressed on its route to Liverpool. As dusk fell, city lights started to switch on in the distance and the landscape lit up. This was not the panoramic view he had seen from above Cave Hill, but it was a sentimental part of Belfast that Shane had come to know and love. The lights of the city, always a beautiful sight, faded further and further into the distance.

Most people headed back into the lounges. Shane remained on

the deck alone with his thoughts. Then a posh English voice called over from behind,

"Mind if I join you?"

"It's a free country. Be my guest."

Shane looked over to the guy who was now like him, leaning on the railing and looking out to sea. It was Captain Green.

"Looks peaceful, Belfast with its lights in the distance," the captain said.

"Doesn't it just." Shane pretended not to know him. "Are you on your way back home?" Shane asked.

"Yes, I've completed my two-year stint. Now back to my hometown of Bur-ming-gum," the captain said delivering the response in his posh English accent but dropping to his local Brummie for the word, Birmingham.

"So, what's next in store for you?" Shane asked.

"I'll have some vacation at home and then onto a beach resort in the Mediterranean. After a month I'll be on my way to East Berlin."

"Grand."

Captain Green turned to Shane. "So, what takes you on a boat over to England?"

"I'm moving to Liverpool University for my degree."

"Very interesting. What subject?"

"Music."

"Do you not prefer to stay in Belfast for your degree?"

"Actually, I started at Queen's, but things are becoming more dangerous now in Belfast as I'm sure you're aware. So, I've transferred to Liverpool to complete my degree."

"Yes, I do understand. Best of luck."

"Thanks."

With the conversation finished, both gentlemen gazed out over the tranquil water broken only by the cavitation of the propellors. It was serene. After a few minutes, Captain Green moved to go. "Must be getting back to my team. Nice to speak with you."

"Same here. Best of luck."

As he started to depart, the captain turned back to Shane. "So how old is your mother?" the captain asked.

Shane smirked and responded,

"The answer my friend is blowing in the wind!"

THE END!

Made in the USA
Columbia, SC
15 April 2023

0f176cda-01a4-463d-8adc-16d7d751d783R01